W9-ARG-516

PITT

PITT

BY

LORD ROSEBERY

AMS PRESS
NEW YORK

Reprinted from the edition of 1892, New York
First AMS EDITION published 1969
Manufactured in the United States of America

Library of Congress Catalog Card Number: 78-106521

AMS PRESS, INC.
New York, N.Y. 10003

This little book has been written under many disadvantages, but with a sincere desire to ascertain the truth. My chief happiness in completing it would have been to give it to my wife; it can now only be inscribed to her memory.

November 1891.

CONTENTS

CHAPTER I

YOUTH

William Pitt the younger was born at Hayes in 1759, in the full splendour of his father's famous ministry; in the year that saw Quebec fall before the dying Wolfe; that saw the glorious but inconclusive victory of Minden; that saw Hawke in a November storm crush the French fleet off Brest; the year that produced Burns and Wilberforce. None, perhaps, has given us names so honoured and cherished by the human race. Of his parents it is needless to say anything, except in so far as they influenced his career. His father, William Pitt, Earl of Chatham, was the most striking figure and the most dazzling statesman of his time; while, if one may judge of his speeches by their effect, he may be held the greatest orator that England has ever produced. Lady Chatham was the only sister of two remarkable brothers. One, George Grenville, the obstinate minister of an obstinate King, did much to involve us in our most disastrous and unnatural war. The other, Richard Earl Temple, welded his family into a disciplined and formidable force, which lasted as a potent factor in politics for at least two generations; and accomplished its persistent object in the third, by obtaining the luckless dukedom of Buckingham for its chief.

With such parents, the younger Pitt was born a politician; his rare qualities of mind were from his earliest childhood directed and trained for parliamentary work. It did not, indeed, at first appear probable that he would survive to realise the designs of his father, who himself had suffered from the gout before leaving Eton. A feeble constitution hardly promised life, much less vigour; but, fortified by floods of port wine—the prescription of Lord Chatham's favourite physician, Dr. Addington, the father of the Prime Minister—it enabled him to live to be forty-seven, and sustain for near twenty years, almost unaided, the government of the country. From six to fourteen, however, his health was so indifferent that for more than half that period he was unable to apply himself to study; and, when at the latter age he went as an undergraduate to Cambridge, it stands recorded that he was accompanied by a nurse. In the autumn of that year (1773) his disorder reached its crisis; he returned home dangerously ill; but, on his recovery, he seems to have secured a share of health sufficient for the purposes of public life, and troubled only by periodic fits of the gout, then the appanage of statesmanship, which he owed less to his original disease than its original remedy.

But this sickly childhood only makes his undoubted precocity the more extraordinary. Delicate health probably confined him to study, as it had confined his father. We know that he bought Hollwood, because he used to go birdnesting there as a child. Otherwise, his nursery annals point entirely to learning. He was, indeed, one of the rare instances, like John Mill and Macaulay, of infant prodigy maturing into brilliant manhood. From his earliest years his parents' letters abound in allusions to his talents and character. "Eager Mr. William," "the Counsellor," "the Philosopher," are their nicknames for the marvellous child. In 1766, when he was seven, his tutor writes: "Lady Hester and Mr. Pitt continue to astonish as much as ever; and I see no possibility of diminishing their ardour either by too much business or too much relaxation. When I am alone reading, Mr. Pitt, if it is anything he may attend to, constantly places himself by me, when his steady attention and sage remarks are not only entertaining but useful, as they frequently throw a light upon the subject and strongly impress it on my memory." At the same age he appears to have displayed the dignity and self-possession that marked him in after life; and a trifling anecdote of his stay at Weymouth in that year records him as having dumbfoundered mature observers by these qualities. Another and a later tutor, Bishop Tomline, says, that "although he was little more than fourteen years of age when he went to reside at the University, and had laboured under the disadvantage of frequent ill-health, the knowledge which he then possessed was very considerable; and in particular, his proficiency in the learned languages was probably greater than ever was acquired by any other person in such early youth. In Latin authors he seldom met with difficulty; and it was no uncommon thing for him to read into English six or seven pages of Thucydides, which he had not previously seen, without more than two or three mistakes, and sometimes without even one. It was by Lord Chatham's particular desire that Thucydides was the first Greek book which Mr. Pitt read after he came to college. The only other wish ever expressed by his lordship relative to his son's studies was that I would read Polybius with him." But his latest and most pregnant study, more important to his career than the "obscure rhapsody of Lycophron," or even Polybius, was the great work of Adam Smith. He, almost alone of the statesmen of that day, had mastered and assimilated the *Wealth of Nations*, before entering public life.

A graceful story has been told in which Pitt is made to declare his indebtedness himself. Dundas asked Adam Smith to dinner, but the philosopher did not arrive till all were seated. When he entered the whole company rose to their feet, and Pitt gaily exclaimed, "We will stand till you are seated, for we are all your scholars." The elder Pitt, who seems to have written many of his letters in a sort of classical nightmare, was, it may be gathered from this very pedantry, no great scholar. It was to his training, however, that Pitt owed, not merely the power to translate at sight, which so astonished his tutor, but that fluency of majestic diction and command of correct expression, which afterwards distinguished him as an orator. His father would make the boy of an evening read freely into English the passage which he had construed with his tutor in the morning. So much did this grow into a habit that, when in later years an ancient writer was quoted, Pitt always rendered the sentence into English, as if for his own use, before he seemed to enter into it. It was to these lessons that he always attributed his ready copiousness of language. What was scarcely less valuable, Lord Chatham, (who, we are told, made a point of giving daily instruction, and readings from the Bible to his children), encouraged his son to talk to him without reserve on every subject; so that the boy, who seems to have returned the boundless affection with which his father regarded him, was in close and constant communication with one of the first minds of the age. How strictly political was the bias that his mind thus obtained, we see from a tragedy, "Laurentino, King of Chersonese," still extant, composed by William at the age of thirteen; in which there is no trace of love, but which has for its plot a struggle between a faithful minister and an unscrupulous conspirator about a regency.

The details of the childhood of great men are apt to be petty and cloying. Hero-worship, extended to the bib and the porringer, is more likely to repel than attract. But, in the case of Pitt, those details are doubly important; for they form the key to his career, which without them would be inexplicable. They alone explain that political precocity and that long parliamentary ascendancy, which still puzzle posterity. For he went into the House of Commons as an heir enters his home; he breathed in it his native atmosphere,—he had, indeed, breathed no other; in the nursery, in the schoolroom, at the university, he lived in its temperature; it had been, so to speak, made over to him as a bequest by its unquestioned master. Throughout his life, from the cradle to the grave, he may be said to have known no wider existence. The objects and amusements, that other men seek in a thousand ways, were for him all concentrated there. It was his mistress, his stud, his dice-box, his game-preserve; it was his ambition, his library, his creed. For it, and it alone, had the consummate Chatham trained him from his birth. No young Hannibal was ever more solemnly devoted to his country than Pitt to Parliament. And the austerity of his political consecration lends additional interest to the records of his childhood; for they furnish almost the only gleams of ease and nature that play on his life. He was destined, at one bound, to attain that supreme but isolated position, the first necessity of which is self-control; and, behind the imperious mask of power, he all but concealed the softer emotions of his earlier years. Grief for the loss of his sister and her husband are the only instances of human weakness that break the stern impressiveness of his life, up to that last year when fate pressed pitilessly on the dying man. From the time that he went to Cambridge, as a boy of fourteen with his tutor and his nurse, he seems, with one short interval, to have left youth and gaiety behind.

All this does not amount to much; but it must be remembered that the life of Pitt has yet to be written. That by Richards Green, who wrote under the name of Gifford, need scarcely be mentioned. That by Tomline has been severely judged, more perhaps with reference to what it might have been than to what it is; for there are worse books. But the shores of biographical enterprise are strewn with the wrecks of the private secretaries of that period. There is Tomline; there is Trotter; there is even Stapleton; and there is Bourrienne. The Life by Lord Stanhope remains a standard book; it was written by one born under the shadow of Pitt, and reared in the traditions of hereditary reverence for his name. But it is no disparagement to those delightful volumes to say that there remains a dormant mass of material, that was not then, even if it is now, accessible, which must throw a new light on this period. There are the papers of Grenville, and Harrowby, and Canning; of Liverpool, and Lonsdale, and Mulgrave; more especially the collections of Buckingham and of Tomline, which, it may be presumed, have been rather tapped than drained. The same surmise may be entertained by those who have read what has been published from the archives of Rose and of Malmesbury. There is also the State Paper Office; which, especially in the Foreign Department, seems destined to elucidate much of Pitt's policy. Lord Stanhope gathered and garnered with unwearied sympathy and acuteness. But the materials which he utilised, appear, on examination, to be scanty enough, compared to those, which, it would seem, must necessarily be in existence; even if the papers of George III., which have so mysteriously vanished, should never again see day.

Pitt was admitted at Pembroke Hall on the 26th of April 1773, when he was not yet fourteen. By the kindness of the Rev. C. E. Searle, D.D., Master of Pembroke College, it is possible to print here the letter with which Chatham introduced his boy to the authorities. It is addressed to Mr. Joseph Turner, then Senior Tutor of the College and Senior Wrangler in 1767:—

BURTON PYNSENT,
October 3, 1773.

SIR—Apprehensions of gout, about this Season, forbid my undertaking a journey to Cambridge with my Son. I regret this more particularly, as it deprives me of an occasion of being introduced to your Personal Acquaintance, and that of the Gentlemen of your Society; a loss, I shall much wish to repair, at some other time. Mr. Wilson, whose admirable Instruction and affectionate Care have brought my Son, early, to receive such further advantages, as he cannot fail to find, under your eye, will present Him to you. He is of a tender age, and of a health, not yet firm enough to be indulged, to the full, in the strong desire he has to acquire useful knowledge. An ingenuous mind and docility of temper will, I know, render him conformable to your Discipline, in all points. Too young for the irregularities of a man, I trust, he will not, on the other hand, prove troublesome by the Puerile sallies of a Boy. Such as he is, I am happy to place him at Pembroke; and I need not say, how much of his Parents' Hearts goes along with him.—I am, with great esteem and regard, Sir, your most faithful and most obedient humble Servant, CHATHAM.

At the University, Pitt led the austere life of a student; never missing hall or chapel or lecture, save when illness hindered. He took his degree, by privilege, at the age of seventeen, but continued to reside at Cambridge for nearly four years afterwards, seeing rather more of his contemporaries, and with habits somewhat less ascetic, than heretofore. He had always allowed himself the relaxation of a trip to London to hear his father speak. "His first speech lasted above an hour, and the second half an hour; surely the two finest speeches that were ever made before, unless by himself," writes the enthusiastic son; and in his nineteenth year it was his fate to support the old statesman to the last scene in the House of Lords. Two months later he was bearing his part as chief mourner in the gorgeous procession that followed

—in the heraldic epithets for once not misapplied—"the noble and puissant William Pitt, Earl of Chatham," to that grave in Westminster Abbey, which, in less than thirty years, was, in still darker days, to open for himself.

His father's disregard of money, as complete as his own, left him with an income of from £250 to £300 a year; nor was this immediately available. His uncle, Lord Temple, advanced the sum necessary to purchase him a set of rooms at Lincoln's Inn. He began to keep his terms early in 1779; and, although continuing his residence at Cambridge, to sip with prudence the cup of London amusements. His share of these mainly consisted in attendance at parliamentary debates; where he became acquainted with Fox, already a star of the first magnitude. Nor did he shrink from a visit to the opera or an occasional rout. He was called to the bar in June, 1780.

His residence at Cambridge began at this time to have an object not less solid than study; for he came to be considered in the light of a possible candidate for the representation of the University in Parliament. The eagerness with which he embraced this opportunity, betokened the mind set steadfastly in this direction by every influence and predisposition of youth. The dissolution came in September 1780, when he stood for the University, and was left at the bottom of the poll. But immediately afterwards, the young Duke of Rutland, who had been warmly interested in Pitt's success, applied to Sir James Lowther for a seat for his friend. Lowther, afterwards Lord Lonsdale, exercised in the North of England a sway which we can now hardly measure or imagine. In 1782 he had offered to build and equip at his own expense a vessel of war with seventy guns. Boswell and Wilberforce have borne almost trembling testimony to the splendour of his court, which exhibited extreme hospitality, tempered by extreme awe, and which northern politicians haunted like a northern St. James's. One of the chief secrets indeed of his power lay in his parliamentary influence, the extent of which was exactly defined in the deferential nickname of the Premier's Cat-o'-Nine-Tails. To one of his nine boroughs he now nominated Pitt; who accordingly in January 1781 took his seat in the House of Commons as member for Appleby. Exactly three years later, he was to enter it as Prime Minister, and hold that post with unexampled power for eighteen years.

At the time that Pitt stepped into public life, the administration of Lord North was in its agony. Its thin-spun life was only preserved by the exertions of the King. The good-humoured cynicism of the minister had long ago given way to the most dismal apprehension; he was more and more determined to retire. But he had to deal with a stern taskmaster.

The character of George III. is one which it is not easy to understand, if we take the common and erroneous view that human nature is consistent and coherent. The fact is, that congruity is the exception; and that time and circumstance and opportunity paint with heedless hands and garish colours on the canvass of a man's life; so that the result is less frequently a finished picture than a palette of squeezed tints. George III., who "gloried in the name of Briton," who obtained his initial popularity by being an Englishman born, and who, indeed, never travelled farther than York, was the German princelet of his day. No petty elector or margrave, not the ruler of Hesse, who sold his people by the thousand as material of war, held more absolutely the view of property, as applied to his dominions or subjects.

He saw in the American war, not vanished possibilities in the guidance of a new world, but the expropriation of an outlying estate, the loss of which diminished his consequence. He fought for it, therefore, as doggedly as a Lord of Ravenswood for his remaining acres. As to his ministers, he regarded them as the mere weapons of a warfare waged on behalf of autocracy. So long as they served him blindly, he lavished caresses on them; from the moment that they showed independence, he discarded them like old coats, and old coats which had become repulsive to him. It is probable that he never liked Bute, and that Bute's direct influence over him has been greatly exaggerated. But, while North was the complaisant grand vizier, nothing was too good for him. The Cinque-ports and the Garter, money, terms of endearment, were all freely given. At the time, however, of Pitt's entry into Parliament, the Minister was flinching under the terrific punishment of the Opposition and the severity of continual disaster; it was clear that he could not long endure; and the affectionate monarch was cooling down to freezing point. From the time of his resignation to his death, Lord North remained a stranger to George III.

It is doubtful whether the King ever regarded Pitt otherwise than as an indispensable officer, of whom, with his "d——d long obstinate upper lip," he stood painfully in awe. For Pitt, alive and in power, the sole bulwark against Fox and the deluge, he was willing to do anything—to pay his bills or to double the peerage; but for the dead Pitt's debts he had not a farthing to spare; and he ungraciously ignored, and even denied, his former promise to contribute £30,000 for that object. At one time he found in Addington the servant that he required; and he wrote to him in terms scarcely less fond, than those which James employed to Villiers, or Maria Theresa to Kaunitz. He adjured the minister to take horse exercise; he waited patiently with his family at Addington's house till Addington should come; the favourite was even admitted to share the royal mutton and turnips. No sooner, however, had Addington, appalled by the reduction of his majority to the not inadequate figure of thirty-seven, hurried from the field of battle, than his intimacy with the King ceased also. The Robinsons and the Roses lasted perhaps longer, for they were perennially useful; nor did Eldon ever give the King the chance of proving that his affections survived office.

It is strange that any sovereign should display so thorough a contempt for the loyal service he received; it is stranger still in one whose popularity rested on his English qualities; on his warm heart, and affectionate disposition. Again, his habits were not less domestic than those of Mr. Perceval; but his home was a hell upon earth. What he cared for in his family relations was to maintain the same power over his children that Frederick William I. exercised over Frederick the Great. As a consequence, they escaped from his roof as soon, and returned to it as rarely, as possible.

This is not a pleasant portrait; but there are better features in it. To his sense of duty, mistaken as we may deem it, he was honestly faithful; he was frugal, and pious, and chaste; though the dulness of his court made virtue itself odious, and his parsimony did not prevent constant and unbounded demands on Parliament for the debts of the Civil List. His talents, like his morals, were not of an attractive kind, but they must not be underrated. He was the ablest political strategist of his day. He had to struggle against men of genius, supported by popular enthusiasm, on the one hand; and an impracticable aristocracy, inured to supreme power, on the other. He had, during his reign, to deal with the elder Pitt and the younger Fox, when they were the idols of the nation; with the haughty alliance of Grenville and Grey; with the intolerable obstinacy of Grenville's father; with the close oligarchy of Whig nobles that had encircled and enchained the throne; and with the turbulent democracy of Wilkes. He defeated or outwitted them all. Pitt impatiently betrayed the truth, after an interview with the King, then just recovering from a fit of insanity: "Never has he so baffled me." By a certain persistent astuteness; by the dexterous utilising of political rivalries; by cajoling some men and betraying others; by a resolute adroitness that turned disaster and even disease into instruments of his aim, the King realised his darling object, of converting the dogeship to which he had succeeded, into a real and to some extent a personal monarchy. At any rate, he indefinitely enlarged its boundaries.

It is necessary to dwell on the character of the sovereign, who played so prominent a part before and after our story. Little, however, need here be said of North; for within fourteen months he had ceased to be minister; and, with the exception of his obscure share in the Coalition government, had retired from prominent public life. But his reputation is below his real merits, though it owes something to the majestic eulogy of Gibbon. In the art of gaining affection, and in debating power, he was second only to Fox. He was courageous and resourceful, cool in adversity, of an unruffled temper; he held, moreover, the first place in the State for twelve years, and left office, with all the unlimited opportunities of wealth that were then offered by war loans, even a poorer man than he entered it. His cynical and easy wit, indeed, covered a higher character than many with greater pretensions; and his good nature, facile to a fault, which made him lend himself to reprehensible acts, and to a policy of which at last he clearly saw the folly and the wickedness, is the main reproach that history has to urge against him; though that is heavy enough. He had apparently formed himself on Walpole; with the unlucky difference that, while Walpole had to deal with a Caroline of Anspach, North found his master in George III.

It was of course inevitable that Pitt should attach himself to the Opposition; more especially, as that part of it, which had constituted the personal following of his father, still held together under the leadership of Shelburne. A month after taking his seat he had made his maiden speech (February 26, 1781), and had been hailed by the first men in Parliament, with the ready generosity of genius, as henceforth worthy to rank with them. He spoke on behalf of

Burke's Bill for economical reform, unexpectedly, being called upon by the House; and his first speech was, what, perhaps, no other first speech ever was, an effective reply in debate. Fox and North and Burke vied in congratulation. "He is not a chip of the old block," said the latter; "it is the old block itself." He spoke again in May on a question of the control of public expenditure with not less success; and for the third and last time in the session, on a motion of Fox's for peace with America. His speeches, therefore, in his first session were devoted to peace and retrenchment, and his main effort in the next to parliamentary reform; the three causes nearest and most congenial to him; the beacons of his earlier, and the will-o'-the-wisps of his later career.

We catch glimpses of him now as a lad about town, leading something of a fashionable life during the season, though dutifully going the western circuit as soon as Parliament rose. A club had been formed at Goostree's of a score of young men who had entered Parliament together at the election of 1780, an idea, which was destined to be revived exactly a century afterwards. Here he supped every night, not, we may be sure, without port wine; here he gambled; until he became sensible of the insidious fascination of the gaming table, and turned his back on it for ever. The example of Fox had been perhaps sufficient. We read of Pitt, in 1780, as going to three parties of an evening; two of them masked balls, one given by a lady of not apparently unspotted reputation, and concluding his evening at the Pantheon. A more remarkable evening was that on which he met Gibbon. The great man, lord of all he surveyed, was holding forth, snuff-box in hand, amid deferential acquiescence; when a deep, clear voice was heard impugning his conclusions. All turned round in amazement and saw that it belonged to a tall, thin, awkward youth who had hitherto sate silent. Between Pitt, for it was he, and Gibbon, an animated and brilliant argument arose; in which the junior had so much the best of it that the historian took his hat and retired. Nor would he return. "That young gentleman," he said, "is, I doubt not, extremely ingenious and agreeable, but I must acknowledge that his style of conversation is not exactly what I am accustomed to, so you must positively excuse me."

It is almost a relief after this to find him in 1781 "waging war with increasing success on pheasants and partridges." He did not even disdain the practical jokes of an undergraduate. "We found one morning," says Wilberforce, "the fruits of Pitt's earlier rising in the careful sowing of the garden beds with the fragments of a dress hat in which Ryder had overnight come down from the opera." In truth, no man was less of a prig. He was so loftily placed in early youth that he was compelled to a certain austerity of demeanour in order to maintain respect; and he had indeed something of the lofty shyness of Peel. But, at this unconstrained moment of his life, he was, says one who knew all that was most brilliant in English society for half a century, "the wittiest man I ever knew."

At the end of Pitt's first session, Fox had declared him to be already one of the first men in Parliament. He was to know no flagging in his onward course; his genius was not to want the opportunity for which genius so often pines; the accumulating calamities of his country demanded the best efforts of the noblest ambition. The session had ended on the 18th of July 1781. On the 19th of October Cornwallis surrendered at Yorktown. The news reached London, late in November; and shattered even the imperturbable ease of North. He took it as he would have taken a bullet in his breast. He opened his arms, exclaiming wildly, as he paced up and down the room, "O God, it is all over!" All was indeed over, as regards the Ministry and their policy. British dominion in the revolted colonies, and the administration which had so long asserted it, existed from that moment only in name. The catastrophe was followed by minor disasters: the retreat of Kempenfeldt, the loss of Minorca, and of many of our West Indian possessions: though these were forgotten in the dazzling victory of Rodney. But the long struggle was over; and had ended in the humiliation of Great Britain. It was the lowest point that she had ever touched. "The sun of England's glory," said Pitt, "is set." Twenty years before, it had seemed at its meridian, and in the course of another generation it shone again with renewed lustre; but now it was totally eclipsed.

Before the end of March, even the King was convinced that he must part with North, and submit to peace and the Whigs. During the fierce contests which raged in Parliament between the surrender of Yorktown and the fall of the Ministry, Pitt bore so conspicuous a part, as to justify the declaration which he made just before the latter event, that he had no idea of forming part of any new administration: "But were my doing so more within my reach, I feel myself bound to declare that I never would accept a subordinate situation." The position that was offered him by Rockingham, who succeeded North, was subordinate, but not undignified. The Vice-Treasurership of Ireland was indeed little more than a sinecure; but it had been held by Pitt's own father, and in point of emolument was one of the prizes of the political world; yet he refused it without hesitation.

That he was wise, there can be no doubt. He retained his freedom, and used that freedom well. The new Government had not been formed six weeks, before Pitt brought forward a motion for parliamentary reform. It took, indeed, a shape, to which, for constitutional changes of gravity, objection has sometimes been raised; for he brought forward no specific plan, but moved "for the institution of an inquiry composed of such men as the House should in their wisdom select as the most proper and the best qualified for investigating this subject, and making a report to the House of the best means of carrying into execution a moderate and substantial reform of the representation of the people."

The speech he delivered on this occasion, much applauded at the time, is worth reading even now and in the condensed, denuded report that has reached us. It is remarkable for its vigorous declamation against the power of the Crown, which Fox and Burke could hardly have exceeded in their speeches on the same subject when Pitt was minister in 1784. He allowed that, under the Rockingham Government, "the injurious, corrupt, and baneful influence of the Crown" had ceased to exist. But it was the duty of Parliament to provide for the future, and to take care that this secret and dark system should never be revived to contaminate the fair and honourable fabric of our Government. At all times, this pernicious influence had been pointed to as the fertile source of all our miseries, and it had been truly said of it that it had grown with our growth and strengthened with our strength. Unhappily, however, for this country it had not decayed with our decay, nor diminished with our decrease. And it had supported North's ministry for a length of years against all the consequences of a mischievous system and a desolated empire.

The irony of political destiny, and the astuteness of George III., could receive no better demonstration than the fact that in less than two years Pitt was defending the prerogative of the monarch against the assaults of North, and of those whom he now described as "a set of men who were the friends of constitutional freedom." Yet in truth the anomaly, as is often the case in politics, was more apparent than real. What he denounced were the crawling race of the Welbore Ellises and the Jack Robinsons, the suspected shadow of Bute and the pervading flavour of Jenkinson, the detailed bribes of Martin, the mingled cajolery and terrorism of Henry Fox. What he defended in 1784 were the rights of the constituencies, betrayed by the formation of the Coalition, against a close and corrupt Parliament, in a struggle where the King had intervened for once as the agent of the people. It was the general election of 1784 that ratified the King's action and cleared Pitt of responsibility: had it turned differently, he might have ranked with Strafford and with Lauderdale.

Pitt, in his first Reform speech, analysed the various

kinds of boroughs, which were either representative shams or, worse still, were open to foreign bidders. Among these purchasers he named the Nabob of Arcot, who "had no less than seven or eight members in this House." Finally, he cited his father, "one of whom every member in the House could speak with more freedom than himself. That person was not apt to indulge vague and chimerical speculations, inconsistent with practice and expediency. He knew that it was the opinion of this person that without recurring to first principles in this respect, and establishing a more solid and equal representation of the people, by which the proper constitutional connection should be revived, this nation, with the best capacities for grandeur and happiness of any on the face of the earth, must be confounded with the mass of those whose liberties were lost in the corruption of the people."

In spite of a speech which was evidently forcible and eloquent, and of the support of Fox "in his very first form," and of Sheridan, then his under secretary, "much above anything he has yet done in the House," the motion was lost by twenty votes. The Government spoke indeed with a divided voice of the subject. The Duke of Richmond, Master-General of the Ordnance and a leading member of the Cabinet, was in favour of annual parliaments and manhood suffrage. Lord John Cavendish was "diffident" of the effect of any such reform, though he voted on this occasion for Pitt. Lord Rockingham gave forth a troubled and ambiguous note, rent as he was between regard for Fox and the dominant influence of Burke, who was vehemently hostile. A few days later, this feeling found overmastering expression when Alderman Sawbridge, Pitt's seconder on this occasion, brought forward a motion for shortening Parliaments, and Burke broke forth in one of his impetuous invectives against Pitt and all who should attempt to touch the sacred fabric of the constitution.

While Pitt in refusing office had retained the positive advantage of independence, he had also gained the negative benefit of not forming part of a Government as divided against itself as its members had formerly been from the Government of Lord North. Under a stormier star was no administration ever born. Furious jealousies broke out during the process of formation. Thurlow, North's chancellor, remained in office, to the open mortification of Loughborough, as an abiding source of suspicion and intrigue. Another legacy of North's, the Lord Advocate Dundas, though less prominent, was not less justly regarded with mistrust as a powerful and unscrupulous politician, whose only connection with the Whigs was the memory of bitter altercation and unsparing conflict; who with a happy instinct sometimes inclined to Shelburne, the proximate Prime Minister, sometimes to the young statesman so soon to follow him and to absorb all the powers of the State. Shelburne himself formed another element of disturbance. Not merely did Fox, his colleague in the Secretaryship of State, cherish an hereditary hatred for him, but he had aroused great jealousy by having been at first entrusted with the task of forming the government. The King dexterously fomented these causes of discord among his enemies, and flatly refused even to see Rockingham; so that all the communications between him and his Prime Minister during the construction of the administration were carried on through the ominous medium of Shelburne, and Shelburne alone. All these germs of mistrust were quickened when Shelburne secured peerages and places for his friends from the King; paid the Chancellor compliments, "which very much scandalised all good men," as Fox writes; and intrigued successfully with Dundas. It is, therefore, not matter for surprise that, within a month of their assuming office, Shelburne and Fox, the two Secretaries of State, had each their separate plenipotentiary at Paris negotiating for peace. Such a condition of affairs had little of comfort or permanency: the Government, ruined by intrigue and under virtuous but incapable guidance, could not in any case have continued to exist: the influenza that carried off Lord Rockingham only accelerated the end of an impossible state of things.

CHAPTER II

SHELBURNE AND THE COALITION

THE political atmosphere was charged with electricity, and the breaking of the storm was not delayed. Rockingham died on the 1st of July (1782). That very day the King entrusted the Treasury to Shelburne, who evidently counted on Pitt, and had, it is clear, good reason for doing so. Shelburne received the royal letter on the 2d, and at once communicated the King's mandate to the Cabinet. There was no ambiguity about its reception. The Fox party declared that the nomination of First Minister should rest with the Cabinet; and, to the mortification of the able but impracticable Richmond, recommended Portland for the post. To this pretension the King at once refused to accede. For two days the contest raged. On the third there was a Court. Fox came with the seals in his pocket, and at once took Shelburne aside, asking him if he was to be First Lord of the Treasury. On Shelburne's affirmative reply, Fox merely said, "Then, my lord, I shall resign," went into the closet, and left the seals with the King.

This rupture was a crisis in the lives of Fox and

Pitt, for it marks the commencement of their undying political hostility. Had it not been for Pitt, Fox must now have triumphed—a fact that neither statesman could ignore or forget. Of Fox's resignation it may be said that he was right to resign, but wrong in the manner of his resignation. It was impossible for him, after what had passed in the Rockingham Cabinet, to remain; he could not have continued to serve with, much less under, Shelburne. It does not signify which of the two was to blame for this mutual mistrust; that it existed is sufficient. It would be too much to maintain that all the members of a Cabinet should feel an implicit confidence in each other; humanity—least of all political humanity—could not stand so severe a test. But between a Prime Minister in the House of Lords and the leader of the House of Commons such a confidence is indispensable. Responsibility rests so largely with the one, and articulation so greatly with the other, that unity of sentiment is the one necessary link that makes a relation, in any case difficult, in any way possible. The voice of Jacob and the hands of Esau may effect a successful imposture, but can hardly constitute a durable administration. But as regards the effort to impose Portland on the King, the case is widely different. It was part of the political system that rendered the narrow selfishness of the close Whig corporation even more odious to the people than the tortuous absolutism of the King. To the men of that day, for whom prerogative was a living force, it was not less distasteful than to us, for whom an oligarchy is odious for opposite reasons. For Fox it may be urged that a dummy Prime Minister offered the only means of keeping the Government together, for he would not serve under Shelburne, nor Shelburne under him. Be that as it may, the attempt to procure the succession of a dull, dumb duke to the vapid virtue of Rockingham, whom George III. had ranked among the meanest intellects in his household, did not recommend itself to any large section of the community, and tended further to alienate from Fox the jealous sympathies of the people.

It is clear that Shelburne would not have undertaken in July the post from which he had shrunk in March, had he not relied upon Pitt. Fox, with rare sagacity, had foreseen this even at the time when Pitt was achieving distinction as a parliamentary reformer and denouncer of the influence of the Crown, and had written of him on the 18th of May: "He is very civil and obliging, profuse of compliments in public; but he has more than once taken a line that has alarmed me, especially when he dissuaded against going into any inquiries that might produce heats and differences. This seemed so unlike his general mode of thinking, and so like that of another, that I confess I disliked it to the greatest degree. *I am satisfied that he will be the man that the old system revived in the person of Lord S.* (Shelburne) *will attempt to bring forward for its support.* I am satisfied that he is incapable of going into this with his eyes open; but how he may be led into it step by step is more than I can answer for. I feel myself, I own, rather inclined to rely upon his understanding and integrity for resisting all the temptations of ambition, and especially *of being first*, which I know will be industriously thrown in his way, and contrasted with that second and subordinate situation to which they will insinuate, he must be confined while he continues to act in the general system."

Pitt was not now to be first. But he accepted the great office of Chancellor of the Exchequer, with practically the lead of the House of Commons. His own letters betray no exultation; they speak the indifference not of affectation or satiety, but of long preparation and habitual self-control. "Lord Rockingham's death took place yesterday morning. What the consequences of it will be to the public cannot yet quite be foreseen. With regard to myself, I believe the arrangement may be of a sort in which I *may*, and probably *ought*, to take a part. If I do, I think I need not say you pretty well know the principles on which I shall do it. In this short time nothing is settled, and I only saw what were the strong wishes of *some* who foresaw the event." These sentences are remarkable not merely for their serene simplicity, but also because they show that Pitt the very day after Rockingham's death wrote of his accession to office as a settled affair between himself and those who had foreseen the event. Both parts of the administration, indeed, had long been preparing for it. Fox and Burke on the one side, who were ready with their candidate for the succession; on the other Shelburne and the King, with Pitt as their trump card. Both sides concealed their hands. "Lord Shelburne," wrote the King, on the morning of Rockingham's death, "must see, I am certain, with no small degree of resentment the total ignorance that those who have governed Lord Rockingham cautiously try to keep both me and him in as to the desperate state of that Lord, which certainly is with a view to some arrangement of their own. From the language of Mr. Fitzpatrick it would seem that Lord Shelburne has no chance of being able to coalesce with Mr. Fox; it may not be necessary to remove him at once, but if Lord Shelburne accepts the Head of the Treasury, and is succeeded by Mr. Pitt as Secretary for the Home Department and British Dominions, then it will be seen how far he would submit to it."

While Fox, then, by a resignation which bore too much the appearance of pique, was alienating the sympathies of the public, which by further indiscretion he was within a few months to lose altogether, Pitt, by blameless accession to high office when just twenty-three years of age, was further to attract popular interest and confidence. It is impossible, henceforth, to separate the lives of the two men: and here, where they first come into collision, there is so much of the contrast of the Idle and Industrious Apprentice between them, that one is irresistibly reminded of Hogarth's famous designs. It is so rare to detect the disciplined youth of Pitt in a slip of judgment. He moves steadily and almost irresistibly onwards, with a cold calmness which seems to govern where perhaps it only skilfully adapts itself to events. On the other hand, Fox, ten years older in age, and fully twelve in political life, who at twenty-three was not less famous, was still, by headstrong impulses and a generous tendency to extremes, committing and recommitting all the errors of his youth. Pitt perhaps was never young, and Fox certainly could never have been old.

So close is the connection of the two lives that it is impossible to sketch the career of Pitt without describing the character of Fox, if for this reason alone, that had it not been for that character and its faults Pitt could certainly not have retained, and possibly could not have obtained, the premiership. It may be said once for all that Fox was the greatest of all debaters, the most genial of all associates, the most honourable of all friends. He was moreover, after Burke, the most lettered man in politics among a generation that affected literature. His public career had been one of expansion. Beginning life as a High Tory, he rebounded briskly into the ranks of Whiggery and ultimately of Radicalism. This final phase may have been partly due to his long exclusion from office and to resentment at the unconstitutional vindictiveness of his sovereign, but it was mainly owing to the genial kindness and warm sympathies of his nature :—" large was his bounty and his soul sincere." His was in truth a large, bountiful, outspoken soul. Wherever he saw what he believed to be oppression, he took part with the oppressed—the American, the Irishman, the Negro : he could not side with what he thought wrong against what he thought right, even though they who seemed to him in the right were the enemies of his country. This extreme abstraction of principle was perhaps unconsciously aided by the fact that his country in these contests was often guided by his political foes. Hence his private correspondence is not always pleasant reading. "An expedition is, after all, gone to France, under General Doyle, consisting of 4000 British, besides emigrants, etc. . . . I think nothing can show the complete infatuation of our Government so much as this desperate expedition, which, *I believe as well as hope*, has not the smallest chance of success." And of Trafalgar he has nothing better to say than that, "by its solid as well as brilliant advantages, it far more than compensates for the temporary succour which it will certainly afford Pitt in his distress." To complete these painful extracts, he writes in 1801: "To tell the truth, I am gone something further in hate to the English Government than perhaps you and the rest of my friends are, and certainly further than can with prudence be avowed. The triumph of the French Government over the English does in fact afford me a degree of pleasure which it is very difficult to disguise."

The cosmopolitan character of his liberalism was thus either above or below humanity, either superhuman or not human enough. This exaggeration was probably due to his oratorical temperament. His nature, apt to extremes, was driven with an excessive reaction to the most violent negative of what he disapproved. We see the same excess in a still greater degree in his still greater master Burke. It is this force of extremes that makes orators, and for them it is indispensable. Few supreme parliamentary speeches have perhaps ever been delivered by orators who have been unable to convince themselves, not merely that they are absolutely in the right, but that their opponents are absolutely in the wrong, and the most abandoned of scoundrels to boot, for holding a contrary opinion. No less a force, no feebler flame than this will sway or incense the mixed temperaments of mankind. The mastering passion of Fox's mature life was the love of liberty: it is this which made him take a vigorous, occasionally an intemperate, part against every man or measure in which he could trace the taint or tendency to oppression: it is this which sometimes made him write and speak with unworthy bitterness: but it is this which gave him moral power, which has neutralised the errors of his political career, which makes his faults forgotten and his memory sweet.

His fatal defect as a statesman was want of judgment: he was vehement, passionate, carried away by the impulse of the day, without a thought of the morrow, still less of the day after. "The present day," Metternich used to say, "has no value for me except as the eve of to-morrow: it is with to-morrow that my spirit wrestles." This sublime disregard of to-day can have no place in the politics of a parliamentary country, but the disregard of to-morrow is scarcely less dangerous. Fox could, indeed, lay down principles for all time, but, the moment the game was afoot, they ceased to govern his conduct. Had it not been for this, he would have been the most powerful and popular minister this country has ever known: as it was, he scarcely held office at all. A life of dissipation, hardly paralleled in that dissipated age, did not leave him the coolness or balance which would have made him a match for Pitt: his private life too much influenced his public conduct. At the gaming table he had indeed learned to endure with dauntless bearing the frowns of fortune, whether in politics or at hazard. He had too discovered the charms of that fascinating freemasonry which made the members of Brooks's patiently pay his card debts: but his experience of play had also taught him a low estimate of human nature, a sort of gambling spirit in public affairs.

It is necessary to recall some of Fox's failings and drawbacks, because otherwise it is not possible to understand how, in a country like England, so great a political force did not obtain political supremacy. To comprehend the full prodigy of his parliamentary powers a single example will suffice: it is enough to read Pitt's great speech of the 3d of February 1800, and the reply which Fox delivered the moment he sate down. The first is a magnificent effort, but the second in dissolvent and pulverising power is superhuman. This is not the place to inquire whether, in these days of verbatim reports and greater pressure on time, Fox would have done so much; but it is clear that, under every imaginable condition of discussion, he must have been a giant, and that powers which could make an audience forget his coarse features, his unwieldy corpulence, his slovenly appearance, his excessive repetition, and his ungraceful action, would have overcome any obstacles.

Putting his fashionable vices aside, he reminds one of another colossal figure; another reformer who, though religious rather than political, was not less bold, not less stormy, not less occasionally wrong-headed. To some it may appear a profanation to compare Fox with the German Apostle of light and freedom. But with his passion, his power, his courage, his openness, his flashes of imagination, his sympathetic errors, above all his supreme humanity, Fox was a sort of lax Luther, with the splendid faults and qualities of the great reformer. Whether he would have been a great administrator, we cannot tell; he had no opportunity and we have no experience: his marvellous abilities were almost always exercised in opposition.

In him, therefore, we have only a portion of the life of a statesman: we judge of him as the limb of a fossil monster or the torso of a Greek god; and it is difficult, in judging from the part we possess, to place any bounds on our estimate of the possibilities of the whole.

It has been said that his private life was conspicuously disordered. And yet even when it was blamable it was lovable, and it mellowed into an exquisite evening. Whether we see him plunged in Theocritus after a bout at faro which has left him penniless; or cheerfully watching the bailiffs remove his last stick of furniture; or drinking with the Jockey of Norfolk; or choosing wild waistcoats at Paris; or building with his own hands his little greenhouse at St. Anne's; or sauntering down its green glades with a book and a friend; or prone without either under a tree in the long summer afternoons; or watching the contests of Newmarket with the rapt frenzy of a boy; or chatting before the races with Windham on the horses of the ancients and the precise meaning of *argutum caput*; or corresponding with Gilbert Wakefield about innumerable other niceties of classical reading; or, when crippled and aged, playing trapball with the children and with more than a child's keenness; or speechless with generous tears in the House of Commons when quivering under the harsh severance of Burke; or calmly on his deathbed reassuring his wife and his nephew;—he still exercises over us something of the unbounded fascination which he wielded over his contemporaries. Scarce one of those contemporaries, whose records we know, but mourned his death as a personal loss. He charmed equally the affections of Carlisle and Fitzpatrick, the meteoric mind of Burke, the pedantic vanity of Parr, the austere virtue of Horner, and the hedgehog soul of Rogers. His nephew, the third Lord Holland, converted his matchless palace at Kensington into a sort of temple in honour of Fox's memory, where historians and poets, and authors and statesmen, vied with each other in burning incense before his shrine. It may fairly be said that the traditional estimate of Fox owes something to Holland House. But without such adventitious aids, he stands forth as the negation of cant and humbug, a character valuable then, invaluable now; as an intellectual Titan; and as the quick and visible embodiment of every lovable quality in man.

The new splendour of his position did not for a moment affect the head of the young minister. He watched with the same cool vigilance the intoxication of his new chief. Shelburne could not conceal his joy. He had dished Fox. He had retained Richmond and Conway, Camden, Grafton, and Keppel. He had secured the champion who was alone capable of being matched against Fox. The negotiation of the peace would rest with him alone. He believed that he enjoyed the complete favour and confidence of the King, and so would be in reality prime, if not sole, minister. Thus infatuated he proceeded to act alone, and to disgust his colleagues, without securing the King. The astute occupant of the throne never trusted Shelburne, but his reasons for supporting him at this juncture are clear. In the first place, it enabled him to knock the heads of the hated Whigs together, and so compass their destruction. In the next place, the man he most detested was Fox, and the selection of Shelburne would be sure to preserve him at any rate for the time from Fox. In the third place, he had some hopes, real or fanciful, of Shelburne's assisting him to resist the concession of American independence, which Fox was determined to declare. On the very day on which Rockingham died and Shelburne succeeded him, the King wrote to his new minister: "I am apprised that Lord Shelburne, though he has gone great lengths at the expense of his opinion in giving way as to American independence, if it can effect peace, would think he received advice in which his character was not attended to, if he intended to give up that without the price set on it, which alone could make this kingdom consent to it. Besides, he must see that the great success of Lord Rodney's engagement has again roused the nation so far that the peace which would have been acquiesced in three months ago would now be matter of complaint." The first sentence is as obscure in construction as a speech of Cromwell's, but the general meaning is clear enough. The suspicion of contemporary politicians pointed in the same direction, probably without reason. But Shelburne's habitual ambiguity, and his resistance to the proposition of Fox that the independence of America should be recognised as a preliminary, and not as an accompaniment of negotiation, gave some colour to the hopes of the King.

Parliament adjourned almost immediately after the new ministers had taken their seats. There was indeed one animated debate in each House. In the Lords, the Duke of Richmond announced his reasons for remaining in office, and Shelburne took advantage of the discussion to make his ministerial statement. Already there seemed a rift in the lute. Richmond had said that the influence of the Crown in Parliament was to be diminished; this was one of the great principles on which the administration was formed. But Shelburne announced that he was there to defend the King's prerogative. He would not submit to see the King of England converted into a King of the Mahrattas, with a peishwah elected by a few great chiefs. As regards the independence of America, he had been charged with changing his opinion. That was untrue. It had indeed been ever his opinion that the independence of America would be a dreadful blow to the greatness of this country, and that when it should be established the sun of England might be said to have set. To nothing short of necessity, therefore, would he give way on that head. As regards the sunset of England which would follow concession, it was his resolution so to take advantage of the twilight that the country might yet see its orb rise again.

The debate in the Commons was already over. Two days previously, in a crowded house, Coke of Norfolk, who was to refuse from Pitt in 1784 that earldom of Leicester which he was to accept from Melbourne in 1837, called attention to the pension of Barré. It cannot be denied that Shelburne's party, though it hardly numbered a dozen persons, had reason to congratulate itself on the partiality of its leader. To Barré had been given a pension of £3200 a year, and though this enormous sum would not after the payment of taxes and fees net above £2100, enough remained to be, even in those days, a fair subject for parliamentary inquiry. Advantage was also taken of the discussion to allude to the acquisitions of Shelburne's other main supporter,

Dunning, who in the course of the three months' administration had, through his patron, pocketed a pension, a peerage, the duchy of Lancaster for life, and a seat in the Cabinet. Fox made of these grants an opportunity for praising Lord Rockingham, whose only two jobs had been for men unfriendly to him in politics. Thence he diverged into the larger question of his resignation. He seems already to have been conscious that he had made a mistake. Four days before, he had written to Thomas Grenville at Paris: "I feel that my situation in the country, my power, my popularity, my consequence, nay, my character, are all risked;" and Temple, a day earlier, had pointed out to him the invidiousness of resigning on a personal question. In his present speech, therefore, he placed his resignation on grounds of public policy—grounds which can hardly be sustained by evidence. But on Conway's challenging him to show in what respect the principles upon which Rockingham had accepted office had been disregarded, and expressing his own adherence to the principle of measures, not men, Fox rose again, and frankly avowed that one of his main reasons for withdrawal was the handing over to Shelburne of the Treasury and its patronage. To Burke, however, fell the more conspicuous discredit of debate. His tirade against Shelburne outstripped both sense and decency. "He was a man that he could by no means confide in, and he called heaven and earth to witness, so help him God, that he verily believed the present Ministry would be fifty times worse than that of the noble Lord (North) who had lately been reprobated and removed. . . . He meant no offence, but he would speak an honest mind. If Lord Shelburne was not a Catiline or a Borgia in morals, it must not be ascribed to anything but his understanding." Pitt took but little part in the discussion, and that not as a minister. He charged Fox roundly with a dislike to men and not to measures. The uneasiness of Fox was apparent. Again and again did he rise and explain, without apparently satisfying himself or his audience. And so closed the first round between these two great combatants of the political ring.

The summer and autumn months were spent in negotiations. Those in Paris were carried on mainly by Shelburne himself. The retention of Gibraltar was the one point in dispute which appears to have been hotly discussed in the Ministry. George III. was in favour of ceding Gibraltar for some substantial equivalent, on the ground that no settled peace was possible while it was withheld from Spain. Grafton and Shelburne adhered to this view; Richmond, Keppel, and Pitt were hostile to any cession of the monumental fortress. Before Parliament met, the disputes had risen so high that negotiation of another kind was seen to be necessary. Richmond, Grafton, and Keppel were on the brink of resignation. Camden and Temple were extremely discontented, and it was evident that, if the Government was to continue, it must seek reinforcement from the followers of North or the followers of Fox. Shelburne appears to have remained in a sort of fool's paradise to the last. If he had to conclude an alliance with either chief, it would be with North; Pitt, on the other hand, who always declined to associate himself with North, leaned to Fox. But in truth the negotiations were carried on with little spirit.

Shelburne may well have felt that combination between North and Fox was impossible, and that by their division he might govern. Moreover, he was a little weary of his colleagues, and they were heartily sick of him. No one, indeed, ever trusted him; no one ever cared to be long associated with him.

The languid overtures of Shelburne were soon obliterated by arrangements of a more practical character. Adam, George North, and Lord John Townshend, under the sinister supervision of Eden and Loughborough, were actively reconciling the two chiefs of Opposition. Already in the previous August Fox had sent civil messages to North. On the 14th of February they met, and the preliminaries of the treaty were agreed upon. In four and twenty hours the Coalition was complete, and within four days a resolution of censure on the Peace had been carried by a majority of 16. Pitt's speech on this occasion was perhaps the least effective of his life; he had the bad taste to taunt Sheridan with his connection with the stage, and brought on himself the famous retort that the dramatist would be tempted to try an improvement on the Angry Boy in the *Alchemist.* Strangely enough, however, it was the victor in this encounter who seems never to have forgotten or forgiven it.

For some unexplained reason Shelburne did not at once resign, though in a conversation with Dundas on the 12th he had intimated that he considered his ministry as over. On the 21st, the battle was renewed. The allied forces, led by their stalking-horse, the worthy but insipid Cavendish, made another assault. On this occasion Pitt made one of the great speeches of his life. While Fox spoke, the Chancellor of the Exchequer stood holding open with one hand the door behind the Speaker's chair to hear the attack, while he held the basin into which he vomited with the other. But, when Fox sat down, Pitt at once replied in a speech of nearly three hours. His defence of the Peace as a work of necessity, though it does not concern this story, was convincing; the cutting sarcasm with which he denounced the Coalition—an unnatural union of which in the public interest he forbade the banns—is classical; and the quotation with which he closed—the *probamque pauperiem sine dote quæro*—is memorable not only for its appositeness, but for the modesty of its omissions: though public opinion supplied the *virtute meâ me involvo.* Nor did he forget a dignified, yet not extravagant, eulogy of Shelburne. But the opposition again triumphed. Their majority of 17, when viewed in connection with the calculated strength of parties, does not seem exorbitant. Eden, no bad judge, had reckoned the forces under North at 120, those under Fox at 90, and those of the Government at 140. It is clear then that the Coalition must have alienated, or the Peace secured, a considerable number of independent votes.

Shelburne, however, lost no time in resigning, and recommended Pitt to the King as his successor. Every effort was employed to induce the young barrister to accept the first place. But he saw that the fruit was not yet ripe. For a moment he seems to have hesitated. It was urged on him that the allied forces could not long hold together. But it was obvious that when once they had so far forgotten the past as to unite at all, there was nothing in public principle that need afterwards dissever them. To the angry disappointment of the King, who described himself as "one on the edge of a precipice," and as apparently resolved to abdicate rather than submit, he declined the proud post.

This is the first epoch of his career. He had already obtained a first place as an orator; he had held all but the highest office. That, though he was but twenty-three, was now not merely within his grasp, but pressed on him, with authority and with enthusiasm, by Dundas and the King, the two ablest political strategists of the time. So acute a critic as Horace Walpole blames his refusal; but with a judgment which can only be described as consummate, and a self-control which few by any experience attain, the young statesman, able, eloquent, and courageous as he was, refused the splendid prize, and prepared to resume his practice at the bar.

In the meantime the monarch was desperate. He caught at any hint that would save him from Fox. Gower suggested to him that Pitt's cousin, Mr. Thomas Pitt, might be a capable minister. The King replied that he was ready to apply to Mr. Thomas Pitt or Mr. Thomas Anybody. For five weeks did George III. hunt for a Premier. At last he was compelled to yield. Portland became Prime Minister; Fox and North joint-Secretaries of State. They had pressed Pitt to join them, but in vain. As they kissed hands, a humorous bystander predicted their early fall, for he observed George III. turn back his ears and eyes, just like the horse at Astley's when the tailor it had determined to throw was mounting.

Thus was formed the Coalition Ministry of which it is hard to say which was the most complete—the infamy of the proceeding, or the retribution that followed. Fox in 1782 had said of North's government: "From the moment when I shall make any terms with one of them, I will rest satisfied to be called the most infamous of mankind. I would not for an instant think of a coalition with men who in every public and private transaction as ministers have shown themselves void of every principle of honour and honesty. In the hands of such men I would not trust my honour for a minute." He had declared that he could not believe even North's announcement of his own resignation without corroborative evidence. He had urged that North and his colleagues should be brought to trial, and if possible to the scaffold. Later, again, on Shelburne's becoming Prime Minister, he had declared his anticipation that the Government would refrain from no corrupt method of maintaining themselves in power even to the extent of allying themselves with the party of North. Political digestion is tough, but it could not stomach these things. What is also notable, though less remarkable, Fox and North at once assimilated and concluded the very conditions of peace on which they had moved a vote of censure —censure which a cool examination of the articles and of the situation must pronounce factious, and, as coming jointly from the incapable administrator and the fierce opponent of the war, incredible. Grattan once observed that none had heard Fox at his best who had not heard him before the Coalition. Afterwards, the ability remained, but he felt that he had done something that required defence; the mouth still spoke great things, but the swell of soul was no more.

CHAPTER III

ACCESSION TO POWER

On the anniversary of his previous motion for parliamentary reform, Pitt repeated it. It was supported by one and opposed by the other of the two Secretaries of State, and was rejected by 144. A month later he introduced a Bill for the Reform of Abuses in the Public Offices. In his speech he produced the famous allegation that North in the last year of his ministry had been credited with the consumption of £1300 for stationery, of which £340 was for whipcord. The Bill passed languidly through the Commons, but was promptly strangled in the Lords, where the Ministry opposed it with vigour; a proceeding on which the country could not but comment.

In the recess Pitt went abroad for the only time in his life. He was accompanied by his brother-in-law, Eliot, and by Wilberforce. They first established themselves at Rheims, with the view of learning the language, residing for six weeks at the Archbishop's palace. Here Pitt was thrown into close companionship with the prelate's nephew, the young Abbé de Perigord. They were to meet again in 1792, when Talleyrand as a lay diplomatist was negotiating with Pitt as an autocratic prime minister. Nor did he make much progress in French, though he proceeded to Paris, and thence to Versailles. The son of Chatham could not fail to make a stir in that volatile and curious court; it is even asserted that he narrowly escaped marriage with the daughter of Necker who was afterwards to talk down Europe and write *Corinne*. The queen, indeed, is said to have considered the young lion awkward and dull, and so called forth the pun of Chastellux: "C'est égal: il ne s'en dépitera pas pour ça," but the politicians came round him "in shoals." Two remarks of his during that visit have been preserved—one on the English, the other on the French constitution. Of the first he said: "The part of our constitution which will first perish is the prerogative of the king and the authority of the House of Peers." Of the second he remarked to a Frenchman, "You have no political liberty, but as to civil liberty you have more of it than you suppose." It was here, too, that he paid his famous tribute, not less generous than true, to Fox. Some one expressed surprise that a man of so little character should wield so great an influence. "The remark is just," replied Pitt, "but then you have not been under the wand of the magician." He is said also to have astonished Franklin not merely by his talents, but by the ante-republican character of his sentiments. For the rest, he seems to have hunted and amused himself. He returned to England on the 24th of October (1783). Parliament met on the 11th of November; on the 18th Fox asked for leave to introduce a Bill for the Better Government of India. That day month the Government had ceased to exist.

Into the merits of the Bill it is not now necessary to enter. North, when he saw it, sagaciously described it as "a good receipt to knock up an administration"; in its scope and audacity it savoured even more of the elder than the younger Fox. The objections to its main provision, which handed over the government of India to irremovable commissioners named for four years, have been perhaps overstated. But it was clear that it furnished an admirable weapon against an unpopular Coalition which had resisted economical reform, demanded a great income for a debauched prince, and which now aimed at securing a monopoly of the vast patronage of India,—patronage which, genially exercised by Dundas, was soon to secure Scotland for Pitt. In the House of Commons the majority for the Bill was over 100; the loftiest eloquence of Burke was exerted in its favour; and Fox was, as ever, dauntless and crushing in debate. But outside Parliament the King schemed, and controversy raged. There was a storm of caricatures. One of these, by Sayer, of Fox as an Oriental potentate entering Downing Street on an elephant, Fox himself admitted had greatly damaged him. When the Bill arrived at the House of Lords, the undertakers were ready. The King had seen Temple, and empowered him to communicate to all whom it might concern his august disapprobation. The uneasy whisper circulated, and the joints of the lords became as water. The peers, who yearned for lieutenancies or regiments, for stars or strawberry leaves; the prelates, who sought a larger sphere of usefulness; the minions of the bedchamber and the janissaries of the closet; all, temporal or spiritual, whose convictions were unequal to their appetite, rallied to the royal nod.

Some great nobles, such as Gower and Bridgewater, the one old, the other indifferent to politics, roused themselves to violent exertion on the same side, keeping open tables, and holding hourly conclaves. The result was overwhelming. The triumphant Coalition was paralysed by the rejection of their Bill. They rightly refused to resign, but the King could not sleep until he had resumed the seals. Late at night he sent for them. The messenger found North and Fox gaily seated at supper with their followers. At first he was not believed. "The King would not dare do it," exclaimed Fox. But the under Secretary charged with the message soon convinced them of its authenticity, and the seals were delivered with a light heart. In such dramatic fashion, and the springtide of its youth, fell that famous government, unhonoured and unwept. "England," once said Mr. Disraeli, "does not love coalitions." She certainly did not love this one.

On this occasion there was neither hesitation nor delay; the moment had come, and the man. Within twelve hours of the King's receiving the seals, Pitt had accepted the First Lordship of the Treasury and the Chancellorship of the Exchequer. That afternoon his writ was moved amid universal derision. And so commenced a supreme and unbroken Ministry of seventeen years.

Those who laughed were hardly blamable, for the difficulties were tremendous. Temple, who acted as Secretary of State, resigned in three days, having demanded apparently too considerable a reward for his services. To the young Minister, his first cousin, this was a cruel blow; but Pitt never faltered, though it gave him a sleepless night; while Temple retired in sullen magnificence to Stowe. On the other hand, the Opposition, already in high and hysterical spirits, were proportionately elated. "This boyish prank," writes Elliot, a shrewd and able Whig, "is already over." Probably "they (the embryo Government) mean to gain a few days' time, and to wear some sort of countenance in order to make a capitulation, if it can be obtained. *They have lost all character*," continues the supporter of the Coalition, "and are considered as a set of children playing at ministers, and must be sent back to school; and in a few days all will have returned to its usual course."

Pitt's friends seem largely to have shared the views of his enemies. Camden, the devoted friend of Chatham, and Grafton, whom Chatham had made Prime Minister, both refused office. For Secretaries of State he had to fall back on Tommy Townshend, now chiefly remembered by Goldsmith's famous line, who had become Lord Sydney; and the young Marquis of Carmarthen, who was upright and well intentioned, but vain and inadequate. He secured, indeed, the scowling hypocrisy of Thurlow and the naval fame of Howe; but the one was insidious and the other dumb. It is always difficult to understand the principles on which the Cabinets of the eighteenth century were formed. Pitt's was a procession of ornamental phantoms. He himself was the only Cabinet minister in the House of Commons. Dundas, the Lord Advocate and Treasurer of the Navy, who was to be his right-hand man from the beginning to the end of this administration, was outside the Cabinet. Of the Cabinet ministers, five occupied in solemn silence the front bench of the House of Lords; while Thurlow on the wool-sack, though he often spoke, as often as not did so in opposition to the Government. Never was there in appearance, to use Charles Townshend's graphic phrase, such a lute-string administration.

There was one remarkable omission; nothing was offered to Shelburne. At first sight this can only seem attributable to gross imbecility or flagrant ingratitude. That Pitt, who was gasping in a famine of capacity, should pass by the ablest statesman available, savours of insanity. That he should deliberately and without any political difference ignore the Minister who had a few months before given him the lead of the House of Commons, on whom at the moment of resignation he had passed significant eulogy, and who had been his father's closest adherent in public life, seems so incredibly ungracious as to leave a stain on Pitt's memory. But his action was deliberate: it had been determined months before. To clear Pitt, one must understand Shelburne. And in any case it is not amiss to pause a moment by the complex character of the politician who introduced Pitt to official life; whose fate it has been to be utilised as a political stage-property by a brilliant novelist, who was also a prime minister; and who is variously represented as a popular statesman crushed in the contest with a Venetian constitution, or a sinister schemer of unusual guile. But he was neither a Canning nor a Dodington, though his career presents strange complications.

The problem may be briefly stated thus. How is it that a noble of high lineage and fortune, of great talents, and of an intelligence superior to his talents, who was a distinguished soldier before he was twenty-four; who was a Cabinet Minister at twenty-five, and a Secretary of State at twenty-nine, when Secretaries of State often represented a greater power than the Minister nominally first; who was Prime Minister at forty-five; and who, to pass beyond dignities, was far beyond his age in enlightenment; a Free Trader, the friend of men like Franklin and Bentham and Morellet, the leader of men like Dunning and Barré; who, if not the friend, had at least the courage to be the admirer, of the successful rebel Washington, with whom he had to sign peace;—how was it that this man, so rarely gifted and with opportunities so splendid, should only have touched power to be compelled to relinquish it, and to spend the remainder of his life under universal detestation and distrust? These phrases are unhappily not too strong. It is not too much to say that, during the last decade of this century, the greatest reproach that could be directed against a statesman, short of calling him a Jacobin, was to insinuate a connection with Berkeley Square, where Shelburne had completed the palace which Bute had been forced to forsake.

The key to the enigma seems to lie in the bitter description which he penned of Chatham in his cynical but priceless fragment of autobiography; when he contemptuously dismisses the popular conception of his leader, and pronounces him to be a mere actor, incapable of friendship, anything but disinterested, studied and artificial in all that he wrote or said or did. This was what the man who had gloried in being Chatham's right-hand man, wrote of Chatham when Chatham was dust and his lieutenant forgotten. Elaborate and picturesque as it is, it discloses the fury of a disappointed man wreaked on the cause to which he attributes his failure. It is the sneer of a worshipper burning the idol which he thinks has betrayed him, and attempting to warm himself at the fire. He had ruined his life by a great mistake; he had misread his lesson and misunderstood his master; but the fault, as is usual, seemed to the pupil not to be with himself, but with his teacher. After a cool survey of Bute and Holland, and the politicians of that kidney, he had decided that Chatham was the grand type, and only discovered too late that it was also an impossible one. He could readily see that he must be satisfied with less eloquence and a paler fire; but what seemed within his reach was the patriotic spirit, the attempt to be above and aloof from party, the combination by which the popular prophet cringed before the King; easy to emulate were the mysterious retirement and the haughty demeanour, easiest of all, the pompous fawning style which befogged and bewildered Chatham's contemporaries. All this Shelburne compassed, but what he never understood, until it was too late, was that these were not Chatham's aids but Chatham's drawbacks. There was something in the man, who almost discovered popular feeling in England, which was akin to inspiration; at any rate there was the occasional flash lighting up all his nature—the low and the dark as well as the brilliant and the sublime, the purlieus as well as the majesty of the structure,—which dazzled the beholder into seeing nothing but a great splendour.

Chatham had and sought no friends. The only shadow of such a relation that he knew was in his wife's unamiable family. Shelburne was, like Camden and Grafton, merely the superior disciple, and he was slow in discovering the difficulty of treading in the teacher's steps. In the meantime, having earlier in life gravely compromised his reputation for sincerity in a transaction which the popular and plausible Holland loudly stigmatised as a fraud, he further confirmed the general opinion of his subtlety by his imitation of his master in a sort of stilted finesse. He himself indefinitely strengthened this impression by his constant professions of guileless simplicity, and of a candour so effusive as to compel him to live in retirement for fear of self-betrayal. Lampoons and caricatures are unanimous on this point.

The testimony of his friends is only different in degree. Bentham extols his heart at the expense of his understanding, and charitably attributes the ambiguity of his patron to confusion of mind. But he admits a "wildness about him," and that he "conceived groundless suspicions about nothing at all." Further, Bentham declares that Shelburne "had a sort of systematic plan of gaining people." The third Lord Holland, who avows his partiality, gives much the same opinion. Rose, who was naturally and officially a judge of character, speaks of his discomfort in acting with Shelburne, who was "sometimes passionate or unreasonable, occasionally betraying suspicions of others entirely groundless, and at other times offensively flattering. I have frequently been puzzled to decide which part of his conduct was least to be tolerated." Perhaps an even more curious confirmation is afforded by Rayneval, who visited England as an envoy during the peace negotiations. "Lord Shelburne," he writes, "is not ignorant of the suspicions which have been, and probably still are, entertained in France as to his straightforwardness, and he feels them—the more in proportion as he believes that he has not deserved them. I venture to be of the same opinion, and if I say so, it is because I consider my personal acquaintance and conversations with Lord Shelburne have placed me in a position to know him personally," and so forth. This was in the middle of September 1782, and in December he writes, "You will perhaps ask me how it is possible to reconcile the character I gave you of Lord Shelburne with his conduct relative to the equivalent for Gibraltar," and then he explains. There lies the whole matter—Shelburne's good faith was always exemplary, but always in need of explanation.

Some people seem to think that a reputation worse than his deserts unfairly encumbered his career. But, had his name been as untainted as Bayard's, his style both in writing and speaking would have accounted for the most inveterate distrust. The English love a statesman whom they understand, or at least think that they understand. But who could understand Shelburne? Whether from confusion of head or duplicity of heart his utterances were the very seed of suspicion. The famous lines in the *Rolliad* are merely the versification of a speech he actually delivered.

> A noble Duke affirms I like his plan,
> I never did, my Lords, I never can:
> Shame on the slanderous breath which dares instil
> That I who now condemn advised the ill.
> Plain words thank Heaven are always understood,
> I could approve I said—but not I would,

> Anxious to make the noble duke content,
> My view was just to seem to give consent
> While all the world might see that nothing less was meant.

In 1792 the King asked his advice, and Shelburne gave it in a memorandum which may be commended to any student of the man. It is a mere labyrinth of stilted ambiguities. Take again his speech on the Irish Union, from which both parties to that controversy to this day extract the strongest opinions in support of their respective views. Even his personal appearance, his sleek countenance and beady eye, imply the idea which is conveyed to the ordinary Briton by the word Jesuitical: and the caricatures of the time represent the outer wall of Lansdowne House as a mere rampart to screen his plots.

The pity of it is that his son, with much the same abilities, but richer by the warning, and aiming lower, achieved the position within the father's reach so exactly as to offer a reproachful contrast: the splendid noble, the patron of arts and letters, playing with rare dignity a public part, from duty rather than inclination; sought, not seeking; a strength, instead of a weakness, to his associates; a pillar, not a quicksand.

It was because Pitt had so truly measured Shelburne's character that he preferred any risk and any reproach to including his late chief in his Cabinet. He thus earned Shelburne's undying enmity; but that, as things stood, was rather an advantage than otherwise.

The composition of the Government was, however, the least of Pitt's embarrassments. The majority against him in the House of Commons was not less than forty or fifty, containing, with the exception of Pitt himself and Dundas, every debater of eminence; while he had, before the meeting of Parliament to prepare and to obtain the approval of the East India Company to a scheme which should take the place of Burke's. The Coalition ministers were only dismissed on the 18th of December 1783; but, when the House of Commons met on the 12th of January, 1784 all this had been done.

The narrative of the next three months is stirring to read, but would require too much detail for our limits. Never was excitement so high; never were debates of more sustained and fiery eloquence. But these are like the wars of Marlborough and Turenne,—splendid achievements, which light up the epoch, without exercising a permanent influence on the world; to us at any rate the sheet-lightning of history. On the day of the meeting of Parliament, Pitt was defeated in two pitched divisions, the majorities against him being 39 and 54. His government seemed still-born. His colleagues were dismayed. The King came up from Windsor to support him. But in truth he needed no support. He had inherited from his father that confidence which made Chatham once say, "I am sure that I can save this country, and that nobody else can;" which made himself say later, "I place much dependence on my new colleagues; I place still more dependence on myself." He had refused, in spite of the King's insistence, to dissolve; for he felt that the country required time, and that at the first blush it could hardly be expected to support so raw a Government. But he was daily preparing for the inevitable dispersal of a House of Commons sworn to hostility. To gratify the independent members, he dallied with some idle negotiations for the conciliation of the Portland Whigs. He was able to show that the House of Lords was with him by a division in his favour of 100 to 53. He displayed the confidence of the King, who had refused to grant any honours at the instance of the Coalition, by the creation of several peerages. The city of London, then the stronghold of Liberalism, vindicated him from the suspicion of being a mere tool of the Court by giving him its freedom. The East India Company spared no exertion. They established a Committee of Vigilance that sate permanently in Leadenhall Street. To every borough in the country they sent a copy of Fox's bill with this message, "Our property and charter are invaded, look to your own."

Two accidental circumstances also occurred to Pitt's advantage. On his return from his city triumph, he was waylaid and nearly murdered by an ambuscade of blackguards opposite Brooks's club. So low had Fox fallen as to be accused of instigating this outrage,—an imputation which no one otherwise would have credited a moment, but against which he thought it worth while to frame an indecorous alibi. This occurrence would, perhaps unreasonably, serve to attract the sympathy of Englishmen to the mob's victim, but another secured it. The Clerkship of the Pells, a sinecure office worth not less than £3000 a year, fell vacant the very day that Parliament met. It was universally expected that Pitt would take it as of right, and so acquire an independence, which would enable him to devote his life to politics, without care for the morrow. He had not £300 a year; his position was to the last degree precarious. If now defeated, it was clear that he would meet with no mercy, and that the King and the country would fall bound into the hands of the Coalition, who might almost achieve a permanent oligarchy to his permanent exclusion. Pitt disappointed his friends and amazed his enemies. He gave the place to Barré, making it a condition that Barré should resign the pension received from Rockingham. To a nation inured to jobs this came as a revelation. They were familiar with great orators, and they had seen most of them provided at one time or another with sinecures and pensions, but here was a youth of equal ability to whom it did not seem to occur to place his own fortunes in competition with the commonwealth—to whom money that could benefit the State was abhorrent. Even Thurlow could not refrain from a growl of admiration.

Above and beyond all was the fact that Pitt, young, unaided, and alone, held his own with the great leaders allied against him. Exposed to the heaviest artillery that wit and fury and eloquence could bring to bear, he was never swayed or silenced. In face of so resolute a resistance, the assailants began to melt away. Their divisions, though they always showed a superiority to the Government, betrayed notable diminution; and, large or small, seemed to produce no more effect on the administration than if they were the votes of a college debating society. Worse than all, they had an uneasy consciousness, ripening daily into certainty, that the country was not with them. Addresses were pouring in, to applaud the conduct of the King in dismissing the Coalition. Fox, moreover, found that his party would not join him in stopping the supplies. His one resource was a short Mutiny Bill, which would prevent sudden or premature dissolution. The current Bill would expire on the 25th of March. Ministers were in a state of perplexity and alarm. Burges, then Under Secretary of State, who was, however, too vain a man to be a perfectly trustworthy authority, relates that they were relieved by a simple expedient. It was found that more than once the Mutiny Bill had been introduced into the House of Lords, and coming thence passed without question in the House of Commons. Such a solution would not be possible now, but it was adequate then. Pitt enclosed the paper of precedents in a note to Fox, asking what course he intended to take. His answer is not known, though sufficiently indicated by the result. When the Committee on the Mutiny Bill was moved, only two members showed themselves in opposition.

This was on the 9th of March. On the 25th of March Parliament was dissolved, the announcement being retarded by the unexplained theft of the Great Seal. When the elections were over, the party of Fox, it was found, had shared the fate of the host of Sennacherib. The number of Fox's martyrs—of Fox's followers who had earned that nickname by losing their seats—was 160. He himself had to await, in the constituency of Orkney, the result of a scrutiny at Westminster, for which he had been chosen. Conway and Lord John Cavendish, two Whig princes, succumbed. Coke, the Lord of Norfolk, shrank before the storm. The unknown and plebeian Wilberforce triumphed over the Whig aristocracy of Yorkshire. Pitt himself forsook the inglorious security of Appleby, and stood in the van of the battle as candidate for the University of Cambridge, which had before rejected him. He ousted the two Coalition members, and secured the seat for life.

He won all along the line, but watched the last and longest contest with undisguised anxiety. Fox was carrying on one of those interminable combats which gave a singular celebrity to the constituency of Westminster. The poll was open for forty days. No effort was spared. Promises and menaces and drink and cash were all lavishly given; the proudest ladies stepped into the purlieus of the ancient city to secure highly flavoured votes; the Heir to the Throne himself participated. In this respect the contest was unequal. On the side of Fox's opponent Lady Salisbury took the field; but her haughty canvass was easily routed by the energy, spirit, and grace of Georgiana, Duchess of Devonshire. At last, the first ministerial candidate headed the poll; but Fox easily distanced the second.

It was his only solace. On the other hand, he was excluded from office, with the exception of a few dying months, for life; more bitter still, he had to witness the complete triumph of the youth whom he could hardly yet consider a rival. Pitt, with the entire confidence of the King and the Legislature, was entrusted with a power such as no minister had ever wielded since the Revolution. And he was not yet twenty-five.

It is well here for a moment to pause and, with an undazzled eye, take stock of this splendid occasion. To idle observers it may appear that Pitt occupied his place by mere prerogative, aided by popular aversion to the Coalition. This is only a fraction of the truth. Fox, who had lately been the idol of the people, would have been supported by the constituencies against the prerogative, never popular, and against the King who had not then attained popularity, had the case been so simple; for they would have forgotten the Coalition in resentment against the arbitrary authority of the monarch. But, as it was, the unpopularity of the King was obliterated for ever by the odium of the Coalition. Nor was North personally an object of aversion. After his resignation, he made a tour in the country, during which he received ovations at once unexpected and unusual. The truth lies much deeper. The King and Pitt were supported on the tidal wave of one of those great convulsions of feeling, which in Great Britain relieve and express pent-up national sentiment, and which in other nations produce revolutions. "The Public," says a shrewd contemporary observer, "and the Public only, enabled Pitt to defeat the powerful phalanx drawn up against him."

The country was sick of the "old lot"—the politicians who had fought and embraced and intrigued and jobbed among themselves, with the result of landing Great Britain in an abyss of disaster and discomfiture, such as she had never known since the Dutch ships sailed up the Medway. For eight years there had been war against scattered plantations of our own race, war ending in complete discomfiture; to which had been superadded the perhaps more poignant humiliation of being compelled to yield, not merely to the colonists, but to the French. And as, when the Dutch were insulting and threatening the metropolis, the memories of men recurred to the supremacy of Cromwell but a few years before, so now there was an additional sting to those still alive who remembered the glories of Chatham. Since then, at an expenditure of a hundred and forty millions, through eight agonising years, Englishmen had seen their armies in a constant condition of capitulation or defeat. They had hired Germans by the thousand to shoot down American Englishmen in vain. They had employed Red Indians to tomahawk their brethren without effect. Paul Jones had harried the coasts of Scotland, and people long remembered how the pious folk of Kirkcaldy had watched and prayed while his ships hove to within a mile of their shore. That night, by an interposition which the least devout hailed as a direct result of intercession, a gale arose and drove the flotilla away; but far in the Firth of Forth the traveller can still perceive, almost lost in a gaunt pier of the great bridge, the little simple fortification, which was erected against the audacious privateer. They had seen the fleet of England retiring before the squadrons of France and Spain, and yielding to them the dominion of the British Channel. Even the splendour of Rodney could not atone for this; while his instant supersession increased their distrust of the Government. They had seen their ambassadors suing for assistance at European courts in terms almost abject, and repulsed in terms of candid contempt. It was universally admitted that Great Britain had sunk to be a second, if not a third, rate Power. And if they were thus considered abroad, what was there to console our forefathers at home? They had beheld their capital half burned to the ground by mobs, which the Ministry seemed as unable to control as the people of New England. They had seen Government, in the sheer shame of impotence, obliged to cede to Ireland whatever of independence the Dublin Parliament demanded, from the impossibility of sending a regiment to defend the island. What might have been an act of grace, was only another abasement. There was not a drop wanting to their cup of bitterness. Was it for this they had spent their treasure and their armies? There was something rotten in the State, and the rottenness seemed to begin in their politicians.

The English mind moves slowly, but with exceeding sureness, and it had reached this point at the election of 1784. The people had looked for a cause of these manifold effects, and had found it in their rulers. Any doubts they may have entertained would have been dispelled by the speeches of Burke on economical, and of Pitt on parliamentary, reform. At the beginning of the reign they had fancied that the Scots were at the root of the evil. But, though Bute had long passed away from the political scene, matters had grown worse. And now they found it authoritatively declared how deep the gangrene of jobbery had eaten into the House of Commons; how one member received a large income as turnspit to the King; and how eight were purchased and nominated by an Indian prince. Taxes might grow, and armies might disappear, and the gazettes might reek of disgrace: still, war loans and war contracts swelled the spawn of corruption: still, successive ministers and their friends filled their bottomless pockets, and found a solid set-off to national dishonour in the pickings of national profusion. Under North, political degradation seemed to have reached its climax. There had been hope, indeed, of Fox, who had denounced North in terms of masculine and indignant invective. But now he too had embraced North; the accuser had sat down with the accused, and both were involved without nice discrimination in the common system of turpitude. As to the Whig figure-heads, they were possibly honest but certainly wooden. In their despair, men looked round for a saviour of society, who should cast the money-changers out of the temple of Government, and restore to Britain, not her former glory indeed, but a decent and honourable existence. At this moment, there appeared before them a young university student; rich with lofty eloquence and heir to an immortal name; untainted in character, spotless in life; who showed the very first day that he met Parliament as Minister a supreme disdain for the material prizes of political life. The auspices under which he obtained power were not indeed popular, but less odious than the combination he succeeded. To a jaded and humiliated generation the son of Chatham came as a new hope and a possible revelation. Here was one who would not be easily corrupted; nay, one who might stem the tide flowing so fast against us at home and abroad. In a few months, the elder Pitt had raised England from the ground and placed her at the head of Europe. Might not something be hoped of his son?

The change was thus not merely an epoch in the life of Pitt, but in English politics. It was hailed by the nation as a new departure. Nor did the situation lack the irony inseparable from great events; for there were piquant elements of miscalculation and anomaly. The anomaly lay with Pitt, the miscalculation with the King. Pitt, who had entered Parliament as a foe to prerogative and the friend of reform, was to become Prime Minister by a violent exercise of the one, and to lose sight for ever, with a faint exception, of the other. On the other hand, the risk run by the King had been immense: and it is only fair to say he had made proof of rare and signal courage. For he had played on the throw all that to him made a throne worth having. The general election of May, indeed, condoned his absolute action of December. But, had it fallen differently, he must have become as much the prisoner of party as Louis XVI. on his return from Varennes. And yet, while he stood to lose so much, his winnings, as he computed them, were small. He had reckoned on finding a minister who would execute his wishes, and be the pliant agent of a powerful monarch. But there is little doubt that in ridding himself of the tyranny of the Whigs, with the assistance of Pitt, he only exchanged one bondage for another. He had worked to procure for Pitt the majority which was henceforth to make Pitt independent of himself. There is evidence to show that from the first he dreaded, and in the end disliked, his too powerful minister. In their correspondence we find none of the fondness with which George III. addressed Addington or Eldon. The King's tone is rather that of a man in embarrassed circumstances, corresponding with the family solicitor. He was sensible that Pitt had him in his power, and that, should Pitt desert him, he must fall bound into the hands of Fox. Later on, he was suspected of meditating a possible resource in Grenville. But we doubt his seriously contemplating an emancipation from Pitt so long as Pitt, and indeed so long as Fox, should last. For the peculiarity of the position was that, apart from his own great qualities, the strength of Pitt lay in the aversion of both King and people for Fox. Just as in the opinion of the shrewd Auckland the opposition of Fox had kept North in office, so now it largely helped to sustain Pitt. Incapacity could not long have reposed on mistrust; but so able and honest a Minister was served to the end of his life by the generous extravagances of Fox and the undying memory of the Coalition.

CHAPTER IV

FIRST YEARS OF ADMINISTRATION

THE first days of Pitt's power are not altogether pleasant to contemplate. His demeanour was unendurably cold and repellent. He felt perhaps that it was necessary for so young a minister to hold mankind at a distance; or what had before been called shyness was now called pride. At any rate, as the kind Wilberforce regretfully notes, he did not make friends. His father had kept two generations in a state of subjection and awe, but Chatham was a consummate actor, and Pitt was not. It is told of Chatham that when he met a bishop, he bowed so low that his nose could be seen between his knees. So appalling a suavity of demeanour inspired probably even more terror than his intolerable eye. But Pitt's haughtiness was less sardonic; at any rate, it was of a different kind.

His unfortunate bearing did him no good. A graver charge against him at the moment of elevation is his behaviour to Fox. Fox had been returned for Westminster. But the High Bailiff, instead of making a return, sent in a statement of the number severally polled, and an intimation that he had granted a scrutiny;—

a proceeding which could not be constitutional, as it might have excluded Westminster from representation for a whole parliament, should the scrutiny be prolonged into a measure of obstruction. Pitt, however, under the influence of Sir Lloyd Kenyon, Master of the Rolls, sustained the action of the High Bailiff, and met with a well merited rebuff. Nor was his action a mere incident of party warfare. He threw into it all his energies, and the passion of a personal cause. Throughout the general election he had concentrated his attention on Westminster; he had been defeated, and now endeavoured to cover his repulse by proceedings which, as they were not adequate to prevent his powerful rival from sitting in the House of Commons, bore the appearance of personal rancour or personal mortification, and the even baser suspicion of an attempt to finally crush that rival's wrecked fortunes. On this issue Fox put forth new resources and splendours of eloquence. He exceeded himself, by delivering what is often considered as the best of his speeches; and, more remarkable still, so well reported that Lord Holland declared in reading it, he fancied he heard his uncle's voice. But the Minister's resolution was worthy a better cause. Every omen pointed to disaster; the most sinister parliamentary portents and the marked hostility of public opinion failed to deter him. In the face of shrinking majorities, of lukewarm friends, and a reluctant King, he persevered. The result from the first was discouraging, and soon ended in collapse. His majority on the address had been 168. But in the first division on the scrutiny it fell to 97. Within three weeks it sunk to 78, at the very moment when his majority on the India Bill was 211.

In the next session he fared worse, for on the 9th of February 1785 it had dwindled to 39. On the 21st of February it was but nine; while on the 4th of March Pitt found himself defeated by 38 votes; and the High Bailiff was compelled to make an immediate return. Pitt had mistaken the temper of the nation, and the complexion of his party. Englishmen delight in a fair fight and a fair victory; but nothing is so revolting to them as anything which bears the semblance of ungenerous treatment of a fallen enemy. The feeling of the country was reflected in his followers, who displayed more independence than Pitt had conceived possible. In this particular case, the demonstration against him was manly and justified. It is one of the rare occasions on which his parliamentary tact failed him; perhaps the only instance of personal pettiness to which he ever condescended. If it is not a surprising lapse of judgment and temper in a man of twenty-four, it is amazing when the general tenor of his character and career is considered.

If Pitt sustained humiliation on the scrutiny, it was forgotten in the general lustre of his statesmanship. In the interval between the 19th of December and the 12th of January he had not merely formed his Government, but he had prepared and procured the consent of the East India Company to a new India Bill. It had met, of course, with no mercy in debate, but had only been rejected by a reluctant majority of eight. He now reintroduced substantially the same measure, and obtained a division of 271 to 60 in its favour. It instituted that complex system of government and that Board of Control, which endured till the Act of 1858.

But in comparing it with Fox's notorious Bill, it is fair to make one remark. Fox had proposed to hand over the patronage and power of India to irremovable Commissioners for four years. It was urged against this scheme that by it, Fox, in or out of office, would have through his appointed Commissioners all the patronage of the East; and that for four years, whoever might rule in England, he would rule in India. The same objection might, however, be urged against any new body of Commissioners appointed under party government; and so far as patronage was concerned, it could hardly have been exercised in a more partisan spirit for four years under Fox's arrangement, than it was under Pitt's for eighteen. Wielded by Dundas in dexterous combination, he so arranged it, no doubt for the mutual benefit of both, that the Eastern Empire of which he was the trustee should be enriched by an unceasing immigration from his own kingdom of Scotland.

Pitt's chief cares and eminent success of this session were, however, connected with finance. He had in a year of peace to bring forward a war budget, having been left with a deficit of six, and a floating debt of at least fourteen millions, besides a debt of two millions to the Bank of England and the usual deficiencies on the Civil List. Moreover, smuggling had grown to such a height that it required immediate and drastic remedies. The leading features of his financial operations were three. Smuggling was chiefly carried on in tea; it was calculated that the consumption of illicit was double that of duty-paying tea. To meet this, apart from more stringent regulations as regards search, he lowered and varied the tea duty so as to take away the smuggler's probable profit; while he met the deficiency of revenue thus caused by an increase of the window tax. He calculated the population of England to be six millions; four millions of whom, by paying an increased window tax, should bring up the revenue to at least the seven or eight hundred thousand provided by the old tea duty, although they would pay less for their tea, both in window and tea tax, than under the actual tea tax; while the remaining two millions, consuming the cheaper teas and living in houses of less than seven windows, would get their tea duty-free.

The second feature of his financial policy was that, for the loans required to meet the deficit and the floating debt, he accepted the lowest tender by public competition, thus abolishing for ever the corrupt and costly favouritism which had disgraced previous loans. By this single measure he probably did more to purify Parliament than he could have effected by his Reform Bill.

The third was the variety of tax by which he raised the additional revenue required. Hats, raw silk, horses, linens, calicoes, candles, licenses for dealers in excisable commodities, bricks, tiles, shooting certificates, paper, hackney coaches, gold and silver plate, the export of lead, ale-licenses, race-horses, and postage were all taxed to produce some £900,000. On the night of his budget (June 30, 1784) he moved 133 financial resolutions. Some of his proposals, among them a coal tax, had to be modified or withdrawn, and the above is their ultimate form; but Pitt's conciliatory method of explanation produced scarcely less impression than the capacity which he displayed in unfolding them.

The recess, after this busy and eventful session, he spent between Putney and Brighton, studying, in conjunction with Irish ministers and British merchants, the proper measures to give effect to his Irish policy. This period was marked by two incidents—one of transient, the other of permanent importance. The first was the entry into the Ministry of the cautious Camden; the other was the postponement of the opening of Parliament from the usual date at the beginning of November till the end of January.

The Houses met (January, 1785) under the cloud of European disturbances, evolved by the restless ambition of Joseph the Second in the Netherlands; a cloud soon dispelled. As regards domestic affairs, Pitt was able to point to the success of his financial measures. The revenue was displaying unwonted buoyancy; it was advancing by leaps and bounds; and the minister was able to promise the early creation of a sinking fund, so soon as he should have been able to dispose of the floating debts which he had inherited from the war. As to the measures for the suppression of smuggling, Fox himself acknowledged their efficacy. Pitt's reputation as a peace financier was established, and was to suffer no abatement.

His other measures were less successful. He suffered his final rebuff on the Westminster Scrutiny. For the third and, as it proved, for the last time, he brought forward (April 18, 1785) the question of parliamentary reform. He proposed to give seventy-two seats to London and the largest counties; these seventy-two seats to be obtained by the voluntary and compensated surrender of their franchise by thirty-six petty boroughs, while permanent provision was made for the future surrender of such boroughs under similar conditions of compensation and transfer. This last enactment would, he conceived, make his measure final, self-adjusting, and complete, and obviate all necessity for any further reform.

He displayed extraordinary zeal and ability on this occasion. He personally canvassed his friends. He summoned Wilberforce from the Riviera. He adjured the Duke of Rutland to influence from Ireland Yorkshiremen of weight in its favour. He declared to this intimate friend that he regarded the success of his plan as essential to the credit, if not the stability, of his administration, as well as to the good government of the country hereafter. Nay, he even implored the neutrality of the hostile King, which was promised with the sarcastic comment that "The conduct of some of Mr. Pitt's most intimate friends on the Westminster Scrutiny shows that there are questions men will not by friendship be biassed to adopt." The motion was defeated, whether owing to the reluctance of members or the significant silence of the monarch it is difficult to say.

But the capital measure of the session of 1785 concerned Ireland. Pitt's Irish policy was at this time repeatedly defined by himself. It was large and statesmanlike. He accepted as irrevocable the settlement of 1782, which gave Ireland parliamentary independence; and he sought to unite the two countries on the sure basis of commercial intercourse and common interest. Were this accomplished, it would, he believed, remove all possible danger and inconvenience from the duality of legislatures. Nor was it a work that admitted of delay; it had to be done while the new institutions in Ireland and their under-growth of tendencies were still plastic, before gristle had hardened into bone. His aim was to follow up this, the most urgent, with two other measures; one a reform of the Irish Parliament, the other the conversion of the volunteers into a militia. But all hung together, all fell together.

His commercial scheme was embodied in eleven resolutions, concerted in the vacation, and passed by the Irish Parliament just before Pitt presented them to the House of Commons. Their object was to allow the importation, without increase of duty, of all produce from other countries, through Ireland into Great Britain and through Great Britain into Ireland; to reduce the duties on the produce and manufactures of both countries to the scale of that country where the duties were lowest; and to provide a contribution from Ireland to the imperial navy by enacting that, whenever the gross hereditary revenue of Ireland (which then stood at £652,000) should rise above £656,000, the surplus was to be applied to that object; only in a saving clause, introduced in Ireland, this last provision was not to take effect in time of peace, unless there was a just balance between income and expenditure.

Their general scope, however, was tersely embodied in the first resolution: "That Ireland should be admitted to a permanent and irrevocable participation of the commercial advantages of this country, when the Parliament of Ireland shall secure an aid out of the surplus of the hereditary revenue of that kingdom towards defraying the expense of protecting the general commerce of the Empire in time of peace."

Pitt's exposition of his policy was worthy of the subject. He denounced in the strongest terms the past treatment of Ireland by England. Until these last very few years, he said, the system had been that of debarring

Ireland from the use and enjoyment of her own resources; of making that kingdom completely subservient to the interests and opulence of this country; without suffering her to share in the bounties of nature, in the industry of her citizens, or to contribute to the general interests and strength of the Empire. This system had counteracted the kindness of Providence and suspended the enterprise of man. It had been a policy of keeping the smaller country completely subservient and subordinate to the greater; to make the one, as it were, an instrument of advantage; and to make all her efforts operate in favour, and conduce merely to the interest, of the other. But this "system of cruel and abominable restraint" had been exploded, and he aimed at a better, a more natural, and a more equitable relation—a participation and community of benefits and a system of equality and fairness which, without tending to aggrandise the one or to depress the other, should seek the aggregate interests of the Empire. On this general basis he moved his resolutions; he had anxiously searched for the "best means of uniting the two countries by the firmest and most indissoluble bonds"; and this was the result.

As to the equivalent to be received from Ireland in exchange for the commercial advantages conceded to her, it was to be in exact proportion to the benefit she derived from them. From the nature of the Irish hereditary revenue, it would be an ingenious measure of the success of the proposal and the advantage that Ireland would reap from it; while, on the other hand, it would be, by the same process of self-adjustment, scrupulously fair towards England. For it consisted of certain customs-duties, levied on almost every species of goods imported; an excise duty upon some articles of the most general consumption; and a house tax levelled on the number of mouths in each. It was obvious, therefore, that this revenue would necessarily increase, as soon as the new arrangement began to take effect, and in exact proportion to that effect: every article of which it was composed being so closely connected with commerce, wealth, and population. So much for the solace of Ireland. And for the satisfaction of England he pointed out that, if little should be given to England, it was because little had been gained in Ireland; so that, whether much or little should be gained from it, England would have no cause to be dissatisfied; if much should be got, she would be a gainer; if little, it would be a proof that little of the commerce of England had found its way to Ireland, so that there would not be room for jealousy.

The policy and the speech were alike ingenious, fruitful, and statesmanlike; but in England the opposition of apprehensive interests was sustained and bitter. Two months were spent by the House of Commons in the examination and discussion of commercial representatives, headed and guided by Wedgewood. As a result, Pitt found that he could not carry his original propositions. On the 12th of May (1785) he introduced a score of remodelled resolutions. But the amendments added to secure English, hopelessly alienated Irish support. All the new, as compared with the original, articles were restrictive of Irish trade; but the fourth resolution attempted a restraint on the Irish Parliament. It enacted that all laws, which had been or should be passed with reference to navigation in the imperial legislature, should also apply to Ireland by laws to be passed by the Irish Parliament. Fox saw his opportunity. He could not now defeat the propositions in England; but he could secure their rejection in Ireland. With extraordinary power and ability, he thundered against the surrender of legislative independence that the minister was demanding from Ireland. Where ministers, he declared, had not betrayed their imbecility they had been insidious; where they had not been insidious, they had been treacherous. It would have been more manly and more honourable to have plainly told the Irish, "that however desirous and happy we should be to serve you, yet, in justice to our own country, we find we cannot grant what we offered. Without being the ruin of many here, we cannot serve an equal number of you. Without exposing our own country and its manufactures and manufacturers to ruin, or without your yielding up the independency of your Parliament, we cannot grant the participation offered to you." And he bade farewell to the resolutions with the impassioned exclamation, "I will not barter English commerce for Irish slavery; that is not the price I would pay, nor is this the thing I would purchase." In that pithy sentence with consummate dexterity he combined the objections of both the English and the Irish. The note he struck readily resounded in Ireland. Grattan denounced the English propositions in a speech which the Viceroy described as incredibly eloquent, seditious, and inflammatory. Orde, the Chief Secretary, did not venture to proceed with them, and Pitt abandoned them for ever.

So passed away another of the rare and irrevocable opportunities of uniting the two countries. It is impossible to blame the Irish, jealous of any reflection on their new legislative independence, and who had seen the resolutions which they had passed suspiciously transmuted in this direction. Nothing, again, can be more admirable than the energy, the foresight, and the disregard of popular clamour displayed by the young minister. There is also some excuse for the opposition of Fox, because Fox openly professed that he had never been able to understand political economy. But when we consider the object and the price; that the price was free trade and the object commercial and, in all probability, complete union with Ireland; that there was, in fact, no price to pay, but only a double boon, to use Pitt's happy quotation, "twice blessed; it blesseth him that gives and him that takes," it is difficult to avoid the impression that there has been throughout the past history of England and Ireland a malignant fate waving away every auspicious chance, and blighting every opportunity of beneficence as it arises.

At any rate, Pitt, though he at first preserved the confident language of persistence, henceforward abandoned this wise and kindly Irish policy. He felt that the jealousy and prejudice, which had driven Burke from Bristol, had abated little of their rigour; and that Irish national sentiment, rooted deeply in the past, regarded with classical apprehension the very gifts of the English. His impressions were excusable, and even natural, in view of the circumstances of the time. But all parties may well regret that Pitt did not display on this occasion something of the same pertinacity that he did with regard to his later Irish projects. In 1786 he included Ireland in his commercial treaty with France, and Ireland made no objection. This, however, did not encourage him to resume his larger scheme. From this time forward, he appears to have turned his attention from Ireland, or at any rate to have looked more to that legislative union for which his most intimate friends, such as Rutland and Wilberforce, openly expressed their anxiety, and to which another juncture was soon to point.

But the abandonment of the Irish commercial propositions suggests a curious question. Why were they relinquished, and why were so many of the principal Government measures abandoned or defeated? We have seen that in May 1784 the Opposition lay crushed and almost obliterated at Pitt's feet. Since then, he had sustained defeat on the Westminster Scrutiny, on Parliamentary Reform, and had first to remodel and then to withdraw his Irish resolutions; he had also been compelled to take back his coal tax. In 1786 he was defeated on the government scheme of fortifications. In 1788, on the East India Declaratory Bill, he was again run hard, and thought to be in actual jeopardy.

Why was this powerful minister exposed to these rebuffs, in a Parliament elected so entirely for his personal support? The reason is partly particular, and partly general. "It is a very loose Parliament," notes Eden, than whom there was no more acute observer, "and Government has not a decisive hold of it upon any particular question." Pitt soon made the same observation. "Do not imagine," he writes this year, "because we have had two triumphant divisions, that we have everything before us. We have an indefatigable enemy, sharpened by disappointment, watching and improving every opportunity. It has required infinite patience, management, and exertion to meet the clamour out of doors, and to prevent it infecting our supporters in the House. Our majority, though a large one, is composed of men who think, or at least act, so much for themselves, that we are hardly sure from day to day what impression they may receive." It is probable that, in view of Pitt's youth, his plans were not at first received with the confidence to which they were entitled, nor does it ever seem to have occurred to his supporters that any number of defeats of this nature could bring about his resignation. There can be no doubt that he bitterly felt these miscarriages; but it is also clear that no thought of resignation crossed his mind. This in itself would show how different was the condition of the House of Commons of those days from the House of Commons of these.

But the difference lay much deeper. The composition of a parliamentary majority at that time was that of a feudal or a Highland army. It was an aggregate of the followings of a few great chiefs, of whom the King himself was the principal. A powerful leader would make a sign and his followers disappear; one bugle call would be followed by another, until one day the whole array would have melted away, and the general be a lonely fugitive. What Clanronald or Lochiel had been in a military, Lord Lonsdale or the Duke of Norfolk were in a political campaign. And of those who were not at the beck of great mongers, fewer then than now feared the loss of their seat as the consequence of their parliamentary vote. Some sate for family boroughs; some who had paid four or five thousand pounds for their seat, knew that for the same price they could always secure another.

Public opinion, in so far as it existed, was a subtle and indirect influence. The cohesive force of a party lay, not in the power of the people, but in the patronage of the minister. And so we shall find in those days many more instances of a sort of personal independence in the House of Commons than now, and a minister much more frequently at the mercy of Parliament, of the personal pique of some baffled noble, of a Duke of Greenwich alienated by a Lord Oldborough's unsealed letter, of a Temple resentful of withheld dignities. In recent times a government, clearly designated by the result of a general election, can generally remain in office for the duration of a Parliament; as the pressure of the majority, instant and weighty, not merely supports but guides. But, in the last half of the last century, a minister obtained comparatively little assistance from public opinion, while he had to struggle with the secret currents of royal and jobbing intrigue.

A curious illustration of parliamentary government at this time is to be found in an analysis of the House of Commons dated May 1, 1788, which has been recently discovered among the papers of one of Pitt's private secretaries. In it the "party of the Crown" is estimated at 185 members. "This party includes all those who would probably support His Majesty's Government under any minister not peculiarly unpopular." "The independent or unconnected members of the House" (a party which seems to have corresponded very much with the Squadrone of the old Scottish Parliament) are calculated at 108; Fox's party at 138; and that of Pitt at 52. Even this unflattering computation is further discounted by the remark that "of this party, were there a new

Parliament and Mr. P. no longer to continue minister, not above twenty would be returned." No document has thrown more light than this on the political system of this period.

In these days, too, a minister would expect some help from his colleagues. But Pitt could depend on no one but Dundas. Timidity at first made able men hold aloof. Afterwards, when Pitt had secured his mastery at the polls and in debate, it may, perhaps, be charged against him that he determined, during eight or nine years, that he should be sole and supreme minister, and that none should be admitted who would threaten that predominance. The ordinary vacancies in his Government were filled by men like Jenkinson—"Jenky," the subterranean agent of the King, who divided his studies between courts and commerce, and well understood both; —or Pitt's brother, Chatham, whose indolence swamped the superiority of his talents and the popularity of his manners. Grenville and Wellesley were not exceptions; for Wellesley only held a lordship of the Treasury, and no more than Grenville, Pitt's first cousin, in any degree menaced the minister's monopoly of parliamentary power. It was not till the great deluge of the French Revolution was upon him, that he summoned to his aid all the men of capacity that he could collect.

Pitt found some consolation for his Irish defeat, which he at first regarded as but temporary, in the purchase of Hollwood: an agreeable imprudence, which marked the beginning of his pecuniary embarrassments. There he planted and planned with all the enthusiasm which had marked his father's operations at Hayes and Burton Pynsent. But the Hollwood of Pitt has long disappeared.

The house he built has been demolished, and the woods he planted can no more be traced. There remains, however, an ancient, memorable oak; stretched under which, Wilberforce and he resolved on that campaign for the abolition of the Slave Trade, which gave honour to the one and immortality to the other.

CHAPTER V

WARREN HASTINGS AND THE REGENCY

In 1786 Pitt returned to a January meeting of Parliament, when the Duke of Richmond brought forward a scheme for the fortification of Portsmouth and Plymouth. This, as has been said, was defeated. On the other hand, the minister reached the culminating point of his financial fame by his plan for the redemption of the National Debt, which his contemporaries regarded as his highest claim to renown, and which is accordingly inscribed on the scroll to which he is pointing in Lawrence's majestic portrait. The merits of his plan were twofold. He created an independent Board of Commissioners for the reduction of the debt, to whom a million was to be annually paid; they were to be officials of the highest character and distinction: the Speaker, the Chancellor of the Exchequer, the Master of the Rolls, the Accountant General, the Governor and Deputy Governor of the Bank of England; and in this form the Board exists to this day. With the million allotted to them they were to purchase stock. This stock was not to be cancelled, and so would continue to bear interest; and this interest would be received by the Commissioners and applied to the purchase of stock, in addition to the annual million at their disposal for the same purpose.

The signal merit of this scheme was that by these means the Sinking Fund so formed was in the hands of a permanent and substantive body, whose action could only be controlled by the direct interference of Parliament, and could not be tampered with for the passing needs of a ministry. There was this further indirect advantage, that there was extracted from the pockets of the taxpayer for the redemption of debt not merely the annual million, but also the amount of the interest of the stock purchased. These were the real benefits; of which the second was not merely subordinate, but kept in the background. The attractions held forth were far more dazzling, but absolutely fallacious. The great discovery was supposed to be the accumulation of the fund at compound interest. This was the golden vision held out by Dr. Price, with the fanaticism of an alchemist; a fanaticism which culminated in the declaration that "war, while such a scheme was going on, would increase its efficacy." The error was not merely fundamental, but disastrous; for the nation was deluded into the belief that it mattered little what was spent in war, if only the Sinking Fund were regularly maintained. As a matter of course, however, the compound interest, as it was called, was only the produce of taxation or loans. To grow of its own virtue and essence, in the manner described by Price, the Sinking Fund should have been invested in some remunerative form of productive industry, with a constant reinvestment of the profits; as it was, it only represented the sums, whether in the annual capital or the interest paid on the stock purchased, that Parliament chose to set apart for the payment of debt. All the money, in fact, came from the same source. Its real value lay in the fact that it was an honest and steadfast method of paying off debt; and experience tells us that debt is in reality only reduced by the patriotic resolve of Parliament; which is rendered doubly efficient when, as in Pitt's scheme, the Fund devoted to debt redemption is placed beyond the casual interference of a needy minister, and when its operations are scarcely perceptible to a public, justly if sometimes ignorantly, impatient of taxation. It is probable that Pitt grasped this truth, and was not for long the dupe of Price's fantastic calculations. Frere, at least, says that this was so, and that Pitt mainly valued his Sinking Fund as a means of inducing the nation to submit to the irksome and unpopular operation of paying off debt.

The most striking feature of the session is the opening of that long campaign against Warren Hastings, which, as regards its duration and the forces brought into play, resembles rather some historic siege of ancient times than a judicial investigation into the conduct of an individual. That great man had returned in 1785, conscious of eminent services, of having strengthened, if not preserved, our Indian Empire; conscious also of having committed acts which might be easily condoned by Eastern morality and by the pressure of dire necessity, but which could hardly bear the most indulgent inquisition of a British Parliament. He had, however, powerful allies; the Court, the East India Directors, and, it was believed, the Ministry with its majority. Indeed, except the leaders of the Opposition, his only enemy seemed to be his own intolerable agent. But he was ambushed by the undying rancour of Francis, and the sleepless humanity of Burke.

The episode may be said to have occasioned more eloquence (including Macaulay's), than any event in history. But we touch it only as regards Pitt's connection with it. On the first charge, that relating to the Rohillas, Dundas was spokesman of the Government, and defended Hastings, though he had once bitterly attacked him with regard to this very transaction. Pitt sate silent. On the second, that relating to Benares, one of less gravity, Pitt's support was confidently anticipated by the friends of Hastings, and he spoke mainly in Hastings's defence. But towards the end of his speech he astonished the whole House by declaring that, while he approved the demand for aid and a fine for non-compliance, he thought the fine too large, and should therefore vote for the resolution; not thereby, he expressly stated, pledging himself that there should be an impeachment, but only, if there were to be an impeachment, that this should be included as one of the articles. The sensation was immense. There was open revolt. Both Paymasters, Grenville and Mulgrave, rose from his side to speak and vote against him. But he maintained his majority. For the Rohilla charge, which he had allowed to be opposed, there had voted 67 against 119; for the Benares charge there voted 119 against 79.

About few incidents of Pitt's long administration has there been so much controversy. Hastings had made so sure of his support, and had, indeed, received it on a more damning charge; the point on which he gave his vote seemed so comparatively insignificant; the occasion for putting himself in direct antagonism, not merely to the King but to his own subordinates, was so small, that a score of reasons have been discovered for his behaviour. He was jealous of Hastings; he wished to draw a red herring across the path of the Opposition; he had had a midnight interview with Dundas; Dundas was jealous of Hastings: we can imagine the hum and buzz of political insects. But there is no necessity for any explanation, except the straightforward one that after a detailed examination of the charges and answers, completed after the Rohilla debate, and discussed at length with Dundas, Pitt was led to the conviction that he could not defend Hastings, or risk the reputation of his Government by associating it with the acts of the Hastings administration. Indeed we now know that this was so. The debate on the Rohilla charge was on the 2d of June; that on the Benares charge on the 13th of June. On the 10th of June Pitt writes to Eden: "I have hardly hours enough to read all the papers necessary on that voluminous article" (Benares). And Dundas writes to Lord Cornwallis, speaking of Pitt and himself: "The truth is, when we examined the various articles of charges against him with his defences, they were so strong, and the defences so perfectly unsupported, it was impossible not to concur." That Pitt was not deeply chagrined at seeing his great foes absorbed in a different campaign, which should engross their energy of attack, may readily be believed; but such a consideration is totally insufficient to explain a course which implied a rupture with his own friends, infinitely more distressing to him than a daily renewal of his accustomed conflicts with the Opposition. It may even be said without extravagance that, habituated as he was to these contests, and confident of success in them, he would have regretted rather than promoted their cessation.

The recess was uneventful but for the signature of a commercial treaty with France, on which Pitt employed the polite perfidy of his most recent convert William Eden. When Parliament met on the 23d of January 1787 its conclusion was announced, and two days afterwards it was laid upon the table. It was at once made the subject of bitter attack by Fox, for reasons which increase our admiration of the superhuman parts that could obliterate such amazing vagaries. In the very language that he reprobated most strongly six years afterwards, he thundered against any connection or friendship with France. It may be said that in one case he was attacking a monarchy, and in the other defending a republic. But it was not a question of government, so far, at any rate, as this speech was concerned. "Past experience proved that whenever France saw this country weak, and thought her incapable of effectually resisting, she seized the opportunity, and aimed at effecting her long-desired destruction. If the minister would look over the correspondence in the Foreign Office he would find the warmest assurances of friendship from France up to the very moment of breaking with us and joining America against us. It was idle, therefore, to hope that she would forget her resentment, and abandon a purpose she had so long and uniformly endeavoured to achieve." This was not the random rhetoric of faction, but the expression of his matured and deliberate opinion. In November 1785 he had written to Fitzpatrick: "The worst of all is that I am far from sure whether the country in general would not like a good understanding with France (from the vain hopes of a durable peace) better than anything. I am sure that any minister who can like it must not only be insensible to the interests of his country, but to any feelings of personal pride: for, depend upon it, whenever you are in such a situation the French will make you feel it enough."

This strange opposition, though supported by the heaviest artillery of Burke and Sheridan and Francis, was absolutely futile; and the address in favour of the treaty was carried by 236 to 116. Nothing in all Pitt's career is more remarkable and more creditable than the bold disregard of narrow prejudices and the large conciliatory spirit which he displayed in framing and concluding this treaty. But the hostility of Fox, though unavailing, was unrelenting and persistent, and indeed, with the charges against Hastings, took up the greater part of the session. The operations with regard to Hastings, so far as they concern the subject matter of this book, may be dismissed in a sentence. After the most famous of all English orations had been delivered by Sheridan, Pitt had spoken in support of the Begum charge. This made the impeachment inevitable. A formal resolution to this effect was unanimously carried, and taken up to the House of Lords by Burke. The episode illustrates in the highest degree the power and probity of Pitt. He had held Hastings in the hollow of his hand. He, and he alone, had pronounced judgment; and pronounced it against his own interest. All the forces of politics, with the exception of a small Opposition, were in favour of the great governor. There can be little doubt that had Pitt given his vote for Hastings, he would have done what many men, as honest as he, were able conscientiously to do, and would have gratified the Court, the Company, and the mass of the Commons. But his amazing authority was not more conspicuous than the purity of his rectitude. He declined to associate himself with those who held that the end could justify the means, even for the construction of an empire or in the atmosphere of the East. He gave his decision as calmly as a judge in chambers; while Britain and India abided meekly by the decree of this young gentleman of twenty-eight.

Probably the most useful work of the session was a plan for the consolidation and simplification of the various duties levied for purposes of revenue. These had gradually lapsed into a condition of confusion and complexity, involving great difficulty in collection and some loss to the Exchequer. The intricacy of the subject may be judged from the fact, that the remedial resolutions were numbered by the hundred, and even the thousand, and the success of the proposal by the eulogy extorted from the truculent hostility of Burke. Further detail is beyond the limits of a sketch like this. So, too, is the scandal with respect to the Prince of Wales—his debts, his lies, and his marriage—which engrossed much of the session, and probably all the attention that what is called Society had leisure to devote to politics. It is merely necessary to observe Pitt's stern attitude, and absolute refusal to agree to any parliamentary address to the King for the payment of the Heir Apparent's debts.

He had not long to wait for the result of his action in this matter.

The health of George III. seemed to promise a long life. As a young man, he had been warned by the precept and example of his uncle, the Duke of Cumberland, that the danger of their family lay in a full habit of body, and he had struggled against the hereditary tendency to corpulence with energy and success. He spent days in the saddle. His passion for exercise wore out his stoutest equerries. The simplicity of his daily fare was such as to excite scarcely less mirth among the wags and wits of London, than the cool solitude of Richmond's kitchen. But he had overdone his remedy. Already, in 1765, he was said to have been attacked by mental aberration. In the autumn of 1788 he was again stricken. Of all imaginable accidents the death or incapacity of the sovereign seemed the only one that could affect the position of the minister. It was known that, in either of those events, the Prince of Wales would at once dismiss the statesman, who had not merely withstood the proposal for the payment of his debts, but who was the foe of all his personal and political friends.

It seemed clear that a regent would have to be appointed, and the question at once assumed several different phases. Pitt maintained that it was for Parliament to name a regent, and to fix his powers; that it was the absolute and undeniable right of the two Houses, on behalf of the people, to provide for the revival of what he erroneously called the Third Estate. Fox imprudently declared that "in his firm opinion the Prince of Wales had as clear, as express a right to assume the reins of government, and exercise the power of sovereignty during the continuance of the illness and incapacity with which it had pleased God to afflict His Majesty, as in the case of His Majesty's having undergone a natural and perfect demise;" an opinion which the Prince of Wales was compelled to disavow. The Parliament of Ireland saw in this difficulty an opportunity of asserting its independence; and, without waiting for the action of the British Legislature, accorded an unconditional regency to the Heir-Apparent.

At Westminster the limitations proposed were strict, but not unduly so when the nature of the case is considered. The view of the Ministry, as stated by themselves, was that, "while they considered the temporary exercise of the royal authority on His Majesty's behalf and during His Majesty's illness as essentially different from the actual possession of the Crown, they have at the same time been anxious to extend that authority which they could conceive essential or necessary for the temporary administration of the King's power." Pitt has been accused of attempting to maintain an authority independent of the sovereign and Parliament, because his Bill handed over the royal household, involving an expenditure of some £200,000 a year, and vast patronage, to the Queen, and therefore presumably to his own control. It was contended that his action was analogous to that of Fox in framing his scheme for India; and that similarly he would retain an irresistible influence and patronage, which could be affected neither by prerogative nor vote.

Those, who argued thus, ignored the keystone of this policy—the opinion of the best experts that the King's disorder was only temporary. No doubt, when the King's madness was declared, the first impression of his physicians was that it was incurable, and under those circumstances Pitt prepared for a prolonged exclusion from public life. But these doctors spoke with almost absolute ignorance of insanity; and, before the Bill for a regency was introduced, Willis, who spoke with almost absolute authority, predicted a speedy convalescence. The regency, then, for which Pitt was making provision, was not one for an indefinite number of years, but for at most a few months, or even weeks. Would it then have been well for the minister to hand over the King's household, his personal surroundings and personal associates, to the caprice of the Prince of Wales; that his old servants might be sent about their business to make way for the pimps and the blacklegs, the Jack Paynes and the George Hangers, who formed the Prince's Court, so that the King's first returning rays of reason might rest upon the faces he most detested—on the parasites and boon companions of his debauched son? Such a state of things might have renewed the disease of the Sovereign, and was, at any rate, wholly unsuited to a fleeting and temporary regency.

The restrictions, however, such as they were, the Prince accepted, though with the worst grace in the world. The appetite of the Opposition was not such as could afford to wait. "I think it certain that in about a fortnight we shall come in," writes Fox, who counted eagerly on obtaining office by the prerogative of the new regent in disregard and defiance of Parliament; the very proceeding which had inspired him with such piercing philippics against his rival five years before. The

Minister prepared to fall with dignity. He had been, indeed, for the last two years, less a prime minister than a dictator; he ruled England, and loomed large in Europe. He now made unostentatious preparations to resume his practice as a junior at the bar. The merchants of London met, and voted £100,000 to place him beyond the accidents of politics. Pitt might without cavil have taken this offering, so honourable to both parties. But he would not even entertain it. He waved it aside with disdain. "No consideration upon earth," he said, "shall ever induce me to accept it." And yet, at the time, he was insolvent.

One may be permitted to regret that he was not allowed to pass for a month or two from his seat of power to a cell in Lincoln's Inn. History, however, was denied so picturesque an episode. While the Regency Bill was passing, the King was recovering. Before it was out of committee in the Lords he was receiving his ministers. The situation was almost ludicrous. A week later it would have been his duty to give his royal dissent to the Regency Bill. The Ministry of Fox, already overdue some weeks, melted into space. English rats, like Aubrey and Queensberry, cursed their evil star. The rats of Dublin Castle endeavoured to return, not wholly without success. As if to show that the humour of the scene was inexhaustible, there arrived at this juncture the luckless Irish deputation with an absolute offer of the regency to the Prince of Wales. They were received with universal hilarity, which their keen sense of the ridiculous made them, we may be sure, the first to feel. Their appearance was the crowning mortification of the discomfited Heir Apparent. The dignity of the delegation in the presentation of their address, which had to be accomplished, was indeed preserved by his genial grace. But no charm of manner could disguise the fact that Pitt once more reigned supreme, and that the Opposition had once more relapsed into outer darkness. For the Minister enjoyed at once the gratitude of the King, the enthusiasm of the masses, and the almost blind confidence of Parliament. It was his highest point of fortune and power; an elevation that no other minister has attained.

Fortune, moreover, had not exhausted her irony. She seemed determined to show how entirely this puissant minister was her plaything. He had found in the plenitude of his power that he held it by the precarious tenure of the King's health. He was now to realise that there was another frail life to be reckoned in that lease of office. While London was illuminating for the King's recovery, Lord Chatham lay mortally ill. So grave was his malady that the hunters after Providence had fixed on Grenville as the new minister. For Lord Chatham's death, by the grim humour of our constitution, would have removed Pitt from the Commons to the Peers. In the prime of life and intellect, he would have been plucked from the governing body of the country, in which he was incomparably the most important personage, and set down as a pauper peer in the House of Lords. It would have been as if the Duke of Wellington in the middle of the Peninsular War had been transferred by the operation of constitutional law to the government of Chelsea Hospital. The system, in which Burke could find no flaw, had ruled that default in the possession of an elder brother should be thus punished, and that the accident of an accident should have power to blight this great career. Fortunately for Pitt and for the country, Lord Chatham recovered. Strangely enough, in this very year, Fox was nearly overtaken by a similar calamity. He was indeed actually addressed as Lord Holland, under the belief that his nephew was already dead.

And elsewhere the fates were spinning new threads, scheming new combinations, and shifting in their most tragic mood the circumstance and destiny of the world. The cauldron was simmering into which all parties and politics and Pitt himself were to be plunged, to emerge in new shapes. Within three months the guns that were fired in London for the King's recovery were echoed in Paris as the first signals of the long agony of a King's downfall; the Bastille had fallen, and the French Revolution had begun. Outside France that event most deeply affected Englishmen, and of all Englishmen Pitt, the spoiled child of fame and fortune.

CHAPTER VI

THE FRENCH REVOLUTION

WHILE the eyes of all Europe were fixed on Paris, Pitt ostentatiously averted his gaze. He was deaf to the shrieks of rage and panic that arose from the convulsions of France. He determinedly set himself, to use the phrase of Candide, to cultivate his own garden and ignore all others. Let France settle her internal affairs as she chooses, was his unvarying principle. It is strange to read the uneventful record of the flat prosperous years as they passed in England from July 1789 to January 1793, and to contrast them with the contemporary stress and tumult in Europe.

The history of England and of Pitt during this period hardly fills a page. Pitt's budgets—to him the most important events of the year—are, with one exception, brief. The salient questions are questions of emancipation. There are two personal episodes, great but not equal: the final dismissal of the intolerable Thurlow, and the heroic quarrel between Fox and Burke. Thurlow had, as Pitt's Chancellor, both publicly and privately, led the opposition to Pitt's Government. The origin of the grudge that produced this scandal cannot now be ascertained: some unguarded phrase probably rankled. Thurlow relied absolutely on the King, and thought himself royally impervious to ministerial change. He had been Chancellor with North, with Fox, and with Shelburne; he could well afford to snap his fingers at Pitt. He was therefore taken by surprise, but growled out the cynical truth: "I did not think that the King would have parted with me so easily. As to that other man (Pitt) he has done to me just what I should have done to him if I could." The schism between Fox and Burke is not merely one of the most dramatic scenes and one of the most interesting personal passages in history, but it marks a great epoch in party growth. A thick crust of Whiggism was sloughed off, and there appeared a first, raw, callow germ of the Liberalism that was to grow in silence for forty years, and then assume a sudden and overwhelming preponderance. There were some revolutionary symptoms in the country, notably in Scotland, where they were most justifiable; but systematised repression had hardly yet begun. It was difficult to listen to Pitt, and believe that there was anything more stirring in the world than the tax on female servants, or the subjection of tobacco to excise. There was indeed in 1790 a dissolution of the Parliament which had now lived six years; but it was uneventful, as it fully renewed the mandate to Pitt. Tranquillity was only occasionally interrupted by the sonorous voice of the Minister, proclaiming, as from a muezzin's minaret, the continued peace and prosperity of the Empire. Historians have hardly done justice to the dogged determination with which Pitt ignored the French Revolution.

So far from this being a period of coercion, it was one

of almost competing liberalism. Attempts were made—reluctantly opposed by the Minister under the pressure of the bishops—to repeal, in the interest of nonconformists, those obsolete clauses of the Test Act which still remained on the statute-book. The demand of Roman Catholics for the abolition of some of the disabling enactments, by which they were oppressed, was actually acceded to. Fox introduced a Bill, substantially the same as one that had been ineffectually proposed by Chatham, for enabling juries to give a verdict as to the character of an alleged libel as well as to the fact of its publication. He naturally received the warm support of Pitt; and the warm support of Pitt as naturally ensured the bitter hostility of Pitt's chancellor. Thurlow, however, was only able to delay the measure for a single session.

On an even nobler stage than that of domestic emancipation, Fox and Pitt were able to display a generous rivalry in the cause of freedom. In 1788 the physicians declared that Wilberforce could not live a fortnight. On his death-bed, as he believed, Wilberforce exacted from Pitt a solemn promise to undertake the cause of the abolition of the Slave Trade. In May, therefore, of that year Pitt, ardently supported by Burke and Fox, induced the House of Commons to resolve unanimously to take the question of the Slave Trade into consideration during the next session; and a Bill for its provisional regulation was actually carried. In 1789 Wilberforce was able to exert his own mellifluous eloquence in the cause. But it was in 1792 that Pitt set an imperishable seal on his advocacy of the question, by the delivery of a speech which all authorities concur in placing before any other effort of his genius; and certainly no recorded utterance of his touches the imaginative flight of the peroration. He rose exhausted, and immediately before rising was obliged to take medicine to enable him to speak. But his prolonged and powerful oration showed no signs of disability; indeed, for the last twenty minutes he seemed, said shrewd critics, to be nothing less than inspired. He burst as it were into a prophetic vision of the civilisation that shall dawn upon Africa, and recalled the not less than African barbarism of heathen Britain; exclaiming, as the first beams of the morning sun pierced the windows of Parliament, and appeared to suggest the quotation—

> Nos . . . primus equis Oriens afflavit anhelis,
> Illic sera rubens accendit lumina Vesper.

Fox was loud in his generous admiration. Windham, an even more hostile critic, avowed that, for the first time, he understood the possible compass of human eloquence Sheridan, most hostile of all, was even passionate in his praise. Grey, who ceded to none in the bitterness and expression of his enmity, ceded also to none in his enthusiasm of eulogy. To those who consider Pitt a sublime parliamentary hack, greedy of power and careful only of what might conduce to power, his course on the Slave Trade, where he had no interest to gain, and could only offend powerful supporters, may well be commended.

It is now, however, necessary to turn from the recital of home politics to the position abroad, where Europe was watching with awe and apprehension the gathering portents which presaged some unknown horror of convulsion.

It is doing Pitt no injustice to say that, in the earlier years of his administration, his mind was given rather to domestic questions than to foreign affairs. The peace of 1783 found the vessel of the State, to resume the ancient and imperishable metaphor, in so perilous a condition that the first object of the captain was necessarily to repair and refit her, so that at some future date she might once more take the seas, though with a less imperial bearing. He had, indeed, to restore vital warmth and consistence to the shattered fragments of empire. He had, therefore, at once applied himself to place on a permanent and workable footing those novel relations, which had been hurriedly adjusted with Ireland under the stress and pressure of calamitous defeat. He had strained every nerve to restore the ruined finance of the country, which was always the darling object of his political life. And, moreover, at the head of a passive and silent host, he had to maintain his position against the most powerful artillery of debate ever directed against a treasury bench. What wonder, then, if he had but little attention to give to those external complications in which Great Britain could at the best play so subordinate a part? Even during the grave crisis in Holland, which first forced foreign affairs upon his notice, the only letter for months that he addressed to our minister at the Hague was to inquire as to the operation of the Dutch succession duties, in the hope that an analogous tax might furnish him with a new financial resource. At the same time it would be unfair to Chatham to suppose that foreign policy, on which he so largely built his own fame, occupied a secondary place in the training of his favourite son. It cannot be doubted that Pitt would learn from his father that a foreign policy required firmness and purpose; that in that, as in other things, vacillation was the one unpardonable sin; but that the arm of this country should never be put further forward than it could be maintained. Even in those days of exhaustion, our means were less inadequate to our ends than now; we were less scattered over the world; and our army, relatively to those on the Continent, was respectable, and even powerful. Nevertheless Pitt, as we shall see, had to draw back, although his first steps on the Continent were marked with something of the happy audacity of Chatham.

It was in Holland that his first complication arose. On that familiar board all the great powers of Europe were moving their pawns—the fitful philanthropist, Joseph the Second, who had opened the game with his usual disastrous energy; the old fox at Berlin; the French monarchy, still bitten with its suicidal mania of fomenting republics against Great Britain; and the crafty voluptuary of St. Petersburg. The game lay ultimately between England and Prussia on one side, and France on the other, though it is hardly worth recalling now. Harris, afterwards Lord Malmesbury, represented the English interest with consummate dexterity, but the final success lay with the big battalions of Prussia. Nevertheless, honour is due to the firm attitude of the British Government; and the treaties of alliance between Great Britain on the one side, and Prussia and Holland on the other, marked the first diplomatic success that England had achieved for a generation.

We obtain, too, in this transaction an interesting

glimpse of Pitt's policy. Lord Malmesbury has preserved for us the minutes of a cabinet held on the 23d of May 1787. Pitt then said that, though war was only a possible and not a probable result of the affair, yet that the mere possibility should make England pause, and consider whether anything could compensate for arresting the growing affluence and prosperity of the country —a growth so rapid as to make her in a few years capable of grappling with any force that France could raise. He was, in fact, nursing England through the convalescence after the American War for the possibility of a great effort; and it was difficult, by any allurements of foreign success, to induce him to forsake the course which he had marked out, until the fulness of time should come.

A second complication arose with Spain. That great country seemed in the last state of decrepitude. Her monarchy and her religion, the bases of her former splendour, were fast rotting into superstitions; but she abated no jot of her highest historical pretensions. Her court was the common ground of priests and gamekeepers; her army, navy, and finance were a vast scene of ruin. Her princes burlesqued even the Bourbon passion for the chase, and shrank from no extravagance in the name of sport. One day they would bombard with artillery the 100,000 head of large game that haunted the vast domains of Aranjuez; on another they would have a solemn battue of all the little birds that fluttered through the gardens and pecked at the fruit. And yet Spain was taken almost as seriously by others as herself. Pitt himself, in giving his reasons for abandoning the Russian armaments, spoke of gaining

Spain as one of the chief objects of the concession. She was now governed by that king who was to hand over Spain and the Indies to Napoleon like a dish at breakfast, and vanish ingloriously out of history with his queen and their favourite at Bayonne. In 1789 an English vessel was seized off Vancouver Island by two Spanish ships of war, and her crew imprisoned on the ground that a trespass had been committed against the sovereign rights of Spain. This was not a matter which the most pacific minister could afford to ignore; one who loved peace less might have easily fanned England into as fierce a flame as was roused by the alleged loss of Jenkins's ears. But Pitt kept his negotiations as secret as he could. At last, in 1790, a vote of credit had to be asked, and the usual measures taken as for a possibly immediate war. The situation was further complicated by the French Government—then a government half-way between the Monarchy and the Terror—fitting out a fleet as a measure of precaution. This menace had at least the advantage of showing the anxiety of Pitt to avoid all interference or contact with France. He pursued a firm but conciliatory course, and the Court of Spain, after one or two mysterious lurches, agreed to a convention honourable to England and not dishonourable to herself.

So far all had been well. Without war the minister had raised his reputation, and England had once more raised her head. It is true that peace had been preserved in the main by the interior complications of France. Spain had appealed to France for aid under the Family Compact of 1762; but the French Assembly, in considering the question, had wandered off into constitutional discussions, which indirectly landed her in peace; to which conclusion a naval mutiny at Brest may also have contributed. On this abstention Florida Blanca, the Spanish minister, had grounded the necessity of his concession to England. It is also true that Pitt had spent over three millions in naval preparations. Yet it seems clear that the powerful fleet, thus produced "in the readiest and most perfect state ever known in the annals of Great Britain," as Auckland writes, was scarcely less effective than the neutrality of France in determining the attitude of Spain; and the heaviest peaceful expenditure of this sort is much less costly than the smallest European war.

So far, then, all had been smooth and peaceful and cheap. But now a change was to come. Pitt was to put out his hand too far, and to be compelled to withdraw it with some appearance of discomfiture. If there is one point on which history repeats itself, it is this: that at certain fixed intervals the Russian Empire feels a need of expansion; that that necessity is usually gratified at the expense of the Turk; that the other Powers, or some of them, take alarm, and attempt measures for curtailing the operation, with much the same result that the process of pruning produces on a healthy young tree. One of these periods had occurred in 1791. The war declared by Catherine II. was running the usual course. The Russians had gained several decisive victories, and were preparing to reap the fruit of them. During the three years and a half that the war had lasted, Pitt had not been inactive. A main result of the operations in the Netherlands had been the conclusion of an offensive and defensive alliance between Holland,

Prussia, and Great Britain. In 1788 these powers had by their attitude prevented the destruction which Gustavus III. of Sweden had brought on himself, at the hands of the Danes and Russians, in rashly attacking the Muscovite Empire. Again, in 1790, they had had no difficulty in detaching Austria, then governed by Leopold II., not merely a prince but a statesman, from the Russian alliance. And now, in 1791, their object was to induce Russia to content herself with a smaller share of recent conquests than was agreeable to her, and more especially to insist on the cession by her of the fortress of Oczakow at the entrance to the Black Sea, which she had taken with an appalling loss of life at the close of 1788.

In this policy of the triple alliance, it is necessary to note that Prussia took an eager part, but Holland none. Pitt himself was strenuous. Chatham had avowed himself "quite a Russ," and the traditions of the Whig party had pointed in the same direction. But foreign policy necessarily varies with the varying importance of states. There is, indeed, no such a thing as a traditional foreign policy in the sense of its being necessary and inevitable, any more than, in all conditions of the atmosphere, a ship carries the same traditional sails, or a man wears the same traditional clothes. The instinct of self-preservation guides the European powers with the same certainty as weather moves sheep on the hill; it has at different periods produced combinations against the dominion of Charles V. and against the dominion of the Ottomans, against France and against Russia, against Venice and against the Pope. On this occasion there was no necessity for Whigs to be friendly to Russian policy. The

Empire of Catherine the Second was a very different affair to the Empire of Peter the Great. It was absorbing Poland, it was threatening the Mediterranean, it had swallowed the Crimea, it had become a European Power. Nevertheless, it might well be questioned, if war, without Austria, and with the aid only of Prussia and the disabled Porte; which would certainly check the recovery of Great Britain and lose the gains of eight years; war which must be carried on in regions so remote, under circumstances so unfavourable, could be justified by any such exigency as had arisen. That the crisis should have overcome the passionate peacefulness of Pitt, his rooted economy, and his devotion to domestic policy, shows at least his overwhelming sense of its importance.

On the 28th of March 1791 a short message was brought from the King to the House, stating the failure of his Government to bring about peace between Russia and Turkey, and demanding an augmentation of the navy "to add weight to his representations." Fox received this announcement with unusual solemnity, and asked for futher information. Pitt haughtily refused to give more than was furnished in the message—an amazing reticence, when the circumstances are considered; and one which the Foreign Secretary, Leeds, himself denounced, after he had resigned. The next afternoon was fixed for the discussion; and before the dawn of another day Pitt had discovered his mistake. The country had had enough of war; the taste of the American campaigns was still hot in the mouth. It had never heard of Oczakow, and was not prepared to renew its sacrifices that that swampy spot might remain a

Turkish possession. More than that, the Baltic trade was of enormous extent; its annual value was computed at three millions sterling; the commercial classes were ablaze. Woronzow, the Russian ambassador, finding out from Leeds what was in contemplation, had gone to Fox and excited all the energies of Opposition.

Nor was the Cabinet by any means united. The measure, planned outside it, had, so to speak, been rushed upon it; and its ministerial opponents remained unconvinced. Richmond, one of Pitt's ablest colleagues, was hostile; Grenville, whose influence over the Premier appeared then to be on the increase, always cold, waxed colder; the mutes trembled and wavered. Pitt, his brother, and the chancellor had been the strongest advocates for action. But Pitt, in spite of his enormous majorities on the message—97 to 34 in the House of Lords, and 228 to 135 in the House of Commons—resolved to recede. He had received some of the secret warnings that forebode the cyclones in which Governments go down. Camden, indeed, thought the Government would go down. Grafton made his sons, both members of Parliament, refuse their support. The action, so hurriedly determined, was as hurriedly withdrawn. On the 22d of March, 1791, the Cabinet had agreed to send fleets to the Baltic and the Black Sea, and to make a representation jointly with Prussia at St. Petersburg, stating that the two allies were under the necessity of at once taking part in the war against Russia, should satisfactory assurances respecting Oczakow not be received within a certain definite time. The messenger, with the joint representation, set off for Berlin on the 27th; the royal message was delivered to Parliament on the 28th, discussed and voted on the 29th. On the 30th the Cabinet met, and showed a disposition to retreat. On the 31st two Cabinets were held, at the second of which there was a general collapse; so general, that Thurlow feigned sleep to avoid being a party to it. It was determined to send a messenger to Berlin to stop the joint representation. Leeds with spirit declared that, if such a despatch must go, it must go without his signature. This, however, constituted the least of obstacles; the despatch went, and Leeds resigned.

The whole transaction, from the very inception of the policy to its withdrawal, including the parliamentary debate, had taken just nine days. Able writers speak of Pitt's being warned to recede by his declining majorities on this subject. Nothing can be more erroneous. The rapidity of action with him had been equalled, as we have seen, by the rapidity of reaction. He resolved to recede in a space of twenty-four hours, during which the one division taken gave him a crushing majority. The cool promptitude and courage of his retreat, after a lease of power which would have made most men headstrong, was rare and admirable. Still, it was retreat, absolute and avowed. To drain the cup of humiliation to the dregs, Fawkener was sent to St. Petersburg to try what he could effect by expostulation. It needs no great experience of affairs to judge that, when menace has been attempted and has failed, expostulation is only an opportunity for insult. It was an opportunity that Catherine was fully qualified to appreciate. Fortunately for her purpose, Adair, the friend of Fox, happened to be at St. Petersburg. On him she heaped every compliment and caress, while Fawkener was sent empty away.

The whole transaction is noteworthy for many reasons. The shortness of time during which the policy was framed and reversed is sufficiently remarkable. So, too, is the unreality of the great majorities in its favour. For it is clear that these votes were reluctantly given, and would have been turned against the Government had the pressure been less, or had the Government proceeded further. The weakness of the support was evidently due to the sudden force of public opinion; which acted with a celerity and a completeness rare in the eighteenth century, and amazing under the circumstances.

The most astonishing circumstance, however, is the undoubted fact that the Government, with all its overwhelming majority, was in imminent danger of dissolution. Storer, a keen watcher of men and events, wrote that, had not Fox been impossible, he could easily have got into office. Auckland, at least equally acute, thought the same: so, as we have seen, did Camden. Pitt himself acknowledged it. In a letter which he addressed to Berlin in explanation of his change of policy, he admits that, had he not receded, he must have fallen. So great, indeed, was the loss of prestige that nothing in all probability saved Pitt, but the fact that Fox was the only alternative.

What was the cause of this catastrophe? High authorities say the Prussian alliance. But it is clear that there was too much reluctance at Berlin itself for this explanation to be adequate. The real rival and enemy on which Prussian ministers kept their eyes fixed then and for near a century afterwards, reigned not at St. Petersburg but at Vienna. The cause was in reality twofold. Pitt saw the danger to the balance of power in Europe from the constantly growing strength of Russia; and emboldened by his pacific successes in Spain and in Holland, did not doubt that the armies of Prussia and the fleets of Great Britain would awe Catherine, then entirely without allies, into acquiescence. It is not impossible that his calculation was correct. Twice had he played the game of brag successfully, and on the whole he had a right to calculate on a third triumph. But his whole plan was nipped in the bud by the one element on which he had not calculated, the hostility of Parliament and of the country.

Why then had not this entered into his calculations? There lies the second cause of his disaster: it was his growing isolation. Always secluded, he had become almost inaccessible. Dundas and Grenville were alone admitted to his confidence. An inner cabinet, indeed, is not unfamiliar to us; and, as the numbers constituting cabinets increase, it must become a recognised institution. But Pitt had not the excuse of numbers; nor, indeed, that of impracticable colleagues. The real reason for the limitation of his confidences was probably his rooted distrust of Thurlow. To summon a meeting of the Cabinet that he might be cursed and betrayed by Thurlow, was not worth the trouble. Nevertheless, his solitude was a grave disability. He was not in touch with his colleagues, still less with the pulse of the people. Had it been otherwise he could scarcely have remained in absolute ignorance of the storm of opposition that his Russian policy was certain to evoke.

And so ends the Oczakow incident. Save a gigantic speech by Fox, it left little behind it. The place itself, like so many spots that have caused, or nearly caused great wars, is forsaken and forgotten. But as an epoch in Pitt's career, as an illustration of his weakness and his strength, the transaction possesses a vital interest, and deserves the most elaborate study. Its political effects endured for a considerable time. It relaxed if it did not dissolve that triple alliance of Prussia, Holland, and Great Britain, which had been so far Pitt's main achievement and object in foreign policy. It caused a grave disparagement on the Continent of Pitt's judgment and Pitt's power. Of this he reaped the fruits later. As Thurlow remarked with complacency of his chief, there could now be no danger of war while Pitt was in office; for, as he had swallowed this disgrace, it was impossible to conceive one that he could scruple to digest in future.

Pitt's reputation did not merely suffer abroad; it was gravely compromised at home. He had rashly menaced and hurriedly retracted. To his proud spirit the mortification was undoubtedly deep. Burges, then under-secretary for foreign affairs, has left a curious record of a conversation he had with Pitt at this time (April 19, 1791). Pitt assured him, "On my word of honour, that my sentiments, notwithstanding everything that has passed, are precisely the same as they were, and as the Duke of Leeds's are now. He has had the constancy and courage to act upon them in a manner which must ever do him honour. Circumstances, dreadful circumstances, have made it impossible for me to do the same. I am under the necessity of remaining as I am, in order to avoid consequences of the most unpleasant nature; but the Duke has acted nobly both to the country and to myself." The exact import of these expressions it is not necessary to seek; in the mouth of Pitt they are sufficiently remarkable.

Another result, as we have seen, was the resignation of Carmarthen, who had succeeded to the dukedom of Leeds in 1789. In itself the fact had no importance. Leeds was a cypher. He had little capacity. He was both vain and pompous. He was incurably indolent. It is not, therefore, surprising to find that he had become a mere channel and signature stamp for despatches drafted by Pitt. The importance of his retirement arises from the fact that his successor was Grenville. Some have thought that Leeds was slighted out of office, to make room for Grenville. But from the conversation between Pitt and Burges just quoted, it is clear that this is not so. Pitt was anxious to appease Burges, and to confide to him the name of his new chief. But Pitt expressly declared "that from the variety of difficulties that have occurred, from the number of claims and interests to be discussed, and the multitude of things to be taken into consideration, it was impossible for him to tell with any certainty what that arrangement was likely to be."

Grenville, who played so considerable a part, has dropped out of history from sheer want of sympathy. It is due to that fatal deficiency, congenital and hereditary with him, that he is now barely remembered as a transient and unnoted premier, as the writer of an obsolete pamphlet, as a partner in a sumptuous edition of Homer, and for his behaviour to Pitt. He was not merely one of Pitt's nearest relations, being by birth his first cousin, and having married a Pitt, but he owed everything to his great kinsman. Yet he pursued Pitt with the most truculent hostility, to the very death. What human feeling he possessed was reserved for the jobs and sulks of his brother Buckingham. It is strange to read his letters to that most contemptible of human beings, who daily required incense or consolation or gossip or apology. It was a grievance against Grenville that, when Prime Minister, he did not daily pay his respects to the brother whom he had made Paymaster-General. Buckingham frowns; and Grenville's protestations of anguish and contrition and devotion rend the air. It was a grievance against Grenville when he did not, regardless of his oath, transmit cabinet secrets to this benignant relative; and again he has to kiss the dust. Great potentates have been found after death to have always worn some mortifying garment next the skin; Buckingham was Grenville's hair shirt.

Grenville was, or became, the typical Whig of his day; for Fox and Burke, with their blaze of passion and genius, were hardly Whigs; they were extremists, one way or another, and the pure Whig hated extremes. They were the gladiators and associates of those sublime personages; they were with them, not of them. Fox perhaps was rather a Liberal than a Whig; and Liberalism represents less the succession to, than the revolt against, Whiggery: Burke was a unique and undefinable factor in politics, for both parties may claim him, and both with justice. The Whig creed lay in a triple divine right: the divine right of the Whig families to govern the Empire; to be maintained by the Empire; to prove their superiority by humbling and bullying the sovereign of the Empire. Grenville was an admirable embodiment of this form of faith. By accident rather than by choice, he became the leader of the Whigs, and Fox's superior minister; he and his brothers each lived on enormous sinecures, Buckingham's amounting, it is said, to £25,000 a year; while his tactless treatment first of the King, and then of the Regent, had much to do with the long exclusion of the Whigs from office. His pride and his principle were so equally unbending that he was apt to confound the two. It is fair to say that it was not only kings that he treated like dirt; for, as he himself acknowledged, not prematurely, when he was Prime Minister, he was utterly incompetent to deal with men; and when he was Secretary of State our foreign relations suffered from that deficiency. Fox, when in the closest alliance with him, groaned under his impracticability. By 1797 it is clear that Pitt found him extremely difficult to deal with. Wilberforce notes in July 1797, "Grenville and Pitt very like breaking friendship." The familiar allusions to Grenville in Pitt's private letters to Wellesley amply confirm this view. Most significant of Pitt's experience of him is the fact, that, in the sketch of a combined administration which he drew up in 1804, he substituted Fitzwilliam as Secretary of State and relegated Grenville to the Presidency of the Council.

It was not only impediments of temper and character that caused Grenville to remain so long out of office. From the time of Pitt's death, it is clear that he ceased to care about politics. Perhaps that blow had really cut deeper than appeared on the surface. Be that as it may, Grenville was obviously not reluctant to leave office in 1807, and certainly never showed any wish to re-enter it. He was not in harmony with his party as to the war. He had achieved all that his ambition sought. He was so amply, but so strangely, provided for by the State, that the very nature of his sinecure, the holder of which was supposed to audit the First Lord of the Treasury's accounts, was an obstacle to his holding the Premiership; while its income made life too easy. More than that, to so proud a man, the Buckingham system, of which he was a part, must have made politics unendurable. To so guide a flying squadron of borough nominees as to compel the change of a marquis's coronet into a duke's, was more than Grenville could stomach, but more than he could avoid. The enchanting shades, the rare shrubs, and the rare books of Dropmore became to him what St. Anne's had been to Fox. Poor devils like Sheridan might groan, but they were of no account. The oligarchy had made up its mind to remain in the country. "Lords Grey and Grenville" had issued their decrees, and would hardly deign to come to London to pick up the seals. It is to Grenville's freezing indifference that we mainly owe the long monopoly of the Tories; disastrous in training to the Whigs, and in loss of power to the country. To him we owe it that Horner never served the public as a minister; that Brougham never knew the cares and responsibilities of such service until too late to benefit by them; that Grey (though he himself was also to blame) was unable to complete his second year of office until he was sixty-six; and that a fair growth of political buds never blossomed at all. With many talents and some qualities, Grenville's career cannot be pronounced fortunate, either for himself or his country.

CHAPTER VII

THE SHADOW OF THE FRENCH REVOLUTION

AFTER the affair of the Russian armament Pitt turned his back upon Europe; and he had good reason for doing so. He had been compelled to swallow a mortification that his proud spirit could not easily forget; he had learned that in foreign affairs Parliament is an unknown quantity; and that in Great Britain the immediate certainties of trade generally outweigh the most elaborate views of ultimate advantage. Moreover, he saw the storm-cloud overhanging France—no man could say where it would break or how far it would extend—and that it was obviously the interest of this country that it should pass over our islands and spend itself elsewhere.

No English minister can ever wish for war. Apart from the inseparable dangers to our constitution and our commerce, his own position suffers sensible detriment. He sinks into a superior commissary; he can reap little glory from success; he is the first scapegoat of failure. He too has to face, not the heroic excitement of the field, but domestic misery and discontent; the heavy burden of taxation, and the unpopularity of sacrifice which all war entails. If this be true of every minister, with how much greater force does it apply to Pitt. The task he had set himself was to raise the nation from the exhaustion of the American war; to repair her finance; to strengthen by reform the foundations of the constitution, and by a liberal Irish policy the bonds of Empire. At this very moment he was meditating, we are told, the broadest application of free-trade principles—the throwing open of our ports and the raising of our revenue entirely by internal taxation. He required, moreover, fifteen years of tranquillity to realise the fulness of the benefit of his cherished Sinking Fund. His enthusiasm was all for peace, retrenchment, and reform; he had experienced the difficulty of actively intervening in the affairs of Europe; he had no particle of that strange bias which has made some eminent statesmen believe themselves to be eminent generals; but he had the consciousness of a boundless capacity for meeting the real requirements of the country. Had he been able to carry out his own policy, had France only left him alone, or even given him a loophole for abstention, he would have been by far the greatest minister that England has ever seen. As it was, he was doomed to drag out the remainder of his life in darkness and dismay, in wrecking his whole financial edifice to find funds for incapable generals and for foreign statesmen more capable than honest, in postponing and indeed repressing all his projected reforms.

To no human being, then, did war come with such a curse as to Pitt, by none was it more hated or shunned. What made his position the more galling was that there could not have been a more inauspicious moment for war. Strangely enough, the fourteen years from the outbreak of the French Revolution to the Peace of Amiens—from 1789 till 1802—formed an almost unbroken succession of bad harvests, and that of 1792 was one of the worst of the series. There was, moreover, a commercial crisis of the first magnitude, unconnected altogether with any prospect of hostilities. For, indeed, up to within a few weeks of the actual declaration there was no sign of apprehension of war in any branch of trade; the country had rightly judged Pitt, and was confident of his determination to preserve peace. From other causes, however, there were, in November 1792, no fewer than 105 bankruptcies—almost double the number recorded of any previous month. And whereas the number of such failures in 1791 had been 769 and in 1792 934, in 1793 there were 1956; of which as many as twenty-six were those of country banks. In April 1793 Parliament had to intervene, and authorise advances amounting to £5,000,000, in Exchequer bills to leading merchants on good security. It was, then, at a moment of acute commercial and agricultural crisis that this most pacific and commercial of ministers found himself confronted with a war of the very first magnitude.

It is probable that on the continent of Europe he still stands higher than any of his contemporaries and successors as having headed the great league against France. Never was there a more involuntary distinction. If we can fancy Lord Eldon complimented for his performance of the Carmagnole, or Wycherley upon his theology, we can form some idea of the feelings with which Pitt up to 1793 would have regarded such a reputation. It is true that, when he was driven to fight, he fought with all his might and main; no prudent minister could do otherwise: that is a matter of conduct and of method, not of principle. But the supreme and salient point is that there was no man in England more resolutely determined on peace and non-intervention; and that he pushed his ostentatious ignorance of the proceedings in France, and indeed of the proceedings of Europe, to the verge of affectation.

Let us see how this matter stands; and take the positive evidence of his own pen and of his own lips. At first it is quite clear that Pitt considered the French Revolution as a matter which concerned France alone; but which by, disabling her, made a peaceful policy more easy for England. On the day of the taking of the Bastile, in ignorance of course of that event, he writes: "This scene, added to the prevailing scarcity, makes that country an object of compassion even to a rival." Fox too in February 1790 delivered a great speech against any augmentation of the peace establishment. "Had France," he cried, "remained in that formidable and triumphant state by which she was distinguished in the year 1783, I should have been the first to applaud such an augmentation." He described her as now, however, "in a state which could neither fill us with alarm nor excite us to indignation." "If fortune has humbled the pride and ambition of this mighty empire, if the anarchy and confusion incidental to such a revolution has struck her people with inertness and inactivity, why should we dread her sudden declaration of hostilities?" Small blame, perhaps, attaches to Fox for this extremely imperfect appreciation of an unprecedented situation; on the other hand, in the teeth of such declarations it is unwise to claim for him any superior policy of prescience. Pitt's reply was no less remarkable. "The present convulsions in France must sooner or later terminate in general harmony and regular order, and though the fortunate arrangements of such a situation may make her more formidable, they may also render her less obnoxious as a neighbour. I hope I may rather wish as an Englishman for that, respecting the accomplishment of which I feel myself interested as a man, for the restoration of tranquillity in France, though that appears to me to be distant. Whenever the situation of France shall become restored, it will prove freedom rightly understood, freedom resulting from good order and good government; and thus circumstanced France will stand forward as one of the most brilliant pioneers of Europe: she will enjoy that just kind of liberty which I venerate, and the invaluable existence of which it is my duty as an Englishman to cherish. Nor can I under this predicament regard with envious eyes an approximation in neighbouring states to those sentiments which are the characteristic features of every British subject." "And," he concluded, "we must endeavour to improve for our security, happiness, and aggrandisement those precious moments of peace and leisure which are before us." It will be observed that the tone of the minister is one of almost patronising friendship. Yet within a year or two he was to be universally denounced as the ruthless and inveterate enemy of the new state of things in France.

In October 1790 he writes to Hugh Elliot: "This country means to persevere in the neutrality which it has hitherto scrupulously observed with respect to the internal dissensions of France, and from which it will never depart unless the conduct held there should make it indispensable as an act of self-defence. . . . We are sincerely desirous of preserving peace and of cultivating in general a friendly intercourse and understanding between the two nations." Again, in July 1791, he writes to his mother: "We are all anxious *spectators* of the strange scene in France," and by underlining the word "spectators" he emphasises the attitude he was determined to maintain.

It is, however, in February 1792 that we obtain the most remarkable view of his mind on this subject. It was then that he delivered that famous survey of the finance of the country which has been noticed as the exception to his commonplace budgets of these four years. In it he repealed taxes, he added to the Sinking Fund, he reduced the previous vote for seamen by 2000 men—from 18,000 to 16,000—he declined to renew the subsidy for the Hessian mercenaries. And to raise hopes of further reductions he declared that: "Unquestionably there never was a time in the history of this country when from the situation of Europe we might more reasonably expect fifteen years of peace than at the present moment." This, it may be said, is a random expression in debate. Even in a budget speech, an eloquent and sanguine Chancellor of the Exchequer may be betrayed into a flash of extravagance by the high hopes that he entertains and excites. On the contrary, this was a speech as to which extraordinary means were taken to supplement the imperfect reporting arrangements of that day. Moreover, this unusually accurate result was submitted to Pitt, and the speech is one of the two, or at most three, which he corrected for publication. So far, then, from this being a haphazard utterance of impulse, it may be considered, delivered as it was after three years of watching and waiting, specially reported and personally revised, as one of the most mature expressions of Pitt's most deliberate opinions. Nothing, perhaps, can more than this impress the reader who remembers that within twelve months the great war between France and England had begun. But Pitt's letter of the 13th of November 1792 to Lord Stafford is, if possible, still more remarkable. He was writing within ten weeks of the commencement of hostilities, and says: "However unfortunate it would be to find this country in any shape committed;" and further: "Perhaps some opening may arise which may enable us to contribute to the termination of the war between different powers in Europe, leaving France (which I believe is the best way) to arrange its own internal affairs as it can." It will be perceived that he still speaks as a mere spectator of the war in Europe, and as a supporter of the sound and wholesome policy with regard to France which he had always advocated: this but a few days before France had declared the Scheldt open, and her readiness to overturn every established government in Europe.

Grenville's language is even stronger. He was at this time, it will be remembered, Pitt's Foreign Secretary. Six days before the letter last quoted, (November 7, 1792), he writes: "Portugal and Holland will do what we please. *We shall do nothing*. . . . All my ambition is that I may at some time hereafter . . . have the inexpressible satisfaction of being able . . . to tell myself that I have contributed to keep my own country at least a little longer from sharing in all the evils of every sort that surround us. *I am more and more convinced that this can only be done by keeping wholly and entirely aloof*:"—and he continues in the same spirit.

This language was fully embodied in action, or rather inaction. In spite of many provocations, the Government preserved a severe neutrality. They would have nothing to do with the expedition of Brunswick, towards which they preserved rather an unfriendly than a friendly attitude. They indeed recalled Gower, the ambassador in Paris, after the events of the 10th of August 1792, but that was because the King to whom he was accredited was actually suspended, and soon afterwards deposed; so that his mission had terminated, and he had no longer any functions to discharge; while the fact that an insult to his person or domicile was possible in the convulsed condition of Paris, made his presence there an actual danger to peace. They ordered Chauvelin, the ex-envoy of France, to leave England after the execution of Louis XVI.; but public sentiment left no choice in that matter, and Chauvelin had been actively employed, since his official character had ceased, less as a diplomatic than what is known in police language as a provocative agent. On the other hand, they saw Belgium, and what is more, Antwerp, seized by France, but they determined not to make either event a cause of war. It may safely be said that few ministries would have remained so passive. They witnessed the promulgation of a policy of universal disturbance, which culminated in the decrees of the 19th of November and the 15th of December 1792.

The first of these decrees promised assistance to all nations that should revolt against their governments, and was accentuated by the constant reception of English deputations to whom the Convention promised early "liberty"; while the second compelled all territories occupied by the French to accept the new French institutions. As the French had seized Savoy and Nice, the Low Countries, and the Rhine Provinces of Germany, there was an ample area for its execution.

By these decrees the French Government had not merely placed all monarchies on their defence, but goaded them into war. Nor were they merely abstract declarations; they were accentuated by constant promises of action. A few days after their promulgation a deputation from Great Britain, which came to intimate its intention of overturning the British Government, was received with rapture by the Convention, which assured the delegates that the day was at hand when France would be able to congratulate the National Assembly of England. These deputations were numerous and frequent, and were invariably received with the same incendiary assurances. France, in fact, would not leave other countries alone—would not leave England alone. By so doing she disarmed the most ardent and powerful advocate in England for peace at almost any cost—the Prime Minister himself.

It can hardly be denied that the Government pushed their neutrality to an extreme point. On the publication of the decrees, however,—these being the open declaration of a proselytising policy which was at the moment being carried into effect by arms,—and when the navigation of the Scheldt was thrown open, this imperturbability began to give way. The navigation of the Scheldt had been assured to the Dutch by the treaty of Westphalia. It had been repeatedly guaranteed by the Powers; by France herself in 1785; and by Pitt in the name of Great Britain more solemnly and specially in 1788. The French now declared these provisions abrogated by the law of nature, and the Scheldt to be an open river. It was impossible for Pitt to pass by his own treaty of 1788, without a violation of good faith, so signal as to be remarkable even at the time of the second partition of Poland. But, on wider grounds, the danger to Europe was more universal. To allow that the French Government were in possession of a law of nature which superseded all treaty obligations, and the copyright and application of which rested exclusively with them, was to annihilate the whole European system. On this point, however, the French were firm. They were ready to explain away the decree of the 19th of November, but on the question of declaring the Scheldt open, and open by the operation of natural law, they would give no satisfaction at all. Moreover, it was certain that an invasion of Holland was being prepared; and the treaty of 1788, barely four years old, compelled Pitt, without any possibility of evasion, to come to the assistance of the States.

It became clear now, even to those most unwilling to see, that war was inevitable. Then came the execution of Louis XVI. A universal shudder ran through England. The nation went into mourning. The playhouses were closed. Maret, afterwards Duc de Bassano, who was secretly in London as a semi-diplomatic agent, said that he could not leave the house for fear of being exposed to the "insults and ignorant ferocity" of the populace. The King could not leave his palace without being surrounded by crowds demanding instant war. A fortnight before, Fox had been nearly turned out of a vestry meeting at St. George's. But the feeling then, which this circumstance proves to have been sufficiently bitter, was faint compared to the horror excited by the death of Louis. Yet Maret wrote days after that event that Pitt was still sincerely anxious for peace. There is something pathetic in this flash of light thrown on the lonely figure, clinging to hope with the tenacity of despair. As it fades, the darkness closes, and the Pitt of peace, prosperity, and reform disappears for ever.

While Maret was writing his report, war was already decreed. On the 1st of February 1793 the French Convention—moved, as Maret said, by stockjobbers, as Roland said, by the necessity of finding employment for armed desperadoes—declared war on the rulers of Great Britain and Holland. Pitt cherished one last sanguine belief. He was confident that the condition of her finances made it impossible for France to wage war for more than a short time; just as a few years later he is said to have assured the House of Commons that he could see his way to one more loan of twenty millions, but that then the credit of England would be exhausted. Both forecasts were probably correct according to experience; but the French Revolution was destined to annihilate the guidance of experience, and to elicit unsuspected powers both in France and in England. At any rate, Pitt entered on the contest under the firm faith that any war with France must necessarily be brief.

Two points remain to be noticed. Why, if Pitt was so much opposed to war, did he not resign? The answer is simple. His resignation would not have prevented war in any case. Besides, he had no excuse or colourable ground for resignation. He could not go to the King or to Parliament and say, "I have resigned because I would not go to war. The case for war has arisen under a treaty I concluded with infinite pains four years ago. Yet, rather than avert the very danger against which it was framed, I wish to resign and let others fight for my treaty." The bare statement of the case needs no further demonstration; he would simply have been succeeded by a minister much more warlike and much less capable than himself.

The other matter is this. A wearisome busybody called Miles has left it on record that George III. bullied Pitt into war. But this story is on the face of it untrue; has, indeed, not the remotest plausibility. The date given for the transaction is 1791. If the story be true, Pitt ought to have been dismissed in that year, for it was not until November 1792 that the bare possibility of going to war occurred to him. The authority given for this preposterous statement is Moira, who declared that he was to have succeeded Pitt at the Treasury. That George III. should dismiss Pitt to take to his counsels the bosom friend of the Prince of Wales, would seem to reveal a fit of lunacy of which we have no other record. The relations between Pitt and George III. were very far from being of this nature. It is no disparagement to either to say that the King would not have ventured to send such an ultimatum to Pitt; nor at first did he feel any great hostility to the popular movement in France. The royal sentiments with regard to the war were transparent enough. It does not need a Rochefoucault to understand that the first humiliations of that French Court, which had so largely contributed to secure the independence of the United States, were observed without poignant displeasure at St. James's. And, up to the last moment, the King, as Elector of Hanover, maintained an absolute neutrality. But when monarchy was abolished, and the monarch a prisoner, the drama became unrelieved tragedy. Then, no doubt, the King was anxious for war; and at the end of 1792 Pitt had lost every weapon by which he could oppose it. That, however, is a very different matter from the King's sending word to Pitt that he must either go to war or make way for Moira.

It is, then, abundantly manifest from every source of evidence that war was forced on the English Ministry; that Pitt carried to an extreme his anxiety to avoid it; that his resignation could not have averted it; and that in any case it was impossible for him as a man of honour, or a serious statesman, to resign. We shall see, when war had begun, his constant endeavours to put an end to it. Whether he was a great war-minister, as he is generally considered, or an incapable war-minister, as he is called by Macaulay, he is certainly the most strenuous peace-minister that ever held office in this country.

CHAPTER VIII

WAR

It does not seem necessary in a sketch of Pitt's career to enter at large into the incidents of the war that raged from February 1793 to the preliminaries of the Peace of Amiens in 1801. Its first incident as concerns Great Britain was that an army was sent to Flanders under the Duke of York, to act in conjunction with an Austrian army under the Prince of Coburg. From February to August, (1793), the French sustained an unbroken series of disasters. Dumouriez was defeated at the battle of Neerwinden, and deserted to the enemy. Belgium fell into the hands of Austria. Mayence with a garrison of twenty, and Valenciennes with a garrison of eight thousand men surrendered to the allied forces. Toulon admitted an English fleet. But the French were stimulated and not cowed by these reverses. They called the whole population to arms. They set in array a million of soldiers. Naturally brave, but now inspired with the last heroism of patriotism and despair, they turned the tide of fortune. York was driven from Dunkirk with the loss of all his heavy artillery. The Austrians were defeated at Wattignies. The internal enemies of the Republic were ruthlessly crushed. Lyons fell, and Marseilles. The royalists of La Vendée were scattered and slaughtered. Toulon was taken and introduced Napoleon to the world;—a heavier blow to the allies than the loss of a score of fortresses or armies. A few months later, by a strange freak of fate, he became a subject of the King of Great Britain, when Corsica proclaimed herself a monarchy under the sovereignty of George III. Prussia began to withdraw from the war, preferring the tangible advantages of an immediate share of Poland to the much more doubtful possibilities of a problematical partition of France. The Austrians were overthrown on the historical battlefields of Worth and Weissenburg; while Brunswick once more displayed his sinister strategy in a retrograde movement.

In the succeeding year (1794) the battle of Fleurus, followed by a retreat of the Austrians, which is explained less by that defeat than the policy of their government, put an end to the campaign of Flanders; Belgium and Holland fell into the hands of the French. The German Emperor, who had come to witness victory, returned to Vienna. Coburg and York were recalled. On their eastern frontier the French repelled the Prussians, and on their southern, the Spaniards and the Portuguese. So great was the effect of their successes that, at the opening of the parliamentary session, on the 30th of December 1794, there were several motions urging negotiation, two of them brought forward by Wilberforce.

As some set-off to this picture, it may be recorded that the English had captured the French settlements in India and a few West Indian islands; while, at the famous battle of 1st June 1794, Lord Howe secured a crushing victory over the fleet of France.

To the British Government also occurred a signal advantage for the future conduct of the war by the adhesion of a number of the principal Whigs. Portland, the ex-Prime Minister, and Windham, a brilliant but fantastic orator; Lord Spencer, an administrator of signal ability, and Lord Fitzwilliam, a great noble of less tact than character, joined the Government, and the moral effect produced by their accession was greater than any personal assistance that they could render. It gave a national character to the Administration and to the war. It reduced the Opposition in the House of Commons to something less than fifty; a little later they were able to travel with comfort in two hackney coaches.

As the war continued, the superiority of France increased. In April 1795 Prussia, in June Sweden, and in July Spain came to terms with the triumphant Republic. A limited consolation might perhaps be derived from the fact that the Court of Vienna continued its readiness to receive subsidies from England; but in other respects it showed little activity, though its armies under Clairfait gained some unfruitful victories in the autumn. Pitt's Government displayed a singular but luckless energy. Windham, the new War Minister, built his greatest hopes on an expedition of French aristocrats and malcontents to Quiberon Bay; but this force, sumptuously provided with money and munitions of war, and supported by a powerful fleet, was pulverised by Hoche as soon as it landed. In the West Indies the English arms lost ground. On the other hand, the Empire was enriched by the splendid acquisitions of the

Cape of Good Hope and Ceylon. Pitt's hopefulness was in no degree diminished. He wrote to Addington (October 1795) that he trusted to open his budget before Christmas. "If that goes off tolerably well," he added, "it will give us peace before Easter."

In 1796 a general election refreshed Pitt's majority. While it proceeded, he sent on his own responsibility a subsidy of £1,200,000 to Austria,—a grave act, fiercely censured by the Opposition, and only condoned by a devoted House of Commons, on the express stipulation that it should not be considered a precedent. He was rewarded by the recall of Clairfait and the substitution of the Archduke Charles,—a young prince whose consummate generalship was sometimes crippled by physical disabilities, and oftener by the pedantry of his own Government, but who stands forth as one of the most brilliant opponents of Napoleon. He at once defeated Jourdan, and drove the French back across the Rhine. In the West Indies, Great Britain also secured some advantages. But all was darkened and eclipsed by the Italian campaign of the irresistible Bonaparte; while Spain and Prussia entered into distinct alliance with France.

This year (1796) began and ended with determined overtures for peace on the part of Pitt. In the previous December (1795), the minister had brought a royal message to Parliament, declaring that the establishment of a new constitution in France (that of the Directory) offered facilities for negotiation. In March, Pitt made an earnest and genuine overture for a general pacification, through Wickham, our envoy in Switzerland; but it was ungraciously received, and was rejected.

Again, in October, Lord Malmesbury, a diplomatist of the highest distinction, was sent to Paris. But as had happened in March, the envoy's instructions to insist on the evacuation of the Netherlands by France rendered negotiation fruitless. On the 19th of December (1796) he was ordered to leave France within forty-eight hours. Four days earlier, a French fleet, with an army under General Hoche, had sailed for the invasion of Ireland. The expedition was, however, wholly unsuccessful. The weather was unfavourable; the fleet was scattered; Hoche was in one portion, the army in another; both returned separately to France, and the hopes of Irish discontent were postponed. A slighter enterprise of a filibustering character directed against south-western England completely failed. A far greater effort was, moreover, crushed in its inception. It had been calculated that by a junction of the Dutch, the French, and the Spanish fleets, another and more fortunate Armada might effect the invasion of England. But the great victory of St. Vincent, fought on the 14th of February 1797, by which Jervis and Nelson crushed the Spanish contingent, blighted these hopes.

The year 1797, which opened so brilliantly, was destined to be the darkest and most desperate that any British minister has ever had to face. In April, Austria, England's last ally, laid down her arms and concluded a preliminary treaty of peace at Leoben (April 7, 1797). France was now free to turn her victorious armies and her inexhaustible resources to the destruction of England; and she was determined to do so.

At this moment Great Britain was paralysed. The

Navy, that had just given fresh courage to the nation, was now to deal a blow which struck at the heart and stopped the circulation of the Empire. In the middle of April, the crews of the Channel Fleet at Portsmouth rose in rebellion, dismissed their officers, and hoisted the red flag. Their grievances were great, their demands were moderate; and these had to be conceded with a full amnesty. By the end of April the mutiny was over. At the beginning of May, however, it broke out again and spread to Sheerness. Here it assumed a graver aspect, and bore all the marks of being inspired by revolutionary agencies outside. There was, indeed, no sympathy between the two movements. The sailors at Spithead sent word to the sailors at Sheerness that their conduct was a "scandal to the name of British seamen." Nevertheless, the Government was as much disabled by the one as the other. The fleet with which Duncan was blockading the coast of Holland joined the rebels, with the exception of two ships. With these the Admiral kept signalling as if to the rest of his squadron: a mild stratagem, on which, however, the safety of England depended, and which was happily successful. In these days the news would have been flashed to every nook of Europe, and Britain would have lain at the mercy of her enemies. Fortunately neither the French nor the Dutch had any idea of our condition.

The mutiny lasted five weeks and spread all over the world. It smouldered in the victorious fleet of Jervis; who, however, suppressed it with a prompt and masterful hand. The crew of the *Hermione*, cruising near Porto Rico, outraged by the inhumanity of their captain, killed all their officers, and delivered their ship to the Spaniards.

At the Cape of Good Hope, the British squadron was in open revolt; but was overcome by the ready firmness of the Governor and Admiral. It began to affect the artillerymen at Woolwich. There was an attempt to seduce the army. What a position for a country engaged in a life-and-death struggle with a triumphant enemy! Never in the history of England was there a darker hour. The year had begun indeed with one great naval victory, and was destined to close with another. But these isolated successes formed the sole relief to a scene of perpetual gloom. Our generals and armies had been so uniformly unfortunate that we had no longer a foot on the continent of Europe. On land our great foe was everywhere triumphant. We were entirely on the defensive. Two invasions of our islands had been attempted. A third was impending; it might at any moment take place, and could scarcely be opposed.

The war had lasted over four years; and had added a hundred and thirty-five millions to the National Debt, or about as much as the whole cost of the American war, for scarce any corresponding advantage. The Funds had fallen to a lower point than in the worst depression of the American war. In December 1796 it had been necessary to propose a further loan of eighteen millions, and three millions and a half of new taxes. The loan, though issued at a price which produced $5\frac{5}{8}$ per cent, was at $15\frac{1}{2}$ discount in March 1797. There had been an unexampled run on the Bank of England. Cash payments had just been suspended. There was a terrible dearth. Not merely were the ports thrown open to foreign corn, but large bounties were paid on its importation. The last of our allies had just made her peace with France; and we were left to continue the contest alone. Our own efforts to come to terms had been so received as to make all hope of truce indefinitely remote. The worst of all wars was raging in Ireland. Scotland, though not harried into open rebellion, was scarcely less discontented. England was maddened by crimps and press-gangs and unprecedented taxation. Pitt was grossly insulted in the streets; he had to be brought back from St. Paul's under an armed guard. And at this juncture our one efficient arm, to which alone the nation could look for solace and even protection, was paralysed by insubordination: the flag of lawlessness had been hoisted; and the guns of the navy were pointed at British shores. But the spirit of the minister was not shaken, though his health had begun definitively to fail. At the height of the crisis, Lord Spencer came to him for instructions so pressing—(for it was said that the marines had joined the revolt and were about to march on London)—that he awoke Pitt in bed. He received them and left; but in a short time he received a contradiction, and returned. He found the minister already asleep.

This crisis has been dwelt on at perhaps disproportionate length, because it represents not merely the darkest period of the war, but the dauntless spirit which faced it, and which enabled this country, in spite of incapacity and blunders and debt, in face of the hostility of a surpassing genius and of a world in arms, finally to surmount its difficulties. And we are thus able to understand why Pitt, with all his share of miscalculation and disaster, remained long after his death the embodiment and watchword of British determination.

Once more this year did he make overtures for peace. "I feel it my duty," he repeated to Grenville, who urged that the French minister was treating him with scant courtesy, "as a English minister and a Christian, to use every effort to stop so bloody and wasting a war." Grenville formally dissented. But Pitt persisted, in spite of the disapproval of his Foreign Secretary and the anguish of the King. He sent Lord Malmesbury, whose instructions Grenville had the irksome task of drawing, to the town of Lille, which had been fixed for the meeting of the plenipotentiaries. These, however, had their eyes fixed on Paris, where a struggle was impending between the extreme and the moderate factions; on the issue of which, and on nothing else—for Pitt was ready for the most considerable concessions—peace really depended. On the 4th of September 1797 the party of extremes and of war gained the upper hand, and on the 18th of September Malmesbury was again ordered to leave the soil of France.

During the next month, (October 1797), the eclipse of the Navy was proved to be only temporary. In a bloody and obstinate battle off Camperdown the Dutch fleet, once so famous and so formidable, took its leave of history. It fought with a splendour of heroism worthy of its ancient renown, but was defeated by Admiral Duncan at the head of the fleet which had returned to discipline; and thus this black year ended well.

In the year 1798, the struggle had ceased on the continent of Europe, with the exception of a brief campaign in the kingdom of Naples. The genius of war in the shape of Napoleon was in Egypt; where

Nelson, by destroying the French fleet in Aboukir Bay (August 1798), seemed effectually to confine him. We were fully occupied at home by the rebellion in Ireland; which might, had timely succour arrived from France, have proved sufficient to tax the entire energies of the Empire. When it is remembered that the population of Ireland was then little less than one-third of the whole population of the United Kingdom; that it was largely in possession of arms, and almost wholly disaffected; it is not easy to calculate what would have been the extreme extent of the danger, had one of the many French expeditions, under such a general as Hoche, arrived to aid and discipline the revolt. Fortunately for us, the French force under Humbert, which landed in Killala Bay on the 22d of August (1798), came two months too late; for the battle of Vinegar Hill, in which the insurgent forces were completely routed, had been fought on the 21st of June. Moreover, Ulster, which had been the province most organised and eager for insurrection, held aloof—deterred by the religious character of the rising; and the rebellion spent itself in the isolated efforts of a war of banditti, distinguished by constant horrors of outrage and reprisal.

In this year Pitt himself engaged in single combat. Tierney had declared that the proposal to carry the Bill for the more effectual manning of the Navy in one day was somewhat precipitate. Pitt, in reply, charged him with a desire to obstruct the defence of the country. The taunt of obstruction, even of obstruction so mild as to be almost imperceptible to the palled palate of our generation, was then an insult to be wiped out with blood. The statesmen met and exchanged shots;

while Pitt's devoted friend the Speaker, Addington, watched the harmless combat from the genial shade of a gibbet on an adjoining hill. Addington was destined to be Pitt's successor; but it is said that Pitt was asked by Ryder, his second, on this occasion, who should succeed him in case of the worst, and that he designated Perceval. This nomination would be inexplicable, did there not exist a letter of Pitt's which shows the extraordinary impression that had been produced on him by a recent speech of Perceval's. Pitt's own account of the combat is still happily extant, in a letter to Lord Wellesley. In it he lightly declares as to Tierney and himself: "I believe we parted better satisfied with each other, than on any other occasion in our lives."[1]

The duel seems childish to us now, and may have seemed so then, for it was followed by a widely circulated report that Pitt was insane,—a rumour less discreditable under the circumstances than such rumours usually are. Though he was not insane, there is no doubt that his health was seriously impaired, to which, perhaps, we may attribute his loss of self-control on this occasion.

The break-up of his constitution is so marked and so important that it deserves a momentary reference; as it marks an era in his career scarcely less critical than the declaration of war in 1793.

It has been seen that Pitt was a delicate child. A careful course of life, except in regard to the large quantity of port that he was accustomed to drink, had enabled him to get through his work and enjoy his holiday without interruption up to 1797. In that year,

[1] See below, p. 210.

the death of his brother-in-law Eliot deeply affected him; and at that very time he began to complain of illness. He suffered greatly from headaches. What is more significant is that he began to speak of retirement, and of Addington as his successor. It is clear that these allusions were due to yielding nerves and broken health; for the reasons which afterwards caused his resignation did not then exist. His condition became worse in 1798. The passage with Tierney reveals a petulance alien to his singular self-command. And when Wilberforce threatened a motion condemning the principle of duelling, Pitt wrote to him that he considered it as one for his own removal. The report of his insanity probably arose from a continuous display of nervous irritability, culminating in the duel. A few days after his letter to Wilberforce, this last notes that his friend was seriously ill. Wine began to produce an effect on his seasoned head. In August 1798, Lord Auckland reports him as much shaken in his constitution. It is clear that 1798 marks an evil crisis in Pitt's health, which accounts for much in his subsequent career. The man is different afterwards. His will seems to shrink; he has less self-control. The illness of princes and ministers is always a subject of hard swearing; and it will be curious to watch if the archives of Pitt's contemporaries, as they yield their treasures, will gradually clear up a certain air of mystery that surrounds his health in this year.

Meanwhile, Pitt was strenuously combining a second coalition against France. He found in the Czar Paul, who had recently succeeded to the throne of Russia, an ardent if insane ally, who was able to contribute not only great armies but a consummate general to the common cause. The Porte, outraged by the French occupation of Egypt, readily lent its aid. Naples, alarmed by the French invasion of Italy, also prepared for war. Austria, who had recently come to terms with the French at Campo Formio, finding herself tricked, was again arming. Thus, with powerful armies commanded by the genius of Suvaroff and the Archduke Charles; with the fleets of Great Britain in absolute supremacy at sea; and with Napoleon blockaded in Egypt; the year 1799 opened with splendid prospects for the new confederacy.

Had it not been for the strange oscillations of Austria, all these bright presages might well have been realised. But the brilliant victories, with which Charles and Suvaroff opened the campaign in Switzerland and northern Italy, were rendered futile by the orders from Vienna. Russia retired disgusted from the contest. Austria persevered for one year more, unequally matched with Napoleon, who had succeeded in returning to Europe. England's share of the war, besides subsidies, was to send another expedition to Holland, then the favourite theatre of English incompetency. It was commanded by the Duke of York, and was, though the Dutch fleet was finally captured, indecisive and even disastrous. Pitt, ever sanguine, derived a whimsical consolation in its discreditable termination from the fact that "it ought to be a great satisfaction to us to know that our valuable army will be restored to us safe and entire." Against this failure it is only fair to set off a great triumph in the East. Tippoo, the sovereign of Mysore and the relentless enemy of Great Britain, encouraged by the presence of the French army in Egypt, had become a serious danger to our dominion in India. Under the command of General Harris, with the guidance of Lord Wellesley and his greater brother, a British army invaded Mysore, and after an obstinate combat stormed Seringapatam. Tippoo fell, and his kingdom was divided.

In Egypt, again, Sir Sidney Smith had held Acre against Napoleon, who, after a pertinacious investment of sixty days, was obliged to retire: the sole check that he knew in his career, until he crossed the Pyrenees.

The last day of the year 1799 brought a letter from Napoleon, who had just become First Consul, with overtures for peace. It was scarcely six weeks since a revolution had placed him in power; and Pitt, dogged in his anxiety for a cessation of warfare though he was, felt that the actual situation of France did not hold out any solid security to be derived from negotiation. He was anxious, however, to express this negative in terms of eagerness for peace, with a hint that that would be best secured by the restoration of royalty.

It was a pity that the task of answering the First Consul's letter devolved upon Grenville. The didactic despatch is unhappily familiar to us in the annals of British diplomacy. England has always assumed the possession of a European censorship, which impels her to administer exhortation and rebuke to the States of the continent through the medium of her Foreign Office, as well as by the articles of her press. It is this peculiarity which has constantly earned for her an unpopularity of the most universal and the most exquisite kind. No British minister or journalist has, however, carried this spirit further than Grenville on this occasion. He did not send any direct reply to Bonaparte's letter, but he enclosed to the Foreign Minister at Paris what was, though called a note, in reality a supercilious and arrogant lecture to the French nation. Harping on a "system" which he did not further describe, but which he said was the source of all the woes of France and of Europe, he informed Talleyrand that "His Majesty cannot place his reliance on the mere renewal of general professions of pacific dispositions." Some further guarantee was required. "The best and most natural pledge of its reality and permanence would be the restoration of that line of princes, which for so many centuries maintained the French nation in prosperity at home and in consideration and respect abroad," and so forth. There is a fine untutored insolence in this communication, addressed to the triumphant head of a victorious republic, that would be difficult to match. Even George III. could not stomach it. He wrote on the draft, "In my opinion much too strong, but I suppose it must go."

To the advice thus considerately offered, Napoleon despatched a conclusive reply. "The First Consul," he wrote, "of the French Republic could not doubt that his Britannic majesty recognised the right of nations to choose the form of their government, since it is from the exercise of this right that he holds his crown; but he has been unable to comprehend how to this fundamental principle, upon which rests the existence of political societies, the minister of His Majesty could annex insinuations which tend to an interference in the internal affairs of the republic, and which are no less injurious to the French nation as to its government, than it would be to England and His Majesty if a sort of invitation were held out in favour of that republican government of which England adopted the forms in the middle of the last century, or an exhortation to recall to the throne that family whom their birth had placed there, and whom a revolution compelled to descend from it." He concluded by proposing to put an immediate end to hostilities, and to name plenipotentiaries to meet at once at Dunkirk or some similar place. Grenville sent a bald and meagre rejoinder saying, what was in fact untrue, that he had no desire to prescribe to a foreign country the form of its government, and refusing the offer.

We may assume from what we now know of the character of Napoleon as it developed itself, that a durable peace could not then have been concluded; but it is melancholy that Pitt, who had grasped at hopes so much more slender, should have declined even to entertain this solid proffer. He was willing to negotiate in the succeeding August; but in January the French Government was not sufficiently established. On this point Fox was especially happy. "We must keep Bonaparte some time longer at war as a state of probation. Gracious God! is war a state of probation? Is peace a rash system? Is it dangerous for nations to live in amity with each other? Is your vigilance, your policy, your common powers of observation to be relinquished by putting an end to the horrors of war? Cannot this state of probation be as well undergone without adding to the catalogue of human suffering? But we must pause. What! must the bowels of Great Britain be torn out—her best blood be spilt, her treasure wasted, that you may make an experiment?" After pointing out that soldiers in other battles, such as Blenheim, at least knew what they were fighting for, he proceeded: "But if a man were present now at a field of slaughter, and were to inquire for what they were fighting, 'Fighting!' would be the answer, 'they are not fighting, they are pausing.' 'Why is that man expiring? Why is that other writhing with agony? What means this implacable fury?' The answer must be, 'You are quite wrong, sir; you deceive yourself; they are not fighting; do not disturb them, they are merely pausing! This man is not expiring with agony—that man is not dead—he is only pausing. Lord help you, sir! They are not angry with one another. They have now no cause of quarrel, but their country thinks there should be a pause,'" and so forth.

This volley of reason and pleasantry was all the more stinging from being directed at what was, indeed, Pitt's real motive, (as we see in a letter to Dundas of the 31st of December 1799), which was to wait, or, as Fox would have said, to continue fighting until the French Government was firmly established. Nothing could be more impolitic than this refusal, except the manner of it. If Bonaparte were insincere, as was said, and only wished to make the French believe that the wish for peace was on his side and not on ours, the negative upon negotiation was playing his game. If he were sincere, the responsibility of the Government was unbounded. Moreover, there was the advantage of dealing with a strong administration, even if its durability was insufficiently proved. It must, however, be acknowledged that the reception of peace proposals in France had hitherto been far from encouraging; that the dealings of the French with other nations even in the act of treaty did not inspire confidence; and that the course of negotiation in the succeeding August shows that Bonaparte rather desired to snap an advantage by parley, than to establish anything like a durable peace.

In 1800, the Austrians, after a succession of disasters, were compelled to conclude an armistice; and Pitt again made overtures for peace through Lord Minto, our ambassador at Vienna, so that a settlement might be arrived at in conjunction with Austria, and not by separate negotiation. But the preliminary conditions of the French stipulated that they should be allowed to send supplies, while negotiations were pending, to their army in Egypt, and to their garrison in Malta, which were blockaded by our fleets. This would have deprived the British Government of the only trumps in their hand. The opportunity, therefore, if it was one, again passed away. But it elicited a curious memorandum from Dundas, showing the fierce divisions that existed in the Cabinet on foreign policy. He traces no less than four factions in a cabinet of a dozen persons, ranging from Windham, the representative of Burke, the apostle of holy and eternal war with the Revolution, to the less exalted views of Pitt, who was anxious for peace on any decent terms. These differences were not abstract, but practical and incessant. It is clear, therefore, that Pitt must not merely have overridden some of his colleagues in his negotiations, but looked to a certain break up of his Cabinet, had they been successful. It is necessary to note that, while the negotiations were proceeding,

Malta fell into the hands of the English (September 1800).

Austria was more successful. She concluded peace at Lunéville in February 1801. That peace, which marks the termination of the Second Coalition, coincides with Pitt's retirement from office.

CHAPTER IX

PITT AS A WAR MINISTER

THE notable points of these years as regards Pitt's conduct of the war and of foreign policy are these :—his two endeavours to combine Europe against the common enemy ; his constant anxiety for peace ; the four direct overtures which he made with that object ; the almost uniform success of the enemy on land, and the uniform triumph of our arms at sea ; finally, the dictatorship with which the country wisely entrusted him, which enabled him to overrule the dissensions of the Cabinet and carry on war, if not triumphantly, at any rate with more success than would otherwise have been possible under the conditions royal, aristocratic, and traditional, which so hampered our efforts.

Pitt's war policy was twofold : it was a naval policy and a policy of subsidy. His enterprises by land were neither numerous nor successful. There he spent himself in scattered and isolated efforts, costly both in money and life. It was calculated that these expeditions had, at the Peace of Amiens, cost us no less than 1350 officers and 60,000 men. But our fleet swept the seas ; and swept all hostile colonies into our net. Something falls now to be said of his subsidies.

At first sight subsidies have a crude appearance, nor have they agreeable associations. They are apt to recall the time when degenerate emperors were buying off hungry barbarians, or the doles that Charles and James II. received from Louis XIV. But they must be judged on their separate merits. A nation that conducts its main operations by sea, and endeavours also to stimulate hostilities by land, has hardly any choice in the matter. She has, on this presumption, no spare army to send; and she must contribute something more substantial than goodwill or despatches. Pitt, it must be remembered, was in the position of being at war with an enemy of more than twenty-seven millions with many vassal states, though the population of Britain was little more than ten millions, while that of Ireland at her side could only be reckoned to the enemy. His policy of subsidies was, therefore, a necessity; for, while the population of France was eminently warlike, that of England was relatively rich. The essential point, however, in advancing money under these conditions, is to receive in return the services for which the payment is made. This is a precaution not free from difficulty; and so Pitt found it.

His subsidies were of two kinds: guaranteed loans or direct gifts, though they were only different in form, as the result to the taxpayer was the same in either case. Of the first description there were two. One was a loan of £4,600,000, made in 1795, under an Act passed to give effect to a Convention between Great Britain and the Emperor of Germany, dated on the 4th of May 1795. By this instrument it had been stipulated that, in consideration of the maintenance by Austria of

200,000 troops in the war against France, Great Britain should guarantee the interest on this loan. As, after the first two years, Austria was unable to provide the requisite sum, the burden henceforth fell on the British Exchequer. This guarantee Fox describes as "the most imprudent measure, all things considered, that ever was carried through."

Again, a similar Convention was concluded on the 16th of May 1797, and a loan of £1,620,000 made on the same conditions. But the charge fell entirely on the British Exchequer, as Austria was unable to pay anything. Besides these loans, it may be of interest to add[1] a list of the subsidies which were gifts during Pitt's governments, as furnished to Parliament in 1815.

But the subsidies, though considerable, formed of course only a small fraction of the cost of the war. On this point something must now be said.

The total addition made to the capital liabilities of the State between the 1st of February 1793 and the 17th of March 1801 amounted in stock to £325,201,460.[2] Stock, however, did not constitute the whole liability. For, in addition to stock, subscribers often received, as part of their security, a certain amount of terminable annuities. These terminable annuities, (which expired in 1860), were known as the "Long Annuities"; and their capital value, if computed at a rate of 5 per cent interest, may be taken to amount to £9,323,976 at the end of the eighth year of war (1800-1). Thus Pitt increased the capital liabilities of the State for war purposes in the course of those years by a total sum of £334,525,436. But it must be remembered,

[1] See Appendix A. [2] See Appendix B.

that, during all this period, Pitt's Sinking Fund was at work. While he was borrowing with one hand, with the other he was still setting aside large sums for the redemption of debt by the purchase of stock. The stock, therefore, acquired during this period by the National Debt Commissioners, amounting to £42,515,832,[1] must be deducted from the total liabilities, if it is desired to ascertain the burden that the war during these years laid upon posterity. The result of the deduction gives a net total of £292,009,604 as the war burden permanently imposed by Pitt in his first and main administration.[2]

Of these 334½ millions Pitt only received about 200 millions in cash. He borrowed in a stock of a low denomination; and, as in January 1797, for example, the 3 per cents fell to 47, it may readily be imagined at what a sacrifice of capital value the loans were raised. For this he has been much blamed. It has been said that he should have borrowed in stock of a denomination more nearly corresponding to the actual credit of the State; by which method the capital would not have been swollen to such an inordinate extent, and the generation responsible for the war would have borne a fairer share of the burden. The answer to this criticism, though convincing enough, would require too much spaciousness of detail to be given here. This much may, however, be said, that Pitt had no choice. He was borrowing on a scale unknown in the history of the world; and he had to borrow, not in accordance with his own views, but with those of the lenders. He made repeated attempts to borrow at 5 and 4 per cent, but

[1] See Appendix B.

[2] The further additions made to the debt by Mr. Pitt in his second administration will also be found in Appendix B.

met with no response. For his very first loan, raised within a few weeks of the declaration of war, he received tenders from only one set of persons, who insisted on 3 per cents. When, again, he funded the Navy and Exchequer Bills in 1796, he offered options in 3, 4, and 5 per cent stock. According to the market price, the option in 5 per cents was the most favourable to the lender; but 85 per cent was taken in 3 per cent stock, and only 11 per cent in 5 per cent stock.

There is overwhelming evidence to show that he repeatedly did all in his power to stimulate public competition, and to raise his loans in stock of a higher denomination. Such stock, however, not only commanded less popularity, but had relatively a less marketable value, owing to its liability to be redeemed on the conclusion of peace and the return of better credit. Consequently, it is open to question whether Pitt would have done better for posterity, even if he had succeeded in borrowing by methods different to those to which he had to resort. Indeed, a high financial authority—Mr. Newmarch—in an interesting monograph on this subject, demonstrates, by actuarial calculations, that borrowing in 3 per cent stock as compared with 5 per cent stock was in reality an economy. However that may be, the plain truth is, that, having to appeal to a limited and abnormal market, Pitt was in no sense master of the situation; and that, had he not offered the temptation of stock which was certain to rise sooner or later in capital value, he could not have secured the requisite means for carrying on the war.

Another cognate objection is that he ought to have raised more by taxation within the year and depended less on loans. There was no more strenuous upholder of this doctrine than Pitt himself. He explored and attempted every source of taxation. He added repeatedly to existing taxes. He even appealed to voluntary contribution; by which he obtained more than two millions sterling in 1798, and a further sum in 1799. He introduced such fertile expedients as the legacy duty, which he borrowed from Holland in 1796.[1] In 1796 he took the desperate measure of trebling the assessed taxes (when the familiar phrase of the "pleasure horse" made perhaps its first appearance); and when this impost fell short of expectations, finding that "the resources of taxation were failing under him," he boldly carried through an income tax of minute and complicated graduation in an oration "which," said a competent French writer, Mallet du Pan, who heard it, "is not a speech spoken by the minister; it is a complete course of public economy; a work, and one of the finest works, upon practical and theoretical finance that ever distinguished the pen of a philosopher and statesman."

Mr. Gladstone demonstrated in a speech fully worthy of this description that, had Pitt imposed the income tax in 1793 instead of 1798, there need have been no debt at all. But he would be the first to admit that what was possible in 1798 would not have been possible in 1793; that what was practicable in the fifth year of war would not have been practicable in the first; and that it was not until all other possible sources of taxation had run dry that he could have persuaded the country to accept a severe

[1] There are no fewer than three claimants for the honour of having called Pitt's attention to these duties: Miles, Harris, and a Mr. Lamb.

and graduated income tax. It was only when the trebling of the assessed taxes had failed, that he determined to attain, by a direct impost, his avowed object, of taking a tenth of the income of the country. The net of the tax was extremely wide, and the mesh extremely small. It operated on incomes of no more than £60 a year, which were mulcted at the rate of twopence in the pound. The tax proceeded by a minute and complicated scale; each £5 of additional income being taxed at a different rate until £200 was reached. From incomes of £200 a year and upwards Pitt boldly took his tenth. The imposition and acceptance of a tithe so novel and exasperating shows sufficiently that all that taxation could do was done, as well as the anxiety of Pitt and his generation to bear the fullest possible proportion of the burden of the war.

Another criticism of a directly opposite import has been raised against him. He has been accused of unduly adding to that burden by keeping up the charge for the Sinking Fund. The main reason for his doing this is that which would have prevented his proposing the income tax in 1793. He was convinced that the war would be so short, that it would not be worth while to derange his scheme of redemption on that account. It is clear from his speech of the 11th of March 1793, as well as from other indications, that he thought it highly improbable that hostilities could continue beyond that year. This expectation was based entirely on the financial condition of France. It would, therefore, have been extravagant, in his judgment, to interrupt a beneficial sequence of fifteen years, for a few months of incidental warfare. Financially, his calculation was correct; but, politically, he was trying to compute a tornado. Nor did these sanguine hopes abate, as the war proceeded. Each year, each month was to be the last. And even had it been otherwise, it may well be that he would have been reluctant to dispel that mirage, which induced the population to bear taxation readily, under the belief that a magic machinery was producing gold as fast as it was spent. The Sinking Fund, in fine, inspired confidence, and enabled the nation to endure with cheerfulness the burden of what he believed would be a short war.

It is, therefore, probable that, in spite of the largeness of the figures, Pitt's finance was well and wisely managed; that, looking indeed to the monetary and political conditions of his time, he achieved as much both in annual payment and in economy of borrowing as could well have been accomplished. That he managed this, too, without crushing commerce by taxation is evident from the fact that our imports and exports went on mounting during the war in spite of deficient harvests with reassuring elasticity. In the year ending 5th January 1793 the total value of all imports into Great Britain had been £19,659,358; and on an average of six years ending at that date £18,685,390. In the year ending 5th January 1799 they were £25,654,000, and on an average of the six years then ending £22,356,296, showing an increase as between the two years of £5,994,642, and as between the two averages of £3,670,906. The total value of the exports of British manufactures in the year ending 5th January 1793 had been £18,336,851; on the six years' average £14,771,049. The comparative figures in 1799 were £19,771,510, and £17,154,323, showing an increase of £1,434,659 and £2,383,274 respectively. Of foreign merchandise exported in the year ending 5th January 1793 the value was £6,568,000, and in the six years the average had been £5,468,014; the corresponding figures in 1799 were £14,028,000 and £10,791,000, showing an increase of £7,460,000 and £5,322,986 respectively. It might be said of him as the grateful citizens of London recorded of his father that under his administration commerce had been united with and made to flourish by war.

But it is not possible to discuss Pitt's war administration, which has been so bitterly attacked, merely by laying down general principles. It must be considered as a concrete record of achievement and failure. As regards the minor and military part, it may at once be admitted to be unsuccessful, and want of success may be held at once to damn it. But the circumstances must be borne in mind. Pitt's catamarans and martello towers must not be compared with torpedoes and Brialmont turrets. It must be remembered that he was dealing with dupes or invalids or self-seekers on the one hand; and with a cosmopolitan convulsion, embodied in a secular genius, on the other. The French Revolution, to borrow Canning's fine figure, was a deluge which submerged the ancient monarchies of Europe; it was long before their spires and turrets emerged once more above the subsiding wave. Most European Courts beheld it in the spirit of wreckers. While Pitt was planning how to check the torrent, they were speculating on the value of its flotsam and jetsam. His and their professed objects were the same; their real aims were totally different and incompatible.

Pitt was, as it were, heading a crusade with a force of camp followers. They took his money, and laughed in their sleeve. He could not believe that they were insensible to their real interest or their real danger. It is probable that some Pompeians saw in the great eruption an admirable opportunity for shop-lifting; so it was, but it cost the depredators their lives. Pitt saw the real peril, though he succeeded neither in averting it, nor in alarming the princes of Europe; they deceived him and themselves, and were overwhelmed.

Europe was rotten. The decay had been demonstrated in France, but the fact was universal. The old systems were moth-eaten. The Holy Roman Empire, never very puissant, crumbled like a corpse under the new light. Prussia, so arduously constructed by the unwearied vigilance of genius, had withered under the single reign of an extravagant voluptuary. Spain was a name, and Italy a geographical expression. Great Britain was neither sound nor particularly great. The nations were indeed a dominant force, but the governments which acted in their name were either unrepresentative or futile. Pitt recognised this after Ulm, when he said that nothing more could be hoped of the sovereigns—there must be a war of peoples. A few weeks afterwards, the overthrow of the Emperors at Austerlitz confirmed his opinion; Spain, then Russia, then Germany, were to fulfil his prophecy.

But it was the governments that Pitt headed. And, if he could not calculate on the selfish ineptitude, which distinguished, not the peoples, but the courts of the continent, still less could he calculate on Napoleon.

To that imperial intellect he had to oppose the statecraft of the Thuguts and the Cobenzels, the Lucchesinis and the Haugwitzs, men pitiful at all times, contemptible at such a crisis: and the military capacity of the aged Melas, the hampered Archduke Charles, the incomprehensible Duke of Brunswick. He himself had no generals. "I know not," said Lord North, when a list of officers was submitted to him for the commands in America, "I know not what effect these names may have on the enemy, but I know they make me tremble." So with Pitt. He discovered the genius of Wellington, but did not live to profit by it. He was obliged to employ the Duke of York, or, as Lord Grenville said, "some old woman in a red riband." Nothing perhaps could have availed against Napoleon, for two Napoleons do not coexist. But Europe never had a fair chance.

It is also just to remark that, while Pitt's efforts on land were generally futile, he was uniformly successful at sea. If France held one element, England held the other. If the responsibility of the one be debited to him, the responsibility of the other must be placed to his credit. Even if it be said that these victories were entirely due to the incalculable genius of Nelson, which would not be true, it must be said that the defeats were due to the incalculable genius of Napoleon; so that the one may be set against the other.

There was, however, another reason for the wide difference between the results achieved by the army and the navy in the last decade of the last century. The army was essentially an aristocratic, and the navy a comparatively democratic service. In the navy a man of obscure origin could rise, and the area of choice was not limited by the circumstances of birth; but in the army, purchase and favour and lineage gave promotion. Our admirals were not born in the purple. Collingwood was the son of a Newcastle merchant, Jervis of a country lawyer, Nelson of a country parson. But when our armies had to be sent into the field, it was necessary that, if possible, a prince of the blood should command them. A military command seemed to require nothing more than exalted rank, or the seniority which often spelt senility. It is difficult to apportion the blood-guiltiness of this proceeding or tradition. Pitt at any rate informed George III. that, so far as the Duke of York was concerned, it could not continue. The King acquiesced with real anguish as a father, and perhaps as a sovereign; but solaced himself by telling Pitt that it was not his son, but Pitt's brother, then at the head of the Admiralty, who was responsible for our disasters. What chance had armies, thus guided by indolence or hazard, against legions of veterans, to whom war was a business and a passion, many of whom had risen, and all of whom looked to rise, by merit? The English generals were brave, and the Duke of York had gallant qualities. But they were engaged in a struggle where this was not enough. The disparity extended from the leaders to the ranks. "The French system of conscription brings together a fair specimen of all classes; our army is composed of the scum of the earth—the mere scum of the earth," said the Duke of Wellington, with more accuracy than gratitude. So it was, and so it was treated. Largely recruited from the refuse of humanity, it was scourged and bullied and abused as if outside humanity. And these were the soldiers we opposed to the regiments in which Ney and Hoche and Massena were serving as privates.

These explanations and reserves are not intended to prove that Pitt was a great War Minister. In that respect it may be said that he has been much underrated without asserting that he was a born organiser of victory. He had dauntless spirit, he had unfailing energy, he evoked dormant resource, he inspired confidence; but his true gifts were for peace. The signal qualities which he had shown in administration did not help him on this new stage. Unsupported and overweighted as he was, he could not in any case have succeeded. Nor in all probability could the greatest of War Ministers,—not Chatham, not Bismarck. It must be repeated again and again that, locked in a death grapple with the French Revolution, he was struggling with something superhuman, immeasurable, incalculable. We do not read that the wisest and the mightiest in Egypt were able to avail, when the light turned to darkness and the rivers to blood.

CHAPTER X

DOMESTIC POLICY

DURING these years of struggle, he was compelled to allow all measures of social progress to remain in abeyance. The note of his domestic policy was to avoid any measure that could embarrass the efficient conduct of the war. That, however short it might be in his anticipation, would in any case require the undivided energies of the country. He had no choice, as has been seen, but to go to war. Suppose that, having done so, he had devoted his energies not to the war, but to measures of emancipation and reform, and had split Parliament, which in a war should be unanimous, into half a dozen parties, would he have done better? War is a hideous engrossing fact; it cannot be paltered with. Too much or too little, as Burke said of property, is treason against it; it must have all; every nerve, every muscle, every fibre. And the nation that gives its whole immediate energy to the war it has in hand will have an incalculable advantage over the nation to whom it is merely an expensive incident, dividing its attention with a number of other agitating and absorbing problems.

Parliamentary reform was, no doubt, loudly and justly demanded. But, while, on the one hand, the enthusiasm of the French Revolution would have demanded a larger measure than Pitt would have granted, the far more general reaction against anything in the shape of change would have denied anything. Reformers then insisted on more than we, after a century of agitation, have attained. To move in the matter, then, could only provoke irritating and fruitless dissension, perhaps disabling anarchy, when the union of the nation was the first necessity. It was absurd to discuss annual parliaments when the Gaul was at our gates. It was indispensable to check the French revolutionary propaganda, of which these proposals were only an instalment, and which were really aimed at the subversion of the entire constitution of which Pitt was the official trustee. Heavy taxation for war with little apparent result, and the maintenance of a narrow system against a popular and reasonable demand for reform, soon bear fruit in what is called coercion. And to coercion Pitt was compelled to resort.

It has been said that the period from 1789 to January 1793—the first part of the French Revolution—was one, not of coercion, but of almost competing liberalism. It is true, no doubt, that in May 1792 a royal proclamation had been issued, warning the people against seditious writings; and another in December of the same year had called out the militia as a precaution against the intrigues of "evil-disposed persons acting in concert with persons in foreign parts"; but these edicts could scarcely be considered as other than storm signals. Even the Alien Bill, which was introduced in 1792 as a measure directed against revolutionary propagandism, though severe and harassing to foreigners, was not extraordinary, when the circumstances and opinions of the time are considered. These measures were, however, followed up by frequent press prosecutions; and juries competed in finding persons guilty of sedition on the thinnest evidence, or on no evidence at all.

More especially was this the case in Scotland, where the judges hounded on the prosecutions; and where Braxfield attempted, not without success, to rival the fame of Jeffreys. The discontent here stopped little short of rebellion. A Convention sat in Edinburgh, which scarcely disguised revolutionary aims. So far as parliamentary representation was concerned, the malcontents were fully justified; their grievance in that respect was immeasurably greater than that of Ireland, for they had lost their own parliament, and had no real representation in any other. But, had their complaints been less founded, their disaffection was justified by the measures taken against them. A brilliant young advocate named Muir, arraigned as a member of the Convention and as a promoter of parliamentary reform, was condemned to transportation for fourteen years. Palmer, a clergyman, was sentenced to seven years' transportation for circulating a paper in favour of parliamentary reform. Skirving, for being concerned in the same address and in the Convention, was transported for fourteen years. Margarot and Gerrald, the London delegates to the Convention, received a like punishment. These trials sank deep into the minds of the Scottish people. Half a century afterwards, a memorial was erected to the victims on one of the loftiest sites in Edinburgh; while Fox expressed in an ejaculation what is still thought of those who sentenced them: "God help the people who have such judges."

So far, these prosecutions had proceeded under the ordinary law. But, in May 1794, a royal message was communicated to Parliament, calling its attention to certain papers that were to be laid before it. A secret committee was appointed in both Houses. Reports were issued by each to the effect that a traitorous conspiracy existed for purposes of revolution. The Habeas Corpus Act was instantly suspended. In that year Watt, who had been a spy, was tried and executed in Scotland for high treason; nor, indeed, did he deny that his designs were rebellious, though the plot was on so small a scale that it might well have been treated as venial. In England, on the other hand, a few weeks later, Hardy, Horne Tooke, and others were brought to trial on the same charge and acquitted. Nothing apparently in the nature of treason was proved against them; they had merely combined for purposes of reform; and they derived an exquisite enjoyment from summoning Pitt and Richmond to testify to their own former participation in similar aspirations. These acquittals cleared the air. They showed, on the one hand, that the alarms of Parliament had been exaggerated; and on the other, that in England, at any rate, justice was still pure and unbiassed.

In 1795, the suspension of the Habeas Corpus Act was renewed, and it was continued till 1801. In this year the King, on the opening of Parliament, was shot at and pelted; his coach was wrecked. These outrages were followed by a Treasonable Practices Bill and a

Seditious Meetings Bill. Both measures were interferences with the liberty of a subject, which only the last extreme of necessity could justify. The first indefinitely enlarged the category of treasonable offences, and dispensed with proof of any overt act of treason; the second forbade all public meetings of more than fifty persons without the superintendence of a magistrate, and contained other clauses of a similar tendency. These bills were voted by great majorities. In 1799, an Act was passed for putting an end to various societies, and forbidding the formation of others under specified conditions. Regulations and restrictions and taxation were also imposed on the press. For some years past steps had been taken with the special object of restraining the circulation of cheap newspapers, of which these burdens were the complement. These various proceedings gave Fox a great advantage, of which he nobly availed himself. Though he thundered in vain against the enactment of such laws, his speeches remain, and embody in the most exact and stirring terms the large polity of a free people. In half a dozen words he laid down the fundamental principle of liberal policy. "Liberty is order," said he, "liberty is strength."

It is not easy in cold blood to defend these proclamations and prosecutions and bills. Still less easy is it for a generation that has so often resorted to coercion to criticise them. Ever since the death of Pitt, all English governments have at times adopted those exceptional measures for which their supporters are so apt to censure him. But he can only be held partly responsible. In Scotland, the ruling and language of the judges were largely answerable. In

England, the early findings of juries under the ordinary law pointed in the same direction. For the extraordinary laws Parliament itself bears the burden. Its secret committees and reports made it impossible for any minister to refrain from proposing coercion bills. The scandal and terror caused by the assault on the King were the cause of others. But more must be acknowledged than this. These laws were passed, and these prosecutions instituted, under the ignorant ferocity of panic. The extremity and brutality of that panic can perhaps best be realised in the accounts of the Birmingham riots, of which Catherine Hutton, one of the chief sufferers, has left so graphic a narrative. The French Revolution was a new portent; none could measure it, nothing could be predicated with regard to it; its terrors consisted not merely in the success of its arms, but in the ramifications of its proselytism. Before any exceptional measures were taken, it was encouraging revolt in England, promising support to rebellion, and receiving disaffection with cordiality and honour. To this the English response took the form of some conspiracies, real, though no doubt exaggerated; but in the main of an intense reaction and dismay. "Repression and severity," says so stout a Whig as Erskine May, "were popular and sure of cordial support."

Mr. Massey supplies from secret records the exact moment when the masculine mind of Pitt succumbed to the plots and rumours of plots with which he was encompassed. In December 1792 three thousand daggers had been discovered at Birmingham; one of them had been flung by Burke on the floor of the

House of Commons. The Government had convincing evidence, or evidence which at any rate convinced them, that this was only a part of a vast and imminent conspiracy. The Cabinet sate till four in the morning. When it had dispersed, Pitt still bent brooding over the fire. Presently he asked the under secretary, who was in attendance, what he thought of the situation; and added, "Probably by this time to-morrow we may not have a hand to act or a tongue to utter." Nor did the gravity of his apprehensions diminish with time. He told Wellesley and Wilberforce in 1795 that, were he to resign, his head would be off in six months; and, shortly afterwards, when Wilberforce borrowed Pitt's carriage, he was informed that, were it recognised, its occupant ran the risk of being murdered. When once Pitt yielded to the public sentiment in this matter, there could be neither pause nor limit. The public in its terror called for more and more; Parliament passed every repressive measure with something like acclamation; it was not the coercion of a people by a government, it was the coercion of a government by the people.

It must, further, be admitted that later ministries have departed from the ordinary law with much less reason. While we were struggling for bare existence with the most formidable enemy that England has ever had to face—an enemy fighting not with armies and fleets alone, but with every art of seduction—we had one-third of our population, that of Ireland, arrayed in avowed disaffection; Scotland was combustible and explosive; and it was impossible to speak with confidence of the population of England. All that was known was an enormous sale of the works of Paine, an extensive manufactory of secret arms, a considerable and indefinable amount of furtive organisation. It was as usual the unknown, the suspected, that was terrible. At any moment we might find the very ground that we were defending from France crumble beneath us. Discontent might burst forth somewhere; and once in view, who could tell, with bad harvests and heavy taxes and press-gangs to foster it, how far it might extend? Making the best front we could against an overwhelming enemy, we might find the country in flames behind us. In so dark and desperate a juncture, men act and strike blindly. In face of so present a peril, it is not the minister who is master. He only attempts to keep his feet in front of a tempestuous crowd; and his responsibility in case of mishap is terrible. It may be that exceptional measures of repression can never be justified. If they can, the justification can only be concrete, can only rest on a solid base of formidable circumstance. If they ever can, a fair plea can be advanced for Pitt; for the crisis was incalculable. Even if it cannot, it is difficult for any extant political party in England to censure him. But the truth, with or without apology, may be best expressed by saying that, while the torrent of the French Revolution demolished monarchy in France, its back-eddies swept Pitt and England into reaction.

Even in this dire time of distress, he turned from a state of war, external and intestine, to those eternal problems where policy and humanity work side by side. Whitbread had brought forward a Bill for regulating and fixing a minimum of wages. Pitt recalled the House to a juster view of political economy. He believed that the true course was to allow the price of labour to find its own level, and that this would best be promoted by a reform of the poor-laws; more especially of that law of settlement which prevented the workman from taking his industry to the best market. But, passing from this criticism, he proceeded to deal earnestly and exhaustively with the whole question of the condition of the poor. He admitted a vast ill, and suggested various remedies, which on a later day he embodied in a measure.

He had spared, he said, no pains to collect information on the subject; and there is a curious tradition as to this. It is said, that on a visit in Essex, (probably to the house of his private secretary, Joseph Smith, at Shortgrove), he was descanting on the prosperity of the country and on the comfort enjoyed by the working classes. His host answered nothing; but took him a walk next day to the neighbouring town of Halsted. The minister surveyed it in silent wonder, and declared that he had no conception that any part of England could present a spectacle of such misery. The scene produced a deep impression on his mind; he at once addressed himself to the question; and not long afterwards he took the opportunity of Whitbread's motion to deliver this sympathetic and thoughtful speech on the condition of the poor; through even the meagre reports of which there breathes a warm spirit of earnestness and humanity, unlike the political deliverances of that day.

He followed it up with a Bill, full of novel and comprehensive propositions: so novel and comprehensive, indeed, that, after several alterations, it sank overweighted beneath the parliamentary wave. A vast new system was to be created; a hierarchy of Justices and

Wardens and Guardians. In every parish or group of parishes were to be established Schools of Industry, which were in fact what we have since known as Ateliers Nationaux. Their conditions were to be settled to some extent by Parish Councils; but they were in all cases to furnish work for the destitute poor. The Justices and other authorities were to have nearly the powers of a private employer of labour in regard to them. They were to buy materials; they were to sell the manufactured article; they were to fix the rate of wages. They could build or hire warehouses; they could buy or hire land. They could enclose and cultivate commons for the support of the workers in the Schools of Industry. Moreover, in every parish or union, a friendly society was to be established. Persons also, having more than two children, or, in the case of a widow, one child, were entitled to claim exceptional relief. A certain amount of visible property was not to debar a person from receiving parochial aid. There were, indeed, some 130 clauses more or less. One—perhaps the most daring in those days—provided that money might be advanced, in deserving cases, for the purchase of a cow or some other animal producing profit. Bentham, in his criticisms on the measure, urged that a cow required three acres of grass, and asked whence these were to come. Though the question was not answered, the proposal will be recognised as the germ of a proverbial policy.

There was a certain crudity in the measure, which makes it all the more remarkable as a sterling and strenuous endeavour to grapple with a great question, without deference to tradition or precedent; and it affords a view of Pitt's character which can nowhere else be found. To some of us it is the most interesting view. For in the boldness of this Bill, in its comprehensiveness, in its very crudity, we see the desperate effort of a man to break through the bonds of circumstance and tradition, through that thin red tape which is mightier than chains, in order to raise his race. Failures of this kind are sometimes more impressive and more honourable than the most polished masterpiece of the parliamentary draughtsman.

The Bill was constantly revised; but the mordant animadversions of Bentham, which, though not published at the time, were communicated and circulated, disheartened the Government. It was probably felt that, if to various vested interests the hostility of philosophical radicalism were added, there could be no hopes for the measure, at a time when all novel propositions were discountenanced as dangerous; but men will long look back with admiration to the hearty spirit, the freedom from conventionality or prejudice, and the genuine sympathy which animate its clauses.

CHAPTER XI

IRELAND

BUT the greatest of Pitt's domestic difficulties has been left to the last. Throughout the whole period of the war, he had by his side the gaunt spectre of the Irish question in its most menacing and formidable shape; an aspect which it retains to this hour. It has never passed into history, for it has never passed out of politics. To take a simile from a catastrophe of nature less ruinous and less deplorable, the volcano that caused that eruption is still active; beneath the black crust the lava torrent burns; so that the incautious explorer who ventures near the crater finds the treacherous surface yield, and himself plunged in the fiery marl of contemporary party strife. No number of previous volumes will suffice to ballast or preserve the innocent investigator; his fate is certain and foreseen; for, the moment his foot rests on 1795 he irresistibly slips on to 1886; and rebounding from 1886, he is soon soused in 1891.

Happily, however, it is only necessary, for the present purpose, to consider the actual personal contact of Pitt with Irish affairs, and not to deal with their general phases and effects; although, even thus, there are episodes so controversial that they cannot be treated so concisely as those in regard to which there is less dispute.

It is needful to remember that Pitt, after the rejection of his commercial schemes in 1785, appeared to despair of a change of system. He sent over Viceroys and Chief Secretaries to occupy Dublin Castle and accept its traditions—Buckinghams and Westmorelands, Fitzherberts and Hobarts; but he turned his own attention, perforce, elsewhere. Then came the Regency question; when the action of the Irish Parliament indicated dangerous possibilities under the settlement of 1782,—contingencies, which once more directed men's minds towards a Union, and furnished arguments in its favour not easy to meet in those times of perpetual apprehension and peril.

The next stage in Irish politics is the emancipation of the Roman Catholics in 1792 and 1793; when measures were passed, which, by admitting the Catholic peasantry to the parliamentary suffrage and to juries, and by relieving them from all property disabilities, exhausted, for the time at any rate, their interest in that question. The delay in granting a full emancipation subsequently gave the admission of Catholics to Parliament and to office, no doubt, considerable importance. But it was accompanied by a reversal of the enfranchisement of 1793, and was therefore so much the less a popular boon than the Acts passed by Pitt. To say that they were passed by Pitt is but the strictest truth; for it was only owing to the persistent pressure of Pitt and Dundas that the violent hostility of the Irish Government was overcome. "I do not believe," writes the Viceroy with plaintive acrimony as regards even the minor measure of 1792, "there was ever an instance in any country of such a sacrifice of private judgment to the wishes of His Majesty" (meaning of course the British Government) "as by the Irish ministers in the present concession." While this was the act of Pitt and Dundas alone, it may be noted that, after the admission of the Whigs, the official protectors of the Catholics, to the Cabinet in the ensuing year, nothing more was done for their benefit.

It was in July 1794, as has been seen, that the Portland Whigs joined Pitt. The Duke, their leader, in this rearrangement obtained the Home Secretaryship; under which department Ireland was then directly, as it is now more nominally, placed. It was also arranged that, so soon as a new opening could be found for Lord Westmoreland, Fitzwilliam should succeed him as Viceroy of Ireland. In this way the two official heads of Ireland would be Whig, under of course the general superintendence of the Cabinet; but it was expressly stipulated that there should be no change of system; and that, in fact, Irish policy should be continuous with that previously pursued by the Government.

We are told that Fitzwilliam accepted the Lord Lieutenancy after long hesitation and with great reluctance. It must, on the other hand, be admitted that all the facts point to an immediately opposite conclusion. He discharged letters in every direction. He published his nomination everywhere. He wrote, three months before he was appointed, to offer Thomas Grenville the Chief Secretaryship. He wrote at the same time to solicit the support of Grattan, and to propose an immediate conference; so that Grattan came at once, accompanied by the Ponsonbys, and full of high hopes, to London. So much did he put himself in Grattan's hands that, after the disputes that ensued, he left to that statesman the ultimate decision whether he should undertake the Lord Lieutenancy or not. The news of his approaching Viceroyalty became common property in Ireland. This premature revelation, of an appointment in contemplation but not actually settled, was the first of Fitzwilliam's disastrous indiscretions. It gave a mortal blow to whatever reputation for prudence he may have possessed, and led directly to the unhappy catastrophe which followed. But he did not limit himself to words. He determined to remove Fitzgibbon, the Chancellor, the most powerful man in Ireland. He determined to find high offices, at all costs and by the violent displacement of some of Pitt's oldest adherents, for the two Ponsonbys, the most prominent of the Irish Whigs.

By this time it is clear that Pitt was becoming thoroughly alarmed at the precipitate proceedings of the reversionary Lord Lieutenant. He had told Westmoreland, the actual Viceroy, nothing of any alteration; he did not contemplate any immediate change of system; least of all, would he countenance the removal of the few devoted adherents who had stood by him during the Regency crisis of 1789. He now discovered to his dismay that Fitzwilliam had already formed his administration, was announcing his policy, and proclaiming from the housetops his future achievements, which included the dismissal of Pitt's principal friends. He uttered a despairing wish that the promised appointment could be annulled; but intimated that at any rate Fitzwilliam could only go to Ireland on the condition that he gave satisfaction on these vital points. The new Whig ministers declared they must resign. Pitt expressed his regret; but he declared that it was impossible for him to consent to the Chancellor's removal, or to leave "either him or any of the supporters of the Government exposed to the risk of the new system." "I ought to add that the very idea of a *new system*, (as far as I understand what is meant by that term), and especially one formed without previous communication or concert with the rest of the King's servants here, or with the friends of Government in Ireland, is in itself what I feel it utterly impossible to accede to; and it appears to me to be directly contrary to the general principles on which our union was formed and has hitherto subsisted." He had nothing to reproach himself with. If the worst came to the worst, "I must struggle as well as I can with a distress which no means are left me to avoid, without a sacrifice both of character and duty." Grenville, one of Pitt's two confidants in the Cabinet, was not less dismayed; for the talk of new systems and a new predominance was entirely strange to him, and resolutely repudiated by him. At last there was a general explosion; salutary, as it would seem, for it disclosed and appeared to settle the grounds of dispute. Pitt declared that Fitzwilliam, in his various communications with parties in Ireland, had entirely exceeded his powers, that nothing would induce him to consent to Fitzgibbon's removal, and that he could give no countenance to the idea that Ireland was to be treated as a separate province, outside the general control of the Government, under the exclusive dominion of the Whig party.

Fitzwilliam appears to have thought that Ireland was

made over to him, as were Lampsacus and Magnesia to Themistocles for his bread and his wine; and that Pitt would have no more to do with its government and the policy pursued there than with Finland or Languedoc. This hallucination was due partly to the idiosyncrasy of Fitzwilliam himself, but mainly to the strange proprietary principles of government, to which allusion has already been made, which were held consciously or unconsciously, though quite conscientiously, by the Whig party.

Burke intervened at this juncture with letters of passionate eloquence and pathos. It is scarcely possible even now to read them unmoved. He acknowledged that he was ignorant of the terms on which Portland and his friends had entered the Government. He had the highest opinion of Fitzwilliam, whose virtues he once described as the highest and the most unmixed he had ever known in man. Nevertheless, he admitted that Fitzwilliam had acted with indiscretion, and that Portland and he had put themselves in the wrong. At first, then, he was doubtful as to what they should do. But at last his mind seemed to be made up. He despatched a letter on the 16th of October, in which he solemnly summed up the situation. He wrote, he said, as a dying man, with all the freedom and all the dispassionate clearness of that situation, and declared, with "infinite sorrow," "with inexpressible sorrow," that the Whigs must resign. Four days afterwards, he pronounced, in a letter not less powerful or less pathetic, a directly opposite opinion. If they went, they must be turned out; they must not resign. "Oh! have pity on yourselves," he broke forth, "and may the God whose counsels are so mysterious in the moral world (even more than in the natural) guide you through all these labyrinths." In truth, he himself was distracted by contending dreads and scorns: with a living loathing of the Irish system of corruption, but with that loathing overborne by his mastering horror of the French Revolution. Rather than that a schism in the Government of Great Britain should weaken the resistance to that pestilence, let even Ireland stand aside. He was, in fact, incapable of giving advice. That the terms on which the Whigs joined Pitt did not include any new system of men and measures, Grenville positively asserted; he was not merely truthful and accurate, but a strong pro-Catholic, and could not have failed to know them. Nor is there a particle of proof, or even probability, that there was any such stipulation; for we may be sure that Pitt would never have agreed to part with so large and critical a part of his prerogative.

At last a settlement was arrived at. A final conference was held, at which Pitt, Portland, Fitzwilliam, Spencer, Windham, and Grenville were present; that is to say, Pitt and one follower with four Whigs. Every detail of patronage and policy was exhaustively canvassed and settled. The results were recorded in a sort of protocol, preserved among the Pelham Papers. Fitzwilliam was to go as Lord Lieutenant indeed; but on the explicit understanding that there was to be no new system of men or of measures in Ireland; that he should, if possible, prevent any agitation of the Catholic question during the present session; that, in any case, on that or any other important measure he should transmit all the information which he could collect with his opinion to the Cabinet; and that he should do nothing to commit the Government in such matters without fresh instructions. Thus, one would have thought, was removed all possibility of misunderstanding.

Here, however, was the fundamental mistake. It was impossible for Fitzwilliam, after his detonations and activities of the autumn, to prevent the agitation of the Catholic question; for he was the prime agitator. It would have been as reasonable for Sir Robert Peel to offer Cobden a seat in his cabinet on the condition that he should exert his endeavours to prevent all agitation for the repeal of the Corn Laws. Fitzwilliam for months past had done nothing but announce his approaching Lord Lieutenancy, and stir up the question. Naturally he found Ireland already in a flame.

Nor did his official action allay it. He landed January 4, 1795. The next day (Monday) he spent in bed. On the Wednesday he summarily dismissed Beresford, a powerful though subordinate officer, a main adviser in Pitt's commercial propositions, and one of Pitt's confidential agents; who was not officially under the Lord Lieutenant at all, but in the Treasury department, that is under Pitt himself. This act, Pitt, who did not speak at random, characterised as "an open breach of a most solemn promise." Other dismissals followed. Cooke, the Secretary for War, and Sackville Hamilton, the Under Secretary of State, were promptly removed. It was a clean sweep. Fitzgibbon alone remained; and he only because Fitzwilliam was specially pledged not to remove him. Every faction in Ireland was astir. One party was to be crushed; the other party was to rule. Those with whom Pitt had constantly co-operated in Irish administration were in consternation; for every act of the new Government was directed against them. It was a *coup d'état*, a stroke of State, justifiable and even necessary on grounds of high State necessity, or on the presumption of a revolution in policy; but only defensible on such considerations, and even then to be executed with care and judgment. It was, however, wholly incompatible with the stipulation of Pitt that there was to be no general change in administration or of system; and with his declared, obvious policy to keep clear of domestic embarrassment, when all his energies were required for the war with France.

As to the condition with regard to the Catholics, it would have been impossible to maintain it, even had Fitzwilliam desired to do so. From the day on which he landed, he bombarded Portland with letters to press for the immediate settlement of the question. To these communications Portland for some weeks gave no reply whatever. It is urged by Fitzwilliam's apologists that he considered that silence gives consent: a proverb, doubtful at all times, but preposterous as a political plea; more especially absurd, when it is relied upon for guidance in defiance of definite instructions. Fitzwilliam asserted that he was permitted to give the Catholic cause a "handsome support," in case they were resolved to bring it forward. The Government, on their side, declared that he was in no way to commit them without fresh instructions. But, even on the assumption that Fitzwilliam's interpretation was correct, it is clear that such instructions would apply only to a spontaneous movement, and not to one excited by the Viceroy himself.

At last, on the 8th of February (1795) Portland wrote to impress on Fitzwilliam the importance of giving no encouragement to the Catholics, or of committing himself in any way: the importance, in a word, of his not doing all that he had been doing for a month. On the 9th, Pitt himself wrote, complaining of the dismissal of Beresford. On the 16th Portland wrote to declare at length his views on the Catholic question, and his entire disapproval of the policy of emancipation at that time. A passage from this strictly confidential despatch Fitzwilliam was afterwards so ill-advised, to say the least, as to publish, with the most disastrous results. Even now he did not resign, but answered these communications at length. In his letter to Pitt, he made the unfortunate assertion that Beresford had been guilty of malversation; a charge for which he never produced the slightest evidence, and which in any case he could scarcely have examined judicially in the forty-eight hours that elapsed between his landing and Beresford's dismissal. To Portland he reiterated long expostulations on the Catholic question. In reply, Portland, who it must be remembered was his party leader as well as his administrative chief, wrote a curt note of censure. The next day (Feb. 19) Fitzwilliam was recalled.

Never was there so hopeless a misunderstanding, or one, after the general exchange of views in October, more incomprehensible. Fitzwilliam published two pompous pamphlets, and declared in his place in Parliament that his recall was due to his having connected himself with Grattan. The Government refused to discuss the matter But it must be admitted that, untoward as was that event, the person most responsible for Fitzwilliam's recall was, as is generally the case in such removals, Fitzwilliam himself. He seems to have been a man of generous sympathies and honest enthusiasm; but not less wrong-headed than headstrong; absolutely devoid of judgment, reticence, and tact. Two months before he set out, Pitt had discovered this, and deplored the decision to send him. His announcements of his appointment before it was made, his unauthorised propaganda, his rash dismissals, his speeches, his protests, his publication from confidential letters after his recall, betoken a man earnest, intrepid, and single-minded, but singularly destitute of the qualities required for a delicate and discretionary mission.

The importance of his recall may easily be exaggerated, although it was, in truth, a political calamity. Because it was followed by some miserable years, it has been held to be the cause of the misery of those years. This is surely a misstatement; it was rather a landmark. What in 1795 was called the Catholic question was rather a sign of grace than a measure of real importance. The mass of the Catholic peasantry already had the franchise under the Emancipation Act of 1792-93, and it imported little to them whether or not a number of gentry of their own persuasion went up to Dublin to be bought and sold at the Castle; it has, indeed, always been a matter of comparative indifference to them whether they were led by Protestants or Catholics. Nor can parliamentary reform, if we may trust witnesses so intelligent and well informed as Emmett and M'Nevin, be said to have been an object of enthusiasm to the mass of the population. What pinched the people were tithes and oppressive rents; with this distinction, that, whereas for rents they got something, though perhaps not much, for tithes they got less than nothing. And what excited them were the new prospects presented by the French Revolution. The importance of the recall of Fitzwilliam lies in the fact that he had, however unwarrantably, excited hopes, not of emancipation and reform alone, but of a completely new system; hopes which were shattered by his peremptory removal. So that the quick revulsion produced the blind fury of despair.

The affair still remains obscure; what is clear is that which alone concerns these pages—the part and responsibility of Pitt. It is evident that there was a total misunderstanding; that there was a hopeless discrepancy between the assertion of Fitzwilliam that the removal of Beresford had been tacitly sanctioned by Pitt beforehand, and Pitt's own statement that he considered it a grave breach of a solemn engagement; that the views, declarations, and policy of Fitzwilliam as to a new system of men and measures were irreconcilable with those of Pitt and his colleagues. It is only necessary, however, to produce one proof that Pitt was in the right, though others are not wanting. All Fitzwilliam's friends in the Cabinet, who loved Fitzwilliam, and who disliked and distrusted Pitt; who had entered the Government reluctantly, and who would have embraced any fair opportunity of leaving it; who had been indeed on the brink of resignation with regard to Irish affairs three months before,—all these men, Portland and Windham, Spencer and Loughborough, three of them men of the nicest honour, and cognisant of the entire chain of agreements and events, all unhesitatingly took the part of Pitt against Fitzwilliam. Who, indeed, was the minister who, having obtained special responsibility for Ireland by the threat of resignation, now recalled Fitzwilliam? Who but Portland, himself Fitzwilliam's political friend and chief. In that very letter to Grattan which has been mentioned, of the 23d of August 1794, Fitzwilliam says, "I shall look to the system of the Duke of Portland as the model by which I shall regulate the general line of my conduct." Portland's lethargy had been blamable in the earlier stages of the transaction. But he showed none now. This is a circumstance which appears to bar further controversy. From the mouths of four unquestionable and unwilling witnesses it establishes Pitt's good faith, and the fact that the mistake lay with Fitzwilliam.

We should, however, beware of the slightest confusion between the cause and the effects of Fitzwilliam's recall. That he himself was the cause alters in no respect the unhappy results of his removal. It seems, moreover, clear that the objection was not so much to his policy as to his methods. It was urged by Fitzwilliam that the Catholic question had nothing to do with his removal, but that his dismissals were the real cause. This statement seems accurate to the extent that the Government was by no means averse to emancipation, but had a rooted distrust of his administrative discretion. Pitt was always ready for concession to Catholics; he showed his readiness before and after, in 1792 and in 1797. There was nothing in 1795 that should change his views. The misfortune was that the Irish could not know his real sentiments, or how he had pushed forward the great emancipation of 1793. They could only surmise that Fitzwilliam had been removed because he was a reformer, and the Government hostile to all reform. Dublin shut its shutters and went into mourning; while ardent patriots made up their minds that any amendment must come from France or from an appeal to arms.

It would seem at first, therefore, that it would have been far better, as it happened, to allow Fitzwilliam to fulfil his own promises, and to carry out his own programme. But a moment's reflection shows that this was impossible. There was the direst of all obstacles—a sunken rock. The King had been approached; his honour and his conscience had been moved by the most insidious and most impracticable of arguments. For he had been told that, should he consent to the admission of Catholics to political office, he would break his Coronation oath, and forfeit the crown. In that narrow, and obstinate, but scrupulous mind, this belief was now irrevocably imbedded. Fitzwilliam's policy would, therefore, have been shattered against the King's immovable and impregnable position on the Catholic question : immovable as regards himself, because he believed that emancipation involved the personal guilt of perjury; impregnable against opposition, because it was based on the passions and prejudices of the great mass of the people of Great Britain. And, as soon as he scented the Catholic question, the King urged Fitzwilliam's removal. So the impartial thinker can only once more lament that the mission of Fitzwilliam adds another instance of that curse of mischance that has always assisted the curse of misgovernment to poison the relations between England and Ireland.

And now things went from bad to worse. In September of this year (1795) the Orange Society arose. The Catholic organisation of the Defenders was already in full operation. The United Irishmen availed themselves of both. Agrarian outrage and the plunder of arms abounded. In Ulster there was an organised persecution to drive the Catholics out of the province—"to hell or Connaught." In 1796 all these evils were aggravated by the enrolment of the yeomanry, an undisciplined and uncontrollable force. In December of that year, a French expedition under Hoche invaded Ireland, but effected nothing. In 1797, the state of the North was hardly distinguishable from civil war. It was placed under martial law. A population, which had long been arming for rebellion, was disarmed by harsh and summary methods. The Government had some 60,000 soldiers and militia quartered in Ireland. There were violent reprisals on the part of the military for the outrages that had been committed by the United Irishmen and Defenders.

The year darkened as it passed. The gaols were full. Men under suspicion were crimped and sent to serve in the fleet. Some even attributed the mutiny at the Nore to the element thus introduced into the Navy. Patrols pervaded the country all night. There was disaffection among the troops. The Catholics fled from Ulster. On the one side there were murders, roastings, plunder of arms, and a reign of terror; on the other, picketing, scourging, hanging—half or whole—house-burning, and a reign of not less terror. The miseries of the Thirty Years' War were scarcely more appalling; for it was civil conflict of the most terrible kind, the worse because it was not declared; it was anarchy inflamed by fanaticism; while the Parliament and Government, that should have remedied and appeased, were themselves beyond help or hope. The first could only acquiesce in the proposals of the last; the last could only appeal for more soldiers to England.

In 1798, the rebellion, in breaking out, lost something of its horror. The rising was fixed for the 23d of May; and on that day it flamed forth in the counties of Dublin, Meath, and Kildare. It does not come within the compass of this narrative to describe that insurrection, its massacres and retaliations. That it was not even more formidable may be attributed to two causes: Ulster held aloof, and the French came too late. As it was, the rebellion lasted barely a month, and was both local and partial.

It is, however, worth noting here what Pitt wrote to an eminent Irishman on this subject. To the account of the duel which he had sent to Wellesley he adds: "You will hear that in Ireland the Jacobins (after many of their leaders being apprehended) have risen in open war. The contest has at present existed about a week. The Government have acted with great spirit, and the troops of all descriptions behave incomparably. We cannot yet judge how far it may spread, but I trust with the present force and some augmentation from hence, the rebellion will be crushed, before any attempt can be made from France: and we must, I think, follow up such an event by immediate steps for a union." As to the behaviour of the troops Pitt was certainly ill informed. But in such a matter he would not be likely to know much. The internal administration of Ireland was entirely independent of England. There he had neither knowledge nor control, unless specially appealed to. After all was over, after, as an Irishman said, "rebellion and its attendant horrors had roused on both sides to the highest pitch all the strongest feelings of our nature," he may have heard of the atrocities in Ireland with the same emotions that later ministers may have experienced in learning the horrors of the Indian mutiny and the horrors of its repression. We know this, that when Clare attempted in his hearing a defence of the malpractices of the magistrates and the militia, Pitt "turned . . . round with that high indignant stare which sometimes marked his countenance, and stalked out of the House."

At the close of the revolt a new Viceroy arrived. Cornwallis, whose career had been marked by one supreme military disaster, had obliterated it by his industry, his honesty, and his public spirit. He had not perhaps conspicuous abilities; but this deficiency only brings into greater prominence the sterling splendour of his character; and he remains a signal example of unsparing, unselfish, patriotic devotion to duty. But here his lines were cast in evil places. The one lesson of the rebellion was that the whole system of Irish government must be remodelled. What form the new experiment should take had long been tacitly admitted, and Cornwallis came over to carry a legislative Union between Great Britain and Ireland.

If the dismissal of Fitzwilliam may be said to touch the rim of a volcano, the Union is the burning fiery furnace of the crater itself. Something, however, is admitted with regard to it on all sides. The Parliament that passed the Scottish Union in 1707 had been elected directly in view of that question, which entirely engrossed the national mind. The Parliament that in

1800 passed the Irish Union had been elected in 1797, with no more reference to the question of the termination of its own existence than to free education or female suffrage. So far from the nation being consulted in respect to the obliteration of its legislature, there was not, even after the conclusion of the treaty, any popular election held for the members to be sent to London; but lots were drawn among those elected under such totally different circumstances and for such totally different purposes. Nor is it denied that this Irish Parliament, so wholly without mandate, and probably without power to terminate itself (though this is still subject of contention), was practically bribed and bullied out of existence. The corruption was black, hideous, horrible; revolting at any time, atrocious when it is remembered that it was a nation's birthright that was being sold. It was perhaps less questionable in those days to buy up the nomination boroughs, or most of them, as chattels at a fixed tariff. Pitt had made a like proposition for England in his plan of parliamentary reform. Close boroughs then represented not merely a vested interest, but property of the most tangible and recognised kind. But what stands without either shame or palliation was the remodelling, in the autumn and winter of 1799, of the House of Commons, after it had rejected the Union propositions.

Between the close of the session of 1799 and the beginning of that of 1800, between June and January, sixty-three seats out of a total of three hundred were vacated. Some of those who had held them were cajoled; some were bribed into office and out of Parliament; the mass departed because the patrons of their boroughs had been bought over to the Union. In this way, without a dissolution, the whole complexion and constitution of the House were changed. ·In the session of 1799 the Irish Parliament rejected the propositions of the Government for a Union. When Parliament was opened in 1800, there was not the slightest allusion to the measure of Union in the speech from the throne; but thirty-nine writs were at once moved. The entire patronage and terror of the Crown were employed to pack Parliament and purchase the patrons of Parliament. It rained honey and gall as occasion required—offices and peerages, or dismissal and disgrace. Castlereagh, now Chief Secretary, and the executive agent in this degrading traffic, pursued his task without flinching or remorse. Not Strafford was more thorough. Cornwallis expressed his loathing and disgust of the whole transaction. Castlereagh neither felt nor expressed any. He, in fact, hoped that corruption would die of a sort of surfeit; that it would perish by this final exaggeration; and that by one supreme, shameless, wholesale effort he could put an end to it for ever after.

Under these circumstances and auspices, the measure was passed in 1800, both in Ireland and in England. The Irish debates produced much fine and significant speaking, in which Foster against, and Fitzgibbon (now Clare) for the Union, bore off the palm; many weighty predictions from such men as Parsons and Grattan, that a Union so forced on would inevitably imperil the entire connection between the two countries; some ominous prophecies of the sinister influence that the Irish contingent would exercise over British politics. Charlemont, indeed, had always opposed any Union, on the ground that no other measure could so effectually contribute to the separation of the two countries. In Ireland itself there was a comparative apathy, produced by the ruinous struggles of the last few years; only in Dublin, the dying capital, was there a last agony of patriotism. On the other hand, all the efforts of the Government, unrelentingly applied, could produce but a few thinly-signed petitions in support of the Bill—not a twelfth of those against it. It passed by purchase. "The whole unbribed intellect of Ireland," says an eminent historian, "was opposed to it." Of the members who composed the majority in its favour, it is computed that only seven voted for it without any "consideration." In the House of Commons the minority set their names to an address recapitulating the evils and ignominies of the measure; in the House of Lords it was followed by an eloquent protest headed by Leinster, the only Irish duke, and completed by such signatures as those of Downshire and Meath, and Moira and Powerscourt. After an easy passage through the British Parliament, it received the royal assent in July.

With regard to the Union two separate questions have to be considered. Firstly, were the means by which it was carried justifiable? Secondly, was it a right measure in itself? On both these points it is necessary to keep in mind the preliminary remark that has been made. It is easy on the brink of the twentieth century to censure much in the eighteenth; but is it candid to do so without placing oneself as far as possible in the atmosphere, circumstances, and conditions of the period which one is considering? Have Pitt's critics done this? Have they judged him by the standards and ideas of his time, and not by the standards and ideas of their own? That is the spirit in which History judges statesmen, and for a simple reason: had they attempted to carry into effect in their generation the ideas of ours, they would not have been statesmen at all. They would have been voices crying in the wilderness; they might have been venerated as well-intentioned visionaries, or imprisoned as agitators, or even lunatics; but statesmen they would not have been in name or in fact. A statesman measures the opinions and forces that surround him, and proceeds to act accordingly; he is not laying his account with remote posterity, or legislating for it. The politician who is a century before his time is hardly more a statesman than the politician who is a century behind it. The man who doses a child with colchicum, or who attempts to cure atrophy by bleeding, is neither in name nor in fact a physician. To apply what is wholesome at one stage of growth or of disease to an age or an ailment totally different is merely dangerous quackery. To the man who attempts such mortal mischief in politics is commonly denied the power; and for this reason doctrines in advance of the age, as they are called, are usually the copyright of philosophers entirely dissociated from affairs. It is in this spirit that History, truly and justly written, apportions blame and praise to men, judging by contemporary canons and not by ours. It is thus that History weighs in her balance Cæsar, and Richelieu, and William III., and Ximenes, and Oxenstiern. Were it otherwise, she would hold the third Duke of Richmond, with his universal suffrage and annual parliaments, a greater statesman than Pitt, or Burke, or any of his contemporaries.

To Pitt alone is meted out a different measure. He alone is judged, not by the end of the eighteenth, but by the end of the nineteenth century. And why? Because the Irish question which he attempted to settle is an unsettled question still. He alone of the statesmen of the eighteenth century, with the exception of Burke and perhaps Chesterfield, saw its importance and grappled with it manfully. Since then many ministers have nibbled at it whose efforts are buried in decent obscurity. But Pitt's career is still the battle-field of historians and politicians, because he is responsible for the treaty of Union; and because he resigned and did not do something, neither known nor specified but certainly impossible, to carry what remained of Catholic Emancipation.

Of the corruption by which the Union was carried something remains to be noted. It was, admittedly, wholesale and horrible. But it must in fairness be remembered that this was the only method known of carrying on Irish government; the only means of passing any measure through the Irish Parliament; that, so far from being an exceptional phase of politics, it was only three or four years of Irish administration rolled into one. No Irish patriot can regard the Union as other than the sale of his Parliament, justifiable or unjustifiable according to his politics; but, for an English minister of that day, the purchase of that Parliament was habitual and invariable. The quotations of the parliamentary market were as well known as the quotations of wheat and of sugar. It is scarcely possible to open a letter from an Irish Viceroy or an Irish Secretary of that time without finding a calculation for the hire, open and avowed, of some individual or influence; or some cynical offer by some hungry nobleman of his interest for a determined price. It was the ordinary daily life of Dublin Castle; it was the air which the Government breathed; the nourishment which alone enabled it to exist. No one condemned it, any more than the neighbours of Washington condemned him for owning slaves. And the reason is simple. The Irish Executive was appointed in England solely with reference to English considerations; the Parliament through which this Executive had to pass its measures was an Irish Parliament, elected, so far as it was freely elected, with reference to Irish considerations. The Government and its policy were entirely exotic; and the attempt to root them in Irish soil was a perpetual strife with nature. An artificial temperature had to be formed for them, and that was corruption. A means of bringing the Government and the Parliament into relations had to be found, and that was corruption. A means of carrying Government measures through Parliament had to be discovered, and that was corruption. For a government which rules in disregard or defiance of Parliament must resort to bribery or resort to force. There was no force available; corruption therefore was the indispensable agency. The absolute severance of the Executive and the Legislature both in nature and origin produced an unnatural and unworkable condition of affairs; it was only by bribery that the machine could be set going at all. The great measure of Catholic Emancipation was only carried in 1792-93 by Castle influence; that is, by direct or indirect corruption through a reluctant Parliament. Had Fitzwilliam been allowed to carry the complement of these bills in 1795, he could only have done it by the same means. The Executive was in no way responsible to Parliament; had Parliament been unanimous in opposition, it could not have changed a minister. Any measure, therefore, that the Government wished to pass was a subject of separate negotiation with the leaders of the country. These were generally recalcitrant in proportion to their power, and had to be purchased accordingly. There were in reality no constituencies for the Government to appeal to. As out of the 300 members of the House 124 were nominated by 52 peers, and 64 by 36 commoners, it was with the owners of the constituencies that the Government had to deal.

It must be understood, then, that corruption was not a monstrous, abnormal characteristic of the Union; it was the everyday life and atmosphere of Irish politics. Was it not better, it may be then urged, that this system should end? Was it not better, at the worst, and once for all, to make a regiment of peers and an army of baronets, to buy the rotten boroughs at the price of palaces, than to go on in the vile old way, hiring, haggling, jobbing, from one dirty day to another, from one miserable year to another, without hope or self-respect; poisoning the moral sense, and betraying the honest judgment of the country, in the futile, endless attempt to maintain the unnatural predominance, and the unreal connection, of an alien executive and a sectional legislature? If the answer be Yes, the means are to that extent justified, for there were no others.

It may, however, be said, that even if it be granted that the system was vile and rightly ended, and ended by the only practicable methods, it might have been replaced by something better than the Union. To some of us now living this seems clear enough; but had we lived then, is it certain that our judgment would have been the same? We were engaged in a war, not of winter quarters and of summer quarters, and of elegant expeditions some way off, and of musketeers in laced gloves and periwigs saying, "Gentlemen, fire first," not a war of the eighteenth century: but naked men were fighting for life and freedom with despair; they were crossing the ice barefoot in rags; they were capturing fleets with cavalry; both we and our foes believed it to be a struggle between existence and extinction. Fortunately, it ended in existence for us, nearly exhausted and in terrible debt, but still existence.

At the end of the eighteenth century, however, such a result was by no means certain. We formed the main object of an enemy, who had conquered half Europe. Thrice had that enemy invaded Ireland, and it was certain that an invasion of England was only a question of time. In so appalling a crisis, a new arrangement had, by the admission of all parties, to be formed for Ireland. Grattan himself had tacitly given up his own Parliament as hopeless; for he had withdrawn from it, and encouraged the discussion of Irish affairs in the British legislature. What wonder, then, if from the natural tendency to draw closer and closer and closer yet, in the presence of an overpowering danger, men's minds should have turned with rare unanimity to the idea of a Union. During a campaign even a single Parliament sometimes seems a superfluity, and a second a danger. What would happen, if in war, as in the Regency question, the British Parliament should take one line, and the Irish Parliament the other? If, however, they became united, it would be safe, in view of the overwhelming Protestant majority in England and Scotland, to give concessions that otherwise would be impossible to the overwhelming Catholic majority in Ireland. Internal free trade would give Ireland material prosperity, but without a Union the British commercial classes would not hear of any such arrangement. Neither concession, neither Catholic relief nor internal free trade, would in the then temper of men's minds have had a chance of acceptance in England, so long as they were made to the independent parliament of a hostile nation. But on Catholic relief and on internal free trade Pitt's mind was set.

Again, if a Union were achieved, there would be no focus for French intrigue. The Executive of the two countries had always been practically one: to make the two Parliaments one would place the conditions of Government on a natural basis. But, above all, was the consideration that Great Britain would now face the world with a united front, with a single Parliament in which the elements of loyalty and stability would be in an incalculable majority.

These arguments, whatever may now be thought of their value, appealed with irresistible force to statesmen, for whom, struggling in a great war, unity and simplicity of government were everything. But Pitt never thought, as some seem since to have thought, that the Union could stand alone; he never deemed it a divine instrument, admirable and venerable by its own natural essence. He considered it as only a part, and not even the most important part, of a great healing policy in Ireland; and that, almost if not quite simultaneously, the other parts should be applied; the last limitations of the Catholics removed; the clergy other than those of the Established Church provided with stipends; the oppression of tithe abolished. These were inseparable constituents of his scheme. Had his hands been free, he might possibly have even dealt with the evils of the land system, at least as regards absenteeism. Who will say that, followed up by large, spontaneous, and simultaneous concessions of this kind, the policy of the Union might not have been a success? Had Pitt, in face of the difficulties that presented themselves, temporarily dropped Catholic Emancipation, and only carried a Tithe Bill in 1801, the Union might at least have had a fair start. Frere, who knew Pitt well, declared that it was not true that Pitt ever regarded Catholic Emancipation as a sop to be offered to the Irish to make them accept the Union. On the contrary, he regarded, as Frere knew, the Emancipation of the Catholics as the more important measure of the two, and he would gladly have carried it at any time. The Union was to pave the way and conciliate British opinion. "The word Union," Pitt's Lord Lieutenant wrote, as he was passing the measure, "will not cure the evils of this wretched country; it is a necessary preliminary, but a great deal more remains to be done." That was Pitt's view. But on this necessary preliminary or foundation succeeding ministries reared either structures he had never contemplated, or no structure at all. He passed the Union with one object; it has been diverted to another.

There was a curse upon it. It drove its very author from office in the full plenitude of his authority, in the very moment of the triumph of passing it. Never did Pitt hold power again, for his last two years of suffering and isolation do not deserve the name. And so all went wrong. The measure of Union stood alone. And it was one of the drawbacks of that luckless measure that it left all the remaining machinery of independence when it took away the Parliament; every characteristic of a separate state, everything to remind men of what had been. It was like cutting the face out of a portrait and leaving the picture in the frame. The fragment of policy flapped forlornly on the deserted mansions of the capital, but there was enough to remind men of what had been. It was impossible, for example, to destroy that Ionian colonnade which remains one of the glories of Dublin. So the Government transformed into a bank the noble hall which had resounded with some of the highest flights of human eloquence, which was indissolubly connected with such names as Flood and Grattan and Charlemont, and which was imperishably imbued with the proud memories of an ancient nationality. Men as they passed murmured that that was the home of their Parliament, which nothing had obliterated and nothing had replaced.

But all that man could do was done to obliterate the rest of Pitt's policy. Addington's Irish Government went over with express instructions to do nothing for the Catholics, nothing for the Dissenters, but to push and promote the Established Church in every way. Nothing but the Union remained even to indicate what Pitt's plan had been; and that was a misleading indication. Catholic Emancipation waited for thirty, and Tithe Reform waited for near forty, embittered and envenomed years. The time for ecclesiastical stipends provided by the State passed away for ever. The bright promises of financial improvement that had been held out to Ireland faded away into bankruptcy. Seventy years afterwards, the Irish Church Establishment, which it had been one of the main objects of the Treaty to preserve, suddenly toppled over and disappeared. With it went the keystone of the Union. And so it is Pitt's sinister destiny to be judged by the petty fragment of a large policy which he did not live to carry out: a policy, unhappy in execution and result, but which was, it may be fairly maintained, as generous and comprehensive in conception as it was patriotic in motive. It was at any rate worth trying, where so many had failed. But it had no trial; the experiment was scarcely even commenced; and the ruinous part that remains, exposed as it has been to the harshest storms of nine decades, is judged and venerated as if it were the entire structure.

CHAPTER XII

PITT AND WELLESLEY

IT may be well here to desist for a moment from the task of description, and to give the reader a glimpse of the true Pitt afforded by himself. His friendships were few, but they were close, and even tender, to a very remarkable degree. Of Wilberforce and him it was said that they were like brothers. A scarcely less affectionate though a later intimacy was that with Lord Mornington, afterwards Lord Wellesley, the great Viceroy whose brilliant rule in India conferred such renown on himself, though it afterwards disabled him to a great extent for the rough and tumble of English party strife.[1] To him the following letters were addressed. The first was evidently written in 1796, when it may be presumed that Mornington was in Ireland.

DOWNING STREET,
Sept. 22*d* (undated, but evidently 1796).

MY DEAR MORNINGTON—I have waited from day to day by no fault of my own, much longer than I wished or expected, in the hope of seeing my way as to our official

[1] These letters, which are in some respects the most interesting that we have of Pitt's, have been made available for this little book by the generous kindness of Mr. Alfred Montgomery.

arrangements, and being able to write you something positive respecting yourself. I am happy now to tell you that there is no obstacle to accomplishing what I have from the beginning eagerly wished to find practicable; and that I shall certainly be enabled to open for you either the office of Joint-Paymaster, or some other equally desirable. A very few days will settle the specific mode. We mean to chuse the Speaker on Sunday, but to defer opening the causes of calling the Parliament till after the members are sworn; probably till Tuesday sennight. This will avoid the inconvenience of making or at least delivering the speech so long before it can be debated, which is very material, at a time that every day produces such important events. We have fresh accounts to-day of continued success up to the 8th, when the Archduke was advanced to Wetzlar. Nothing can equal the rapidity of his progress. "Nec vero disjunctissimæ terræ citius cujusquam passibus peragrari potuerunt, quam suis non dicam cursibus, sed victoriis illustratæ sunt."[1] Our overture has been sent to Paris above a fortnight, but we have got no answer, nor any late accounts of what is passing there yet.—Ever sincerely yours,

W. PITT.

The next two refer to Mornington's desire for a peerage of Great Britain before setting out for India. As regards that wish nothing need here be said, nor does Pitt seem able to comprehend the frame of mind in which such a desire could be formed. But his hearty zeal in his friend's cause is surely a pleasant feature. The second of these notes was written on the very day (October 4, 1797) on which Mornington was formally appointed Governor-General of India.

[1] Slightly altered from Cicero, pro M. Marcello, Oratio II. 5. The present reading is, I am informed, "lustratæ."

HOLLWOOD,
Tuesday, Oct. 3d, 1797.
½ p. 9 P.M.

MY DEAR MORNINGTON—I cannot easily say how much gratification I felt, in opening and reading your letter, from knowing that as far as depends upon me, I had anticipated both your reasoning and your wishes. I had written to the King some hours before, requesting as strongly as I thought myself at liberty to do, that you should be included in the List of Peers. I will not pretend to you that I had quite convinced my judgment; but I certainly felt it one of the occasions on which I had the best right to consult my inclination; and I could not reconcile myself to the idea of leaving to such uncertain chance as belongs to these times my hope of being able to contribute to the success of what seems with you so favourite a wish. You will of course know the result from me to-morrow. I have put it in the way I thought most likely to overcome objections, but I cannot venture to state the thing to you as what you can count upon till I receive the King's answer; as he seemed most strongly bent against every extension of the List, and it is one of the points on which he is most apt to adhere to his opinion.

I trust from what I hear from Dundas that there is very little chance indeed that the second part of your case (your not going to Bengal) will arise. As we shall know the result on that so soon, I will say no more about it.—Ever affly. yrs.,
W. P.

The King's resistance did not last long.

DOWNING STREET,
Wednesday, (evidently *Oct.* 4, 1797,) ½ p. 1.

MY DEAR MORNINGTON—If you happen to be disengaged I shall be very glad to see you here at dinner to-day soon after five.—Yours ever, W. P.

I am most happy to tell you, the King agrees to your peerage.

The next letter gives a long and elaborate account of the state of affairs as it appeared to Pitt's sanguine apprehension. His sarcasm on the Crown lawyers is characteristically cold and cutting. The allusion to Grenville shows that the somewhat crabbed character of that minister was recognised by his colleagues as a difficulty to be reckoned with. In this letter, too, occurs that account of a speech by Perceval which so impressed Pitt as to make him on the morning of the duel name Perceval as probably the most available man to succeed him. His genial pleasure over the young man's success explains perhaps what the ordinary view of Pitt's haughty reserve does not: the idolatry with which so many of his followers, particularly the junior ones, regarded him.

WIMBLEDON,
Jan. 26th, 1798.

MY DEAR MORNINGTON—You will hear I trust from various other correspondents who have more leisure, a much fuller history of all that has been passing since you left us, than I can pretend to give you. But I think you will like to hear from me even if it is only to tell you as to myself, that in spite of six weeks of more fatigue and anxiety than have attended almost any other Parliamentary campaign, I am greatly better than you left me, and I trust, equal to fighting the battle as long as may be necessary. Our great measure of the assessed taxes was for some time apparently in great danger of failing, less from any real difficulty or even general dislike to it than from the impression of local and partial clamour, and from the effect of a very great degree of panic which infected too many of those who are generally most free from it. It became necessary to shew that *at all risks* I was determined to persevere in it; and by those means alone I believe it was carried. Opposition I think added to the odium and disgrace of their secession by returning from it on this occasion, and by the whole of their conduct and language upon it. Our last debate (to my great joy) produced a speech from Perceval, which was in all respects one of the best I ever heard; and was an attack upon Fox pointed and galling enough to have drawn forth one of Grattan's warmest encomiums. It certainly sent him home very sick to his supper. Since this effort we have heard nothing of him but from the celebration of his birth-day two days ago, in which the two most distinguished traits were a speech from the Duke of Norfolk, which I think even the Crown lawyers will hardly prove to be much short of treason, and a public profession from Horne Tooke of reconciliation and coalition with Fox, with which I think you will be delighted. On the whole the line now taken by the whole of what calls itself Opposition (with the exception of Grey and Whitbread, whom we neither see nor hear of) and especially by Fox, is a compleat and undisguised avowal of the most desperate system ever acted upon, and I think it seems to be understood and felt as it ought, both in Parliament and in the country. The two great objects of our attention and exertion now are, to endeavour to raise spirit enough in the country to contribute voluntarily to the expense of the war, such a sum as in addition to the assessed taxes may bring our loan within a moderate shape, and next, to be prepared both by sea and land for the invasion which I have little doubt will be attempted in the course of the year, tho' the latter is much the easier work of the two. And I hope we shall have to make the option between burning their ships before they set out, or sinking them either on their passage or before their troops can land, or destroying them as soon as they have landed, or starving them and taking them prisoners afterwards. Indeed the scheme seems so romantic (without the prospect of any naval force to support it) that at any other moment it would not be credible; and it can hardly be attempted on any other notion but that it may be worth the enemy's while to devote two-thirds of an immense army to immediate destruction, for the sake of the mischief which the remainder may effect before they share the same fate. In the meantime however (tho' on the whole I think the attempt will be made) there are two possible events which may prevent it. One is if there should be fresh confusion in France, which seems not distant, and of which the issue cannot be even conjectured. The other is, if the new King of Prussia and the powers of the North should at last awaken, of which there is just now some appearance, but it is not yet decided enough to rely upon. The new decree aimed at our commerce but tending to annihilate a large part of the profit of neutral nations may perhaps (added to the danger of Hamburgh and the North of Europe) bring Denmark at least if not Sweden or Russia, to be ready to enter into an effectual concert with Prussia. And this prospect may tempt Prussia to take a decided part, which if it does, Europe will at last be saved. On the measure of voluntary contribution you will not wonder to hear that all our friends have not thought alike. But at so extraordinary a moment I have felt it so decidedly right, that I have determined as far as depends on me, to push it to the utmost; and tho' it has begun but languidly, I have now good hopes of success; as I have been enabled to-day to announce to the Bank, the

King's intention of giving one-third of his privy purse; and am besides furnished with such particulars as will enable me to satisfy the world, that he has *no other* fund from which he can command a shilling. We in office have thought it right to give an ample *fifth* of our income. And to my great satisfaction, Grenville has concurred very readily in giving his personal share, tho' very adverse in his general opinion to the whole measure. I am very happy to be able to add too, now that I mention his name, that I have not seen a cloud on his brow since the commencement of the session, and that every thing has gone on as pleasantly and cordially as possible. I have now mentioned all that I think it will be most interesting to you to learn. And you must at least for the present accept this picture of the times (which is as much as I can compleat at one sitting) as a substitute for that which I owe you from Hopner and which I hope will come one day or other. I conclude you will have heard from different channels of the anti-Jacobin; and I hope you will sometimes wish you were within reach of supporting it by your voluntary contribution. I have desired a compleat set to be sent you, lest you should not otherwise receive it.—God bless you.—Ever affy. yours,

W. Pitt.

The next, dated three months later, is not less sanguine; more especially in reference to finance and the French Invasion. It is noteworthy that Sheridan's speech in defence of the war was made after a good deal of private negotiation, to which in these years, at any rate during the Addington government, Sheridan seems to have been addicted. The use of the word "Plug" in this sense must be explained by more learned commentators. Grose and other kindred lexicographers throw no light.

WIMBLEDON,
April 22d, 1798, 9 P.M.

MY DEAR MORNINGTON—Lord Auckland has sent me word, by a messenger who came just before dinner, that he is sending (I know not how) some packet to you to-night. I had just before learned that a neutral ship from the Cape brings an account to-day of your arrival there and of your being perfectly well, which I hope we shall soon have verified by yourself. I have not time to write much this evening; but I am very glad to have an opportunity of telling you shortly how much the state of things has been improving since I wrote to you last. The voluntary contribution has succeeded to a great extent. The spirit and courage of the country has risen so as to be fairly equal to the crisis. I am to settle my loan to-morrow, to the amount of fifteen millions, which will leave us without a single difficulty in finance, and I have no doubt of making it on better terms than last year. The plan for the sale of the land tax (which I think we talked of before you went) is going on. The Bill is to be read a second time to-morrow, and in spite of many *Plugs* from Sir Wm. Pulteney will certainly pass, and there is every reason to think the effect will be very considerable. In addition to these favorable circumstances our traitors at home (those chiefly of the lower class) have given us the means of seizing them to such a number as I believe to disconcert effectually whatever were their plans; and the Habeas Corpus Act has been suspended by a Bill passed in both Houses in one day. Our division 183 to 5. Sheridan came (after long notice in *general* conversation and some *private*) to make an excellent speech against the French, and his own friends here. But he was foolish enough to oppose the suspension, and divide in the minority in which the little of opposition that was in the House, left him and voted with us. He did us some good, gained some credit to himself and not too much, and added to the disgrace of the seceders. Of the last class, Fox, Grey, and Whitbread remain, the first, I believe, for ever, and of the latter I cannot judge. The French go on, I believe in earnest, with plans and demonstrations of invasion; but the effect here, is only to produce all the efforts, and all the spirit we can wish. In addition to all this state of things at home, there is a chance (and a better than has appeared for a long period) that the monarchs remaining in Europe will awake before their thrones are taken from under them, and will think it better to lay aside interested jealousies among themselves than to remain any longer a prey to their common enemy. We shall of course encourage and incite this to the utmost, and if they are true to themselves, Europe will still be saved. If this should fail us, I think you may still count fully on finding England a country to receive you when you return from India; and I think you will find our friend (who quoted Pompey upon you at your departure) in better spirits and temper than you left him. He is doing every thing that is right. I have tried to tell you all I could in a short time, and perhaps unintelligibly.—Ever yrs., W. PITT.

The next letter gives Pitt's account of the duel. To us his reference to Irish affairs is more interesting than his light-hearted account of the somewhat boyish escapade.

PRIVATE.

DOWNING STREET,
Thursday, May 31st, 1798.

MY DEAR MORNINGTON—I have not time to write you a very long letter; but as you will hear of me from others, I think you will like to be told by myself that I was under the necessity last Sunday of meeting Mr. Tierney in consequence of some expressions I had used in the House of Commons, on the Friday preceding, and which I did not feel it right to explain. I enclose you a short statement of what passed, taken down by the seconds before we left the ground. The business has ended to my perfect satisfaction, and I must say that Tierney conducted himself with the greatest propriety. I believe we parted better satisfied with each other, than on any other occasion in our lives.

You will hear that in Ireland the Jacobins (after many of their leaders being apprehended) have risen in open war. The contest has at present existed about a week.

The Government have acted with great spirit, and the troops of all descriptions behave incomparably. We cannot yet judge how far it may spread, but I trust with the present force and some augmentation from hence, the rebellion will be crushed, before any attempt can be made from France; and we must I think follow up such an event by immediate steps for an union. The French will probably try a magnificent project of invading Ireland from Toulon; but will be surprised at meeting Ld. St. Vincent in the Mediterranean where they least expect him. I have not time for another sheet.—Ever yours, W. PITT.

ENCLOSURE.

May 28th.

WE are authorised to state that in consequence of what passed on Friday last, Mr. Pitt, accompanied by Mr. Ryder and Mr. Tierney, accompanied by Mr. George Walpole, met at three o'clock yesterday afternoon on Putney Heath.

After some ineffectual attempts on the part of the seconds to prevent further proceedings, the parties took their ground at the distance of twelve paces. A case of pistols was fired at the same moment without effect. A second case was also fired in the same manner, Mr. Pitt firing his pistol in the air. The seconds then jointly interfered, and insisted that the matter should go no further, it being their decided opinion that sufficient satisfaction had been given, and that the business was ended with perfect honour to both parties.

The next contains the innocent offer of the Irish marquisate which caused such dire offence.

DOWNING STREET,
Nov. 6th, 1799.

MY DEAR MORNINGTON—I was in hopes to have atoned in some degree for my long silence by writing to you at large on all the interesting subjects on which you will wish for information, but I have been continually interrupted till the last moment and must now confine my letter to a few lines. They must naturally be employed in the first place to tell you what however I trust you are sufficiently assured of already, how warmly and sincerely I rejoice in all the success and glory which has attended your Indian Government. In the midst of the agitations of Europe, the remoteness of the scene of action has not prevented the value of your services from being felt and estimated by the public as your warmest friends would wish. An Irish marquisate, which the King confers on you, by the title of Marquis Wellesley of Norragh, (which is pitched upon on Bernard's authority) will I hope be satisfactory as an ostensible mark of approbation, and the further provision which Dundas will have explained to you is in contemplation, besides operating as a further acknowledgment of your services, is likely I trust to set your mind wholly at ease in what relates to the interest of your family. I must not attempt in the haste in which I write to enter into any particulars on the wide field of politics, many of them, I know, you will hear from Canning, and probably from

Grenville. In general, much indeed has been gained in the course of the present year, notwithstanding the failures and reverses of the latter part. If Austria can be made to act in earnest next year, and to aim at gaining her own objects thro' the medium of saving Europe instead of destroying it, everything we wish seems within reach of being accomplished in two campaigns more. The decision of Vienna is however wholly uncertain and our best comfort is that if it fails us we can return to our defensive system with unbroken spirits and resources, and trust to our own anchors to ride out the storm. I cannot end without thanking you for the particular accounts you sent me of our gallant friend Cooke, about whom I am more interested than I can express. We are at this moment in great anxiety about him, as the accounts we had received of his being perfectly out of danger, have been followed by others of a later date mentioning his death, but as these last come by Bombay and are only in general terms, I trust there is still some room left for hope.—Ever affectionately yours,

W. PITT.

Wellesley's reply to this letter is well known. It is dated April 28, 1800, and is printed, though not at length, in Lord Stanhope's *Life* (vol. iii. p. 232). He speaks in the bitterest terms of the anguish of mind he felt; that the impression produced in India would be fatally detrimental to his Government; and that the slur inflicted by this "Irish," "pinchbeck" reward affected both his health and his spirits. Pitt's letter in reply, here subjoined, is the most interesting of his that we possess. It seems to combine an admirable specimen of his persuasive power in debate with the soothing affection of a brother ministering to a sick and overburthened mind. It is in itself a final and conclusive answer to the allegations of haughty heartlessness.

HAMPSTEAD,
Saturday, Sept. 27th, 1800.

MY DEAR WELLESLEY—I received last Wednesday your letter of the 28th April, and painful as were its contents to me in many respects I had at least great consolation and satisfaction in the proof of your continued kindness and friendship which I derived from the unreserved communication of your feelings. You will I am sure wish me to use the same frankness in return. I certainly most deeply lament that the particular mark of the King's favor which you have received is so little adequate to your wishes and expectations, but I must fairly own to you that on the fullest reflection I cannot concur in your view of the subject. In the first place I have always felt that in every question of reward for services, the manner in which it is given, and that in which it is received determine its value in the eyes of the public much more than its own specifick nature. But you must allow me to state freely that independent of this general feeling there are particular circumstances in the present case to which you do not appear to have given the weight which I think they deserve. Nothing but the duty of stating to you exactly what I feel with the sincerity of a friend would bring me to refer to the topic I am going to mention. It was certainly to me a most sensible gratification to be able previous to your going to India, to secure to you an object on which you set so much value as the British peerage. But surely considering the circumstances under which the King was induced to give it, it must be considered rather as an anticipation to no small extent of the reward for distinguished service than as a foundation for higher claims when those services should have been actually performed. In this view of the subject to have given you an English marquisate would have been to have conferred in the short course of your Indian Government four steps in the British peerage ; a scale of promotion certainly very unusual. The step in the Irish peerage was precisely the same proportional advancement as was given to Lord Cornwallis for his services in the same quarter ; and from the manner in which you have yourself referred to them, I am sure you will join in the general feeling that to adopt such a proportion had nothing in it disparaging. The truth really is that in my mind and I believe in that of almost all your friends (all feeling the same cordial and zealous interest in your just fame and consideration) the natural question seemed to be whether to recommend to the King to give you an English earldom, or the Irish marquisate. From many quarters I was led to believe that you would prefer the latter ; and particularly the circumstance of Barnard's being in possession of the memorandum specifying the title to which you had looked decided my opinion. I have hitherto confined myself only to the point of promotion in the peerage ; but in estimating the value of the ostensible marks of approbation and honour which you have received, and by which the public both here and in India would judge of the sense entertained of your services, there are other circumstances to be considered much more important than either an Irish or English marquisate. The unanimous thanks of both Houses of Parliament, in the marked terms in which they were conveyed, if they had been accompanied by no other distinction, would in my judgment alone have placed you on ground on which few servants of the public have ever stood. In addition to this decisive testimony, the provision proposed to be made by the company independent of its intrinsic value to your family, is to be considered as a public tribute to your merits, which makes it impossible to suppose that they were depreciated in any quarter. The King's speech to which you refer (however you may perhaps consider it in India as with us in the House of Commons as the speech of the minister) is at least as direct an indication of the sentiment of the sovereign and as much his act, as any title which he confers. Combining all these considerations, I really cannot conceive how the public in India should feel (what I will venture to say the public *in Europe* have never felt, and never I believe will be brought to feel) that there has not been in every quarter (the *highest* included) the most cordial and liberal disposition to bear full testimony and do ample justice, to the extent of your claims upon the public. Still less can I imagine, that with all these marks of approbation from England and with the impression which your conduct must have made on the minds of those who were nearer witnesses of it, it can have been a question whether you were likely to continue possessed of that respect and estimation from all the civil and military servants in India which is necessary for the full support of your authority. Forgive me if I add, that if any such feeling has found its way into their mind or into their conversation, it can only, I believe, have originated from some suspicion of its being entertained by yourself. That idea is at any time enough to make any but the most real friends, admit that a man is mortified and ill used. But it will hardly ever happen (unless in cases very different indeed from the present) that the opinion and language of the person most interested and of those immediately connected with him will not decide that of the public. I have now fairly stated to you my view of the subject. I cannot hope to change an opinion which I fear has taken so deep a root in your mind. But I am sure you will give a candid consideration to what I have stated, and I trust that the plainness and sincerity with which I have expressed myself will appear to you the best proof I could give of real friendship. With these sentiments on the subject as it stood originally, you will not wonder if I do not see the possibility (however anxiously I wish it were possible) that anything should be now done to repair your disappointment. Indeed your own wishes do not seem to point at any additional mark of favor, unless it had taken place on our receiving the news of the final settlement of Mysore. That period is elapsed, and I think you will agree with me that (if no other objection were felt here) whatever was done now would want the *grace* which belongs to rewards of this nature only when they are *gratuitous*, and would be liable to a construction neither creditable to Government nor to yourself. I have said nothing on the little intrinsic difference under the present circumstances, between an English and Irish marquisate, because I conceive you look rather to the public impression than to the thing itself. But as far as in itself it may be an object, it will certainly not escape you that under the circumstances of the Union, the difference to any person already possessed of a British title is little more than nominal; scarcely extending further than to a question of stile in the journals and debates of the House of Lords or of relative precedence as to four or five individuals; objects on which I do not believe such a mind as yours can set much serious value. I have not time to add anything more to this long letter, except the assurance of the cordial and unabated friendship and attachment with which I hope ever to remain.—Sincerely and affectionately yours, W. PITT.

Both Dundas and myself enter into and applaud the justice and delicacy of your feelings with respect to the particular fund out of which your grant was intended to be made, tho' the objection is rather in appearance than in substance. I am persuaded some other mode will be found of carrying into effect what was intended.

MARQUIS WELLESLEY.

The last two letters were written when Wellesley was at war with the Board of Directors, and are interesting mainly as showing the tender delicacy with which Pitt soothed the sore and sensitive spirit of his friend. The great Viceroy, it remains to be added, landed in England in January 1806 just in time to give a farewell grasp to the emaciated hand of the great minister. The note in which Pitt writes to Wellesley of the inexpressible pleasure with which he had received the note announcing Wellesley's return is dated January 12, 1806, and is given by Lord Stanhope (*Life*, vol. iv. p. 373).

PRIVATE.

PUTNEY HILL, *August* 30*th*, 1804.

MY DEAR WELLESLEY—The letters which you will receive by this conveyance will inform you that the King has conferred a peerage on General Lake, and an extra red ribband on your brother Genl. Wellesley. I hope these marks of honour will prove that a just value is attached to the brilliant and extraordinary successes which they have obtained under your auspices and direction, and I congratulate you most heartily on the advantageous and honorable peace which has been the fruit of your victories, and on a series of events which has produced so large an accession of personal glory to yourself and of power and reputation to the country. You will have heard from others the general history of our political situation at home, and will have seen in what has passed and in the state of parties which it has produced, much to regret, and much I believe to wonder at. I have very much wished to write to you at large on the subject; but you will not wonder that I found it impossible during the session, and in the weeks that have elapsed since to the present moment, the details of military preparation under the constant expectation of an immediate attempt at invasion, have in addition to the common course of business furnished me incessant occupation. We are *now* I trust in a state in which we may meet with confidence any enterprise to which even the largest scale of French exertions is equal; and I believe the thing most to be wished is that they may speedily make the trial. It seems probable from what I collect of the last letters received from you, that you will be on your passage home before any further accounts from hence can reach India. Indeed unless any more time should appear to yourself to be necessary for winding up compleatly the result of all your labours, or unless any new or great scene should unexpectedly open for fresh exertions, I hardly think that you would be tempted to prolong your absence. If either of those cases, however, should arise it cannot be necessary for me to assure you that every additional period for which you remain in India, will be considered by us (I mean the Government, for I certainly cannot answer for the Court of Directors) as so much gained for the public; and that everything of course will be done which is practicable on our part, to give you the fullest and most effectual support. With the knowledge of these sentiments, you will I am sure decide on whatever may be the state of circumstances before you at the moment, in the way most for your own honor and the public service; without suffering that decision to be influenced by the sense you may naturally entertain of the petty cabals, and narrow views and prejudices which too often operate at the India House, and which frequently lead to an ungracious return for the services they ought most to value.—Believe me at all times, my dear Wellesley, sincerely and affectionately yours, W. PITT.

DOWNING STREET, *Dec.* 21*st*, 1804.

MY DEAR WELLESLEY—Your brother, I find, thinks it most probable from the last letter he has received from you, that before the present packet reaches India, you will have embarked for Europe. Even if that should not be the case, what you will learn by the present conveyance of the temper and disposition which prevails at the India House, will naturally lead you to a determination not to remain longer than you may find necessary to compleat such arrangements as you may think it most material to bring to a conclusion before your departure. Indeed the advantage which the persons hostile to your measures have derived from your long silence on some of the most important transactions of your Government, and particularly from their being now left without any communication from yourself respecting the war with Holkar has made it difficult to keep them within any bounds ; and things are brought to a point at which it seems to be the clear opinion of your brother and of Lord Melville and Lord Castlereagh as well as my own that you could no longer have the means of carrying on the Government in a way either creditable or satisfactory to yourself, or advantageous to the public service. It therefore seems to us clearly desirable that you should carry into execution the intention you have expressed of returning home (if you have not done so at an earlier period) in the course of next year ; and on that supposition it will probably be thought that whoever should be pitched upon to be your successor, should sail from hence so as to arrive about September or October. Our intention of course is if possible to select for this nomination some person of high rank and consideration at home; which I trust you will agree with us in thinking a much more desirable arrangement, than letting the Government devolve to a company's servant, even in the instance of one of so much distinguished merit as Mr. Barlow. You will I trust readily believe that it must be my earnest wish that you should not take your leave of India without receiving some additional public mark of the cordial sense entertained of your very transcendent services. That which I should be most anxious to obtain because I believe it would be most agreeable to yourself, would be the blue ribband; but partly from personal wishes of the King, and partly from political engagements which in these times it has been impossible to avoid, I much fear that I may find it impossible. In that case the English marquisate, seems to be the only other mark of honor that can be proposed, and I hope in the view with which it will evidently be given, it will not be unacceptable. But whatever you may feel as to rewards and honors for the past, I hope the termination of your Indian career will restore you to us with health and inclination to take as distinguished a share as your talents and exertions entitle you to in the agitated and anxious state of politics in which you will find us involved on your return. It is of course impossible now to foresee how circumstances may change or what arrangements may become necessary within the next twelve months. But if the King's health should continue unshaken (of which at present there seems the fairest prospect) I am convinced we have nothing to fear from all the activity and ability of the combined opposition tho' much indeed to lament in the description of some of whom it is composed. And if on your arrival you should be as much inclined as I trust you will to give your assistance to my administration, and an opening can be found to give you as active and important a share in it as I should wish, I need hardly tell you that such a circumstance would from every public and private feeling be more gratifying to me than I can express. At all events I look forward with eagerness to the moment when I shall find myself again in your society, and to a renewal of all the habits of friendship and confidence from which for so many years I derived so large a share of happiness and comfort.—Believe me always, my dear Wellesley, affectionately yours,

W. Pitt.

CHAPTER XIII

FALL OF THE GOVERNMENT

THE Union was considered a great triumph for Pitt, but it was the cause of his immediate fall. He was anxious not to delay an instant in pushing forward the large and liberal policy of which the Union had only been the prologue. The Act of Union received the royal assent on the 2d of July 1800. At the first Cabinet (September 30, 1800,) after the summer recess, Pitt developed his Irish policy. It included the substitution of a political in lieu of a religious test for office, a commutation of tithes, and a provision for the Catholic and Dissenting clergy.

Pitt had now to learn that, in choosing a successor for the impracticable Thurlow, he had managed to find an even more treacherous colleague. Loughborough, as he sate at council with him, had already betrayed him. During this month of September, while staying at Weymouth, the Chancellor had received a confidential letter from Pitt with reference to these different points, and had at once handed it to the King, whose prejudice on this subject had already been revealed in connection with the Fitzwilliam episode. Thus fortified, the Chancellor at the Cabinet of the 30th of September proclaimed his virtuous scruples. The question was adjourned for three months, during which time it was hoped that the good man would reconsider his objections and prepare a complete measure on tithes. Loughborough had no idea of thus wasting his time. He spent this interval in working on that royal conscience of which he was the titular keeper. He sought the congenial alliance of Auckland, valuable not merely on account of remarkable powers of intrigue, but as brother-in-law to Moore, Archbishop of Canterbury. That prelate was now stirred by some occult inspiration to address a letter of warning to the King. Stuart, the primate of Ireland, was moved by a simultaneous impulse to exert his pastoral influence on his sovereign. Pitt was undermined. His colleagues began mysteriously to fall away. Chatham and Westmorland, Portland and Liverpool commenced to side against the Catholics in a Cabinet which had been supposed to be unanimous in their favour.

In January 1801 the mine was sprung. At a levée in that month, the King stormed audibly against the proposals, which neither the First Minister nor the Cabinet had laid before him. He sent Addington, the Speaker, to remonstrate with Pitt, who indeed could not have failed to hear at once of the scene at Court. He immediately addressed a statement of his policy to the King, tendering his instant resignation if he were not allowed to bring forward these different plans as Government measures. The King in reply begged him to remain and be silent. Pitt immediately resigned, and the King with apparent anguish acquiesced.

The parting honour that he awarded his minister is notable. He knew that it was of no use to offer Pitt money or ribbons or titles. So he began a letter to him "My dear Pitt": a circumstance which throws a little light on the character of both men.

The transaction has brought bitter censure upon Pitt; it is not easy to see why. What more could he do? What war is to kings, resignation is to ministers: it is the *ultima ratio.* He was, perhaps, open to censure for not having himself prepared the King at an earlier stage of the proceedings for the projected policy, instead of leaving it to others with a hostile bias. But a minister who had served George III. for seventeen years may be presumed to have understood the King's times and seasons better than any retrospective intelligence. It must be remembered also that, after the adjournment in September to promote union in the Cabinet, he was obliged to wait, in order to speak on behalf of a united Government. Further, it may well have been that, from his knowledge of the King, he thought that the best chance of obtaining his consent was to lay before him a completed measure, and not a projected policy. Nor could he foresee the black betrayal of Loughborough.

It is not, however, necessary to dwell on the charge of negligence, for the real accusation is much graver than one of negligence: it is one of treachery. The accusation, so far as it can be ascertained, (for it is vaguely and diffusely expressed), imports that Pitt held out hopes to the Irish Catholics by which he secured their support to the Union, and that, instead of fulfilling these pledges, or doing his best to fulfil them, he resigned: a mock resignation which he endeavoured to recall. But when and how were these hopes held out? There is absolutely no trace of them—none, at least, of any Cabinet authority for them. Cornwallis and Castlereagh were indeed strongly pro-Catholic. What they did on their own responsibility is not known, nor is it now in question. But the most recent and the best informed of historians of the Union, and the most hostile to Pitt, expressly admits that: "It is in the first place quite clear that the English Ministers did not give any definite pledge or promise that they would carry Catholic Emancipation in the Imperial Parliament, or make its triumph a matter of life and death to the Administration. On two points only did they expressly pledge themselves. The one was, that, as far as lay in their power, they would exert the whole force of Government influence to prevent the introduction of Catholics into a separate Irish Parliament. The other was, that they would not permit any clause in the Union Act which might bar the future entry of Catholics into the Imperial Parliament; and the fourth article of the Union accordingly stated, that the present oaths and declaration were retained only 'until the Parliament of the United Kingdom shall otherwise provide.'"

The actual hopes held out were these. Castlereagh on returning from London in 1799, where he had gone to gather the sentiments of the Cabinet on the Catholic question, had written to Cornwallis that he was authorised to say that the opinion of the Cabinet was favourable to the principle of relief, though they did not think it expedient to make any public promise or declaration to the Catholics, or any direct assurance to the Catholics; but that Cornwallis would be justified, so far as the sentiments of the Cabinet were concerned, in soliciting their support. And, in his speech of the 5th of February

1800, Castlereagh had further said that "an arrangement for the clergy, both Catholic and Protestant Dissenters, had long been in the contemplation of His Majesty's ministers." These were the pledges—what was the performance? That at the very first Cabinet, held after the passing of the Union Bill, Pitt produced his policy, which more than embodied them; that he urged it on his colleagues with all his influence; that the King learned it surreptitiously, and opposed his veto to it; and that Pitt thereupon promptly and peremptorily resigned.

It is difficult for the most acute critic to perceive what more he could have done. It was impossible to convince or compel the King; his mind was too fixed and his position too strong. But, it is urged that, had Pitt insisted, the King, who had given way to him before, would have given way to him again. The answer is simple; he did insist, and the King did not give way, and would never have given way. For in this case, unlike the others, George III. was convinced that he would incur the personal guilt of perjury under his Coronation oath; and he knew that he would be supported in his resistance by the great mass of his subjects.

Under the strain of this agony, for it was no less, torn by the separation from Pitt and by the pangs of his conscience, his mind once more gave way. The new ministry was already formed; and so, clear of all suspicion of interest, Pitt allowed the King's physician to soothe his old master's shattered mind by the assurance that the Catholic question should never more be raised by him in the King's lifetime. The promise was natural; George III. was old and breaking fast (two years later he was in fact at the point of death); the promise would probably not long be operative. But it has been insinuated that this was a mere renunciation on Pitt's part of a high principle in order to retain office; and that he was only too glad to be rid of an embarrassing pledge by a resignation which he hoped in this way to recall. Those who take this somewhat paltry view omit to state that Pitt's successor was appointed, that he himself declined to lift his finger to return to office, and promoted in every way the strength and efficiency of the Government that replaced him.

Facts of this kind can of course be always dismissed by a knowing wink or a sarcastic smile. But it is not possible even thus to dismiss the letter written, late in December 1801, by Bishop Tomline. The Bishop tells his correspondent, with a groan, that he had just had a long conversation with Pitt; who had told him that he looked forward to the time when he might carry Catholic Emancipation, and that he did not wish to take office again unless he could bring it forward. "Upon the Catholic question our conversation was less satisfactory. He certainly looks forward to the time when he may carry that point, and I fear he does not wish to take office again, unless he could be permitted to bring it forward and to be properly supported."

This, the striking testimony of a most reluctant witness with regard to Pitt's innermost views, ten months after he had resigned and given his pledge to the King, must convince all those who are capable of conviction, that Pitt's Catholic policy and consequent resignation were not less steadfast and straightforward than the rest of his career. It seems also clear from this significant narrative that Pitt's promise to the King was given under the persuasion that the King had not long to live, though George III. survived his great minister just fourteen years. So much for human computation. On the other hand, if the King's death or madness could be attributed to the Catholic question, that reform would be indefinitely postponed. If the mooting of the question renewed the Regency discussions or produced a Regency, it would be too dearly bought. Compassion, nature, and policy pointed in the same direction.

So obvious was the necessity of the pledge that Fox gave it at once and spontaneously on assuming office in 1806; though he had ten months before pressed the Catholic petition in a long speech, raising a fierce debate and division. "I am determined," he said, "not to annoy my sovereign by bringing it forward." This promise on the part of Fox, after harassing his rival with the question a short time previously, has always been held to be venial, and perhaps chivalrous; but, given by Pitt, it forms an item in this inscrutable impeachment.

Another is this. The resignation was a sham, because Pitt urged his friends to join and support the new ministry. The reason, however, is obvious enough. We were at war, and the first necessity of that state of things was to form the strongest possible government. It could not be strong, for the best men of Pitt's Government were out of it, and the area of choice was in no wise extended. But it was the only possible Government; and as it was by Pitt's act that the Government of the country was so weakened, a heavy responsibility lay on him. His critics appear to think it was his duty to have declared war on the new Administration; to have harassed it with Catholic resolutions; to have bidden his friends hold aloof; and to have presented to France the spectacle of a political chaos, of fierce faction fights for power at the moment of vital struggle with a foreign enemy. Fox was impossible. No sane minister could have recommended as his successor in the midst of a war the fiercest opponent of that war, a leader of some fifty or sixty followers at the moment when the most powerful Administration available was required, to a monarch who less than two years before had struck him off the Privy Council with his own hand. Pitt could only be followed by a Government formed out of his own party; one which he could support, putting the Catholic question aside. The choice lay between making his successors strong or weak. His paramount duty was to the war, and he preferred to make them strong. It surely requires a lively prejudice to blame him for this, and the mere formulation of the charge implies considerable ingenuity. As for Catholic Emancipation, that did not enter into the calculation; for, if Pitt could not carry it at that time, it would have been mere folly for any one else to attempt it. We may leave the whole transaction with the words in which Sir James Graham admirably summed it up: "Mr. Pitt was prepared to do the right thing at the right moment: but genius gave way to madness; and two generations have in vain deplored the loss of an opportunity which will never return."

Addington, the new Prime Minister, was a friend of the King's, and a sort of foster brother of Pitt's. The son of the respected family physician, who had prescribed colchicum to the elder and port to the younger Pitt, Addington carried into politics the indefinable air of a village apothecary inspecting the tongue of the State. His parts were slender, and his vanity prodigious. A month after Pitt's resignation, but before he had given up the seals, some of his ardent followers, cognisant of his pledge to the King on the Catholic question, attempted a negotiation to keep him in office. Among them was Canning, who sang—

> Pitt is to Addington
> As London is to Paddington.

This was true, and the minimum of truth; but Addington did not see the matter in that light. The emissaries found him happy and immovable. After a short tenure of high office, the holder almost invariably thinks himself admirably fitted for it. But this was a strong case. Addington had never held political office at all, not an Under Secretaryship, not a Lordship of the Treasury; and yet, before he had even received the seals, he felt himself a meet successor for Pitt. To counterbalance this deficiency in modesty, he had a handsome presence and warm family affections. It must also in fairness be laid to his credit that he was, Heaven knows why, the favourite minister of Nelson. All that can be advanced on his behalf has been forcibly urged in the valuable vindication which Dean Milman addressed to Sir George Lewis. But it amounts mainly to this, that many country gentlemen preferred him to Pitt, because he had bland manners, and because they were not oppressed by his intellectual superiority. It is lamentable to think that, if Pitt had to resign his power, it should devolve on Addington and not on Fox to succeed him. It is, however, pleasant to know that Loughborough received his due reward. The seals were taken from him. Still the wretched man hung on. He continued to attend the Cabinet, until Addington was forced to tell him plainly to begone. He continued to haunt the Court, with the result that on his death George III. composed this epitaph for him: "He has not left a greater knave behind him in my dominions."

Pitt's retirement from office lasted three years. His first duty, like that of most ex-ministers, was to examine his private affairs; and, like most ex-ministers, with a distressing result. He was heavily in debt. He had to sell Hollwood. That Tusculum was heavily mortgaged, and realised little surplus. His distress became known; for he was in danger of arrest. It was proposed to ask Parliament for a grant. The merchants of London offered him a free gift of £100,000. Pitt instantly put an end to such projects. He could not hold office again with the consciousness of such obligations. The King begged him to accept £30,000 from his Privy Purse. Pitt, with some emotion, declined this offer also. Finally, he condescended to take a loan of some £12,000 from a few personal friends. This discharged the most clamant and petty creditors. But it left a heavy balance, and the loan was never paid off; for nearly all the contributors refused to include it in the debts paid by Parliament at Pitt's death. And to the last day of his life executions were threatened and even levied in his house.

This is not altogether a pleasant picture. He had enjoyed fully £10,000 a year for many years from his various offices;[1] although it is only fair to remember that at his death his salary as First Lord of the Treasury was no less than seven quarters in arrear. He had no expenses except those of homely hospitality. But his ideas of public and private finance differed widely. We are told that, when he could not pay his coachmaker, he would order a new carriage, as an emollient measure. And so with the other tradesmen. His household was a den of thieves. While he watched over the Treasury like Sully, he conducted his own affairs like Charles Surface.

In other respects, this year redounded greatly to his credit. He not merely gave an ardent support to Addington, but conducted the negotiations for a peace. By this he pledged himself to the preparation and defence of a treaty, any honour from which would entirely benefit his successor, and of which the blame only could devolve on himself: an episode surely rare in the annals of ex-ministers.

The preliminary articles were signed on the 1st of October 1801. We restored all the colonies that we had taken, except Trinidad and Ceylon. We agreed to give up Malta to the Knights of St. John. The fisheries in Newfoundland and in the Gulf of St. Lawrence were to be replaced on the same footing as before the war. Egypt, from which an expedition, despatched by Pitt, had driven the French just after his resignation, was given back to Turkey. In return, the French did little more than withdraw from Southern Italy. It was a treaty which could only be justified on the plea of imperious necessity. Much was conceded, for it was necessary to concede

[1] See Appendix D.

much. A prolonged armistice,—for with Napoleon it could be little more,—was absolutely needed. At any rate, it was hailed by the public with rapture, and it greatly strengthened Addington's Administration.

Grenville and Windham were, however, furious. They were joined by Spencer. Pitt's following was rapidly breaking up. Already Auckland, who was under every conceivable obligation to Pitt, and whose daughter Pitt had nearly married, had snapped and yelped at the heels of the departing minister. The new Government had succeeded to Pitt's majority, which they maintained at a general election in 1802; he had, indeed, pressed all those whom he could influence to join or support the Administration. Consequently, his personal following consisted only of those adherents, such as Rose and Canning, who would not take his advice.

The years of Pitt's retirement were mainly spent at Walmer, with occasional excursions to London and Bath. From April 1802 to May 1803 he does not appear to have entered the House of Commons. In May 1802, he received the greatest compliment that has ever been paid to an English statesman. Sir Francis Burdett had moved an indirect, and Nicholls, the author of some paltry *Recollections*, a direct vote of censure on the late Government. Both were rejected by immense majorities. But such rejection did not satisfy the House; a mere negative was insufficient. By an overwhelming majority, against a minority of 52, it was carried: "That the Right Hon. William Pitt has rendered great and important services to his country, and especially deserved the gratitude of this House." And immediately afterwards, there took place that spontaneous celebration of his birthday, which was repeated for a full generation afterwards. It was for that first banquet that Canning composed the exquisite verses, "The Pilot that weathered the Storm."

Under honours so unparalleled, Pitt could well remain in contented quiet at Walmer. That repose was greatly needed for his health, which, as has been seen, gave way in 1798, and now continued slowly declining to the end. He who had been at work by nine had become a late riser, he had ceased to answer letters; and the visits to Bath, commenced in October 1802, became a frequent and periodical necessity. In September 1802 he was again seriously ill. But his enjoyment of Walmer was intense. No "disencumbered Atlas of the State" ever returned to country life with a keener relish. Shooting, and laying out his grounds, and the society of a very few old friends were his main amusements, and perhaps he was equal to no more. But, in the summer of 1803, the apprehensions of a French invasion gave a novel employment to his active mind; for he construed his office of Lord Warden in its ancient and most literal sense. In August of that year he raised and drilled a volunteer corps of 3000 men. Amid the derision of his enemies and the apprehensions of his friends, he spent his days in feverish activity, riding and reviewing and manœuvring along the coast committed officially to his charge. He would not even go to London, unless the wind was in a quarter that prohibited a hostile landing.

Meanwhile, Addington and his colleagues drew their salaries with regularity, and, so long as peace lasted, there was no objection to the process. Pitt, indeed, pricked his ears at Addington's budgets; but he had promised support as long as possible, and remained silent rather than disapprove. It was not, however, in the nature of things that these relations could continue. Both men were surrounded by friends, whose interest it was to set them against each other. Addington's followers saw that they could only keep their places, under his Administration, and by the exclusion of Pitt. Pitt's followers were indignant that his post should be so inadequately filled. There were, moreover, little causes of irritation; want of zeal in defence, inspired pamphlets, the petty political smarts so easily inflamed into blisters by the timely assistance of toadies. The Whigs of course stimulated Addington with extravagant eulogy to prevent his thinking of making way for Pitt; and the minister purred under the process.

When, however, it became clear that there was no possibility of preserving peace with Napoleon, all eyes, even Addington's, instinctively turned to Pitt. Men, so different as the Russian Ambassador and Wilberforce, spoke of ministers with undisguised contempt. "Their weakness is lamentable," wrote the philanthropist. "Si ce ministère dure, la Grande Bretagne ne durera pas," remarked the more caustic Woronzow. In March 1803, Addington sent Dundas (become Lord Melville) to Pitt, to propose that he should enter the ministry. Lord Chatham was to be Prime Minister,—a recognition of primogeniture which may fairly be called extravagant; Addington and Pitt joint Secretaries of State. Pitt, however, never learned the post destined for himself, for Melville never got so far. Already, no doubt, sufficiently conscious of the absurdity of the proposition, he broke down at the beginning. "Really," said Pitt with good-natured irony, "I had not the curiosity to ask what I was to be."

It was profoundly galling to Addington to admit that Pitt could be more than his equal, and might possibly be his superior. But under stress of circumstance he went that length. In the ensuing month (April 1803) he renewed the negotiations in person. He offered the Premiership to Pitt; who in exchange requested Addington, with cruel ignorance or heedlessness of the Prime Minister's opinion of his own qualifications, to return to the Speakership, the duties of which he had so admirably discharged; but, as the Speakership of the House of Commons was filled, he proposed to create a similar position for him in the House of Lords. Addington concealed his mortification; but begged that Grenville, Spencer, and Windham should not be included in the new Cabinet, as they had spoken disrespectfully of himself. Pitt declined all exclusions. On this the negotiation broke off, and with it all friendly relations between the principals.

In the succeeding month, war was declared against France, and a few days later Pitt resumed his attendance in the House of Commons to defend that measure. His reappearance created a unique sensation. There were some 200 new members in the House of Commons who had never heard him; many of whom had never seen him. As he walked up to his seat, the feeling was irrepressible, and there was a cry of "Pitt, Pitt," as if proceeding from the very helplessness of showing emotion in any other way. Whitbread and Erskine were heard with impatience, and then he rose, greeted with a renewed storm of acclamation.

He spoke for two hours and a half, and the termination of his speech was received with round upon round of enthusiastic applause. But keen observers noted with pain his altered appearance and the sensible signs of his weakened health. The House immediately adjourned. On the succeeding night, Fox delivered a speech of three hours in reply, of which he says simply, "The truth is, it was my best." There is little doubt that Pitt's was his best also, and that the fortunate members who sat in the House of Commons on the 23d and 24th of May 1803 heard the highest expression of English eloquence. During Pitt's speech, however, the reporters were unluckily excluded, and we have only a jejune abstract of Fox's. Our regret must be for ourselves and not for the orators: as few speeches which have produced an electrical effect on an audience can bear the colourless photography of a printed record.

Some days afterwards, a vote of censure was moved on the ministry. Pitt interposed, and proposed that the House should proceed to the Orders of the Day, for he would not censure and could not defend. He found himself in a mortifying minority of 34 against 275, a curious contrast to his triumph less than a fortnight before. The same motion was defeated in the House of Lords by 106 to 18. Such was the influence of the King; for, in truth, Addington represented nothing else. The strange contrast was between the moral and the voting power. A few days before this last division, Fox had proposed to accept the mediation of Russia. Hawkesbury, the Foreign Secretary, followed him and warmly opposed the proposition. Then Pitt rose and supported it. On which Hawkesbury at once assured the House that the Government would readily agree to it. A month later, Addington brought forward a plan for a renewal of the income tax, which he had abolished on the conclusion of peace. On this Pitt moved an instruction, aimed at a distinction that Addington had drawn between landed and funded property on the one hand, and all other forms of property on the other. Addington resisted this instruction with vigour; sharp words passed between the minister and his predecessor; Pitt was beaten on a division by three to one. But the next day Addington came down to the House and accepted Pitt's suggestion. "His influence and authority in the House of Commons," writes Romilly, a strong opponent, "exceed all belief. The Ministry seems in the House of Commons, in comparison with him, to be persons of no account."

In the session which began in November 1803, the predominance of Pitt was equally apparent. On the question of the Volunteers he made some drastic proposals; and, the next evening, the Secretary at War brought in a Bill embodying them. But his relations to the Government were becoming more and more tense. He declined, however, to ally himself with others in opposition; for he felt that his position was unique and must be maintained free from unnecessary complications. Grenville, always more extreme in hostility, and anxious, some thought, to be independent of his late leader, entered into a definite alliance with Fox, and pressed Pitt to do the same. Pitt steadily refused. This was in January 1804, and was in fact the last confidential communication that passed between them; for the interchange of letters in May was of a very different character.

In February 1804 the King's mind once more gave way. Meanwhile, Addington's Ministry was drawing steadily to an unlamented end. He became peevish and irritable; his majority began to waver; the Whigs, formerly so friendly, openly ridiculed him; and his Chancellor, with the prescience then inherent in the woolsack, prepared for a change. In March, Eldon sent a communication to Pitt, and they met. In the ensuing month Addington himself sent a message to Pitt, begging him to state through a common friend what could be done. Pitt haughtily replied that to the King alone, or to any person deputed by the King, would he make such a communication. This was Addington's last signal of distress; it occurred on the 17th or 18th of April (1804). He now agreed to advise the Sovereign to commission Eldon to see Pitt. On the 21st of April Pitt sent a long letter to the King, which was put into the royal hands on the 27th. By that time the division had taken place, which was to end the Ministry. On the 25th of April their majority had shrunk to 37—a majority, which many administrations would hail with pious rapture, but which betrayed so great a shrinkage as to convince Addington that his position was untenable. On the 26th of April he communicated this decision to the King, and on the 29th to his colleagues. They concurred; and on the 30th Eldon called on Pitt, by the King's orders, to furnish a written scheme for a new Government.

In reply, Pitt urged the claims of Fox. He had drawn up the scheme of a cabinet on a broad basis, which still exists in his autograph. He was to hold the Treasury; but two out of the three Secretaryships of

State were to be made over to Fox and Fitzwilliam, and Grey was to become Secretary at War, while for Grenville he reserved the significant sinecure of Lord President. But he had also formally stated in a letter to Melville, dated on the 29th of March 1804, that he could not force the King, recovering from an almost mortal malady, mental and bodily, to take as ministers persons he had so long proscribed. "From various considerations, however," he wrote, "and still more from this last illness, I feel that a proposal to take into a share of his councils persons against whom he has long entertained such strong and natural objections ought never to be made to him, but in such a manner as to leave him a free option, and to convince him that if he cannot be sincerely convinced of its expediency there is not a wish to force it on him. I should therefore at the same time, let His Majesty understand distinctly, that if after considering the subject, he resolved to exclude the friends both of Mr. Fox and Lord Grenville, but wished to call upon me to form a government without them, I should be ready to do so, as well as I could, from among my own immediate friends, united with the most capable and unexceptionable persons of the present Government; but of course excluding many of them, and above all, Addington himself, and Lord St. Vincent."

This passage has been given at length; because it succinctly defines Pitt's position in Pitt's own words. Once more his kindness for the aged King, slowly sinking into permanent darkening of sight and mind, was to prove a cruel obstacle in his path. The monarch himself received Pitt's letter with cold displeasure; he answered it in a letter, which betrayed the lingering influence of mental disease, in its violence and want of courtesy. He at once saw the weak joint in Pitt's armour, (the tenderness for himself); and loudly refused to have anything to do with Fox or Grenville; the mere proposal of their names was an insult. He even ignored Pitt's request for a personal interview. He could not get over the separation from Addington; poignant indeed must have been the parting between those congenial mediocrities.

At last, by the intervention of Eldon, a meeting with the King was arranged. The Sovereign, who had passed his former minister without notice the year before, now received him with astute cordiality. But, when they came to discuss the formation of the new Government, they were both put on their mettle. The contest raged for three hours. Never was Pitt more urgent; he seems to have forgotten in the heat of argument the limitations which he had set himself in his letter to Dundas. But never was the King more stubborn. The contest ended in a compromise, which was in reality a victory for the sovereign. Grenville was admitted, but Fox excluded, though it was conceded that Fox might receive a foreign embassy. The monarch afterwards went so far as to say that he should prefer civil war to Mr. Fox. But the exclusion of the one confederate entailed the exclusion of the other, and so the King carried both points.

The new Minister at once communicated the result to Fox and Grenville. Their answers were characteristic. The lifelong enemy said that he did not care for office, but that he hoped his friends would join Pitt. The lifelong friend, colleague, and kinsman, persuaded Fox's friends to stand aloof, and stood aloof himself. It was the finest moment of Fox's life, and not the most auspicious of Grenville's.

It is fair to say that Grenville might well be sensitive to the charge that would have been brought against him of having used Fox as a ladder to return to power. But from this imputation he was released by Fox himself. The very objection urged against Addington's Administration was that the crisis required the strongest possible Administration. Grenville's action rendered the new one deplorably weak. Had he entered it with Fox's friends, it would have been exceptionally powerful,—a ministry of all the talents save one;—and the admission of Fox himself must soon have followed. These considerations would make Grenville's action difficult to explain; but there is another circumstance which makes it wholly inexplicable. Exactly a year before, he had urged upon Pitt precisely the course which he now resented, and which Pitt now proposed to adopt. At the end of March, or the beginning of April, 1803, he went down to see his former chief at Walmer; and had a conversation or negotiation so elaborate that he himself wrote out and preserved an account of it. "After this," he says, "I suggested to Mr. Pitt the great advantage which, in my view of the state of the country, he would derive from endeavouring to form a government on a still more extensive foundation than that of which he had spoken, and from trying the experiment of uniting in the public service, under circumstances of extreme public danger as the present, the leading members, not of the three parties who had been in his view, but of all the four into which public men were now divided. I stated the reasons I had for believing that, with regard to the old Opposition, this might be done by including in his arrangement only Lord Moira and Grey, and perhaps Tierney (the latter in some office subordinate to the Cabinet), *and that Fox would be contented not to take any personal share in the government so formed*; and on a subsequent day . . . I took occasion from that circumstance to renew this suggestion." It is clear, then, that the plan of forming a Cabinet of all parties, excluding Fox, was so far from being repugnant to Grenville that it was his own proposal. It was supported by Fox's own wishes; it was at the moment the only practicable method of forming an efficient Administration. Grenville, however, threw over his own plan, and put every possible obstacle in the path of his old chief, who the year before had refused the Premiership at the price of Grenville's exclusion. In this gloomy crisis of the fortunes of his country, he thought that the proper course was to hunt down the new Ministry with inveterate hostility, so that he might succeed it at the head of a mongrel, dubious assortment of all the extremes of politics, and with the public men whom he had most bitterly denounced. But Pitt was not to be cowed. "I will teach that proud man," he said, "that in the service and with the confidence of the King I can do without him, though I think my health such that it may cost me my life." As indeed it did.

It must also be borne in mind as one of Pitt's greatest difficulties that the inclusion of Fox would have been profoundly repugnant to his own followers both in Parliament and in the country. It would have been a coalition enough to try any faith. In Scotland this feeling was strangely strong. Nothing less than Pitt's authority could have restrained it. Nevertheless, he persevered again and again in attempting to persuade the King to receive Fox.

To all such efforts, however, if politics be indeed an affair of principle and not a game to be played, there is an obvious limit. There is, moreover, a point of honour involved. A minister may find it necessary to yield to political forces beyond his control, and to change his policy. In doing so, he may ask for the admission to office of the representatives of that policy. It is a very different matter, however, for a minister pursuing consistently the policy which he has carried out for years, to demand, as an administrative necessity, the inclusion of his principal opponent in a Cabinet of which that opponent has been the inveterate enemy during its entire duration; who has criticised and resisted its every measure, tooth and nail, in letter and substance, in sum and in detail. Such a proceeding is lacking in common sense and common dignity; it is a surrender in the present and a reproach to the past; no hostile vote can carry a deeper condemnation than so self-inflicted a blow. In an acute crisis, and for the pressing purpose of some supreme juncture, such a sacrifice may be made. But Pitt, who had administered Government for eighteen years, not merely without Fox, but under the unrelenting fire of Fox's opposition, could hardly say in the nineteenth that he could not and would not enter office without him. Such a declaration, carried to extremes, would have been a confession of previous error and present impotence that would have gone far to prove he was not fit to be a minister at all.

CHAPTER XIV

THE END

So began Pitt's Hundred Days; for his second Administration can only be compared to that second impotent reign of Napoleon's, after their triumphant dictatorships. His new Cabinet was deplorable. So null was it that it was wittily called "the new Administration composed of William and Pitt"; for, though some of its members afterwards attained eminence under the shade of Pitt, they displayed no such promise. There was Melville indeed, but Melville was in the House of Lords; and his intimacy with Pitt was much less close than in the former Cabinet, presumably since he had accepted a peerage and an embassy to Pitt from Addington. He was, moreover, to be the means of inflicting on his chief a mortal wound. There was Harrowby, who twice afterwards refused the Premiership; and Hawkesbury, who held it for fifteen years as Lord Liverpool; but the first soon retired from illness, while the other had so far displayed little promise, and was indeed something of a butt. Castlereagh was Pitt's only Cabinet colleague in the House of Commons, and he in debate was disastrous. And there was of course the ordinary domestic furniture of Pitt's cabinets; the Portlands and Montroses and Westmorlands, the Camdens and the Mulgraves.

There was also Pitt's brother, Chatham, an underrated figure. He was, no doubt, indolent and extravagant; as a general, he was a conspicuous failure; he was useless as the head of a department; he had no trace of the oratorical abilities of his father or his brother; but, as a minister in Cabinet, he was of singular value. Eldon, who was shrewd, and in such a matter neither paradoxical nor biassed, gave it as his deliberate opinion that "the ablest man I ever knew in the Cabinet was Lord Chatham. He sat apparently inattentive to what was going on, but when his turn came to deliver his opinion, he *toppled* over all the others." As a wretched general, a wretched administrator, a mute senator, and yet a Cabinet minister, Chatham represented to the world a glaring example of Pitt's partiality. They could not know those qualities of counsel that preserved him, as they have many indifferent orators, in the Cabinet. Men forget that judgment is at least as much wanted in a government as agile fence; that the possession of eloquence by no means implies the possession of the other requisites of government; and that, for instance, any minister would prefer as a Cabinet colleague Godolphin to St. John, or Althorp to Brougham. There have been orators like Pulteney, who have shrivelled at the first contact with power. There have been statesmen like Cromwell, who could not frame an intelligible sentence. The qualities, indeed, of action and counsel and speech are absolutely distinct, and rarely combined in one man, but a Cabinet requires all three. Pitt's second Government was endowed with neither a Cromwell nor a Pulteney; but, curiously enough, although so universally derided, it contained no less than four future Prime Ministers—Portland, Perceval, Liverpool, and Canning—while Harrowby might, had he chosen, have made a fifth.

Pitt took his seat in the House of Commons as Prime Minister on the 18th of May 1804. That same day his supreme foe, the First Consul, was proclaimed Emperor of the French. Shortly afterwards Livingston, the American minister in Paris, escorted by Fox and Grey, brought Pitt a vague and dubious overture for peace, which came to nothing. This was the last of the rare occasions on which Pitt and Fox met in the same room. The Minister's military and financial measures (the latter including, as usual, another of the shocking demands of £500,000 to pay off debt on the civil list) he carried by majorities, varying from forty to fifty, in the same House which had furnished him in the previous session with the modest contingent of thirty-three followers. The session closed without incident on the 31st of July. In the recess he continued to discharge his military duties; and, in view of the army that Napoleon had assembled at Boulogne for the invasion of England, no precaution could be superfluous.

His political preoccupations were scarcely less urgent. He resolved to gratify the King and increase his parliamentary support by the admission of Addington. Their mutual feelings were softened, and they returned to something of their early intimacy. Addington became Viscount Sidmouth and President of the Council. A place was also found in the Cabinet for his principal adherent, that Earl of Buckinghamshire who had married Eleanor Eden, Pitt's only love. Another domestic incident occurred, which was curious if not important. The Archbishop of Canterbury had long been dying, and Pitt was determined that his tutor, secretary, and friend, Bishop Tomline of Lincoln, should be the next Primate. The King was equally determined that the succession should not fall to that too acquisitive prelate. Having received early news of the Archbishop's death, George III. hurried across to the Deanery at Windsor, the residence of Bishop Manners Sutton. The Bishop was at dinner; and was informed that there was a person outside, who wished to see him and would not take a denial. He went out and found the King, who had come to offer him the Primacy. The business was settled in a moment, and at the front door; the Sovereign went off chuckling at having outwitted Pitt. It is said, however, that, when they met, language of unprecedented strength passed between King and Minister. It cannot, though, be doubted that the King was right.

The royal speech, at the opening of the session in January 1805, announced that we were at war with Spain: one of those measures, founded rather on secret knowledge than on open rupture, which were then not uncommon, and which were rendered necessary by the multiplicity of occult policies and subterranean agreements then prevalent in Europe. The British Ministry were aware that a secret alliance had been concluded between Spain and France, and determined to strike the first blow. Fox, who had been silent for the last four years, and was to be silent ever afterwards on the question, thought fit now to urge complete Catholic Emancipation as pressing and indispensable; but was easily defeated. The Budget provided for enormous expenses. It became necessary to find forty-four millions for the current year. The army figured for eighteen millions and a half, the navy for fourteen millions and a half, the Ordnance for close on five millions; and five millions were taken for probable subsidies, though little or none of this last sum was spent. To meet these war estimates, Pitt proposed a new loan of twenty millions. Besides, therefore, continuing the existing war taxes, he had to find another million for interest. For this he principally relied, in the spirit of modern finance, on an increase in the death duties.

The supreme event of the session was the successful attack upon Lord Melville. That statesman was now first Lord of the Admiralty, where he displayed his wonted vigour and ability. But he had previously held for many years the office of Treasurer to the Navy, to which, it was afterwards remarked, he had always clung with strange persistence. A commission of naval inquiry had been sitting for three years, and now presented a report on Lord Melville's conduct as Treasurer. It showed that his paymaster had used the public balances for his private purposes. Although the public had not thereby sustained any loss, the Commissioners rightly visited this proceeding with the severest censure. It was also admitted by Lord Melville that he had sometimes, as a confidential minister of the Crown, advanced monies from these balances for the purposes of secret service. The Opposition alleged that he had used these sums to his own profit; but of this charge there was never the slightest proof, nor indeed any probability. Still, he had shown blamable laxity in a matter which requires the nicest precision of scruple. Whitbread brought forward in the House a series of resolutions condemning Melville's conduct. Pitt would have wished to meet them with a negative. But Addington hated Melville, and would consent to no stronger amendment than a reference to a Select Committee. Even that motion was not carried. It was a case in which the House of Commons vindicated its independence. It passed beyond party leaders and party considerations, and sought unbiassed guidance. The speech of Wilberforce was, therefore, eagerly looked for; he was one of Pitt's dearest friends, but one also whom, in a matter of public morals, friendship could not sway. As he rose, Pitt bent forward and fixed an eagle glance of inquiry upon him. Wilberforce felt all that that mute appeal implied, but did not waver. He declared that he must vote for Whitbread. Not in his Slave Trade triumph did he hold a prouder position.

The numbers were equal. The Speaker, as he announced them, turned white as ashes, for the responsibility of decision devolved upon him. After a painful silence of many minutes, he gave the casting vote against the Government. Then arose a shout and turbulence of victory such as this generation has once at least witnessed, when senators behaved like schoolboys, and passion ran uncontrolled. There were view-halloas. "We have killed the fox," shouted one sturdy sportsman with some confusion of idea. Pitt pressed his hat on his head, and it was seen that this was to conceal the tears trickling down his cheeks. Some unmannerly Whigs pressed up to see how he bore his friend's political death. But a little band of his younger followers rallied round him, and thus unconsciously encompassed he moved out of the House. It was the greatest blow that he had ever received. Some have ascribed his death to Ulm, and some to Austerlitz; but, if the mortal wound was triple, the first stab was the fall of Dundas. "We can get over Austerlitz," he said to Huskisson at Bath, "but we can never get over the Tenth Report."

Melville of course resigned at once. He was succeeded by an octogenarian member of his board, Sir Charles Middleton. Addington, who wanted the place for one of his followers, retired in dudgeon; and, though this difference was patched up, his secession was only deferred. After the Easter recess, the attack was renewed. The report was referred to a Select Committee. Whitbread moved an address to the Crown, praying that Melville should be removed from the Privy Council. Pitt at first resisted; but at the request of Melville himself erased his name before the motion could be put. As he made this announcement to the House he almost broke down. Traces of this emotion, so rare in him, were not, indeed, uncommon during the short remainder of his life. The report of the Committee was unfavourable, and, after Melville had addressed the House of Commons from the bar, an impeachment was resolved upon. He was ultimately acquitted, but the divisions on the question of impeachment, in which Addington's friends voted strenuously against Pitt, produced Sidmouth's final resignation. An ex-premier is usually found, by any Cabinet in which he may serve as an ordinary member, to be a fleeting and dangerous luxury. Addington was no exception to the rule.

The fall of Melville was chiefly felt in Scotland. There he had long reigned supreme, with general popularity and good-nature, by the exercise of a double patronage. While he had Scotticised India, he had orientalised Scotland. He had imported into India a splendid staff of Scottish adminstrators; he had imported into Scotland the absolutism of a Guicowar or a Nizam. When he fell, the air was cleared, and men, who had sat in darkness under his shadow, saw the light once more.

The Prime Minister's arrangements to supply the places of Sidmouth, Buckinghamshire, and Melville were only temporary. He still clung to the hope of inducing the King to consent to the admission of Fox and Grenville and their friends. With that object he set out for Weymouth, where for hours he urged upon his sovereign every plea and argument for such an arrangement. But the King was obstinate. It was not necessary, he said; Pitt could do well enough without them. He knew, in fact, that in the last resort he could always rely on Pitt's pride; that Pitt would never resign on account of gathering difficulties or hostile coalitions. But, had he yielded now, he might have saved Pitt's life. With a melancholy foreboding, the Minister said, a fortnight before his death: "I wish the King may not live to repent, and sooner than he thinks, the rejection of the advice which I pressed on him at Weymouth." For the burden fell now solely on the enfeebled shoulders of the dying Premier: the brilliant chiefs of opposition might have relieved him of much. As it was, "if Pitt has the gout for a fortnight," said Rose, "there is an end of us." And so it proved.

The Minister was thus at bay, but never had he shown a richer conception or a greater energy of resource. He had determined to oppose to Napoleon the solid barrier of the European concert. For that purpose he had been maturing a gigantic alliance, which should employ the fleets and treasure of England, and the vastest armies that Russia, Prussia, and Austria could put into the field. He commenced with Russia. On the 11th of April 1804, a treaty was concluded at St. Petersburg. Five hundred thousand men were to be arrayed against France. Great Britain was to contribute ships and men and money. On the 9th of August, Austria signified her adherence. This was the Third Coalition. Prussia, ruled by covetous incapacities, wavered; and was wavering when the Coalition was crushed. So she escaped that fall; but a worse fate awaited her.

At this moment (August 1805), Napoleon was still bent on striking a mortal blow at England. He only awaited the fleet which was to give him command of the Channel for the fatal twelve hours. Daily he gazed intensely at the horizon, till the tidings came that his admiral had retreated into Cadiz. There was no time to be lost, for he was well aware of the new league. He instantly moved his collected legions to Germany. The Empire which possessed the Archduke Charles preferred to oppose to him General Mack; a strategist of unalloyed incompetency, and unvaried failure. In a few marches Napoleon cut off Mack from Austria, and surrounded him at Ulm; and the first event in the history of the Third Coalition was the absolute surrender of thirty thousand of their choicest troops.

This was on the 19th of October. At the end of October, and in the first days of November, there were rumours of it in London. Pitt almost peevishly contradicted them. But on Sunday, the 3d of November, came a Dutch paper, which Pitt brought to Malmesbury to translate, and which told the worst. He went away with a look in his face which never again left it. But his spirit did not quail. On the 5th of November a despatch was on its way to Vienna, in which Pitt made a supreme appeal to Austria not to flinch. He had already, he said, sent Lord Harrowby to Berlin "to urge the early activity of the Prussian armies. There seems at present every reason to hope that this mission will be effectual. . . . Great as have been the pecuniary efforts which His Majesty has made for the common cause, he is ready still to extend them to such a farther amount as may enable those Powers to bring an active force of from two hundred to two hundred and fifty thousand men; and His Majesty has no doubt of being enabled himself to augment his own active force . . . to not less than sixty thousand men." With objects so paramount in view, with such vast means in reserve, these efforts could not fail. And in a glowing sentence, so like one of Pitt's perorations that one can almost hear his voice in it, he says that, even should the enemy plant his standards on the walls of Vienna, he is sure "that the antient spirit of Austria would still remain unshaken and undismayed"; and that Napoleon would still "have to encounter the concentrated energy of a great and loyal nation and the united efforts of powerful allies."

A few days afterwards, the news was eclipsed by the tidings of Trafalgar. Nelson had attacked with an inferior force the combined French and Spanish fleets, consisting of thirty-three ships of the line and seven frigates. Of these no less than twenty struck their flag. But even this consummate achievement was overbought by the death of England's greatest warrior. It is for this reason, perhaps, that Trafalgar is inscribed as a victory in the Museum of Arms at Madrid unto this day.

The nation was profoundly moved by the double intelligence, but triumph predominated. The minister himself, once so equable, when roused at night to read the despatches so full of joy and sorrow, could not resume his rest. The day afterwards, he was present at the annual dinner of the Lord Mayor. The populace had forgotten Ulm, and could think only of Trafalgar. Once more, and for the last time, they received him with acclamations, and drew his chariot in triumph to the Guildhall. There his health was drunk as the saviour of Europe. Pitt replied in the noblest, the tersest, and the last of all of his speeches. It can here be given in its entirety: "I return you many thanks for the honour you have done me. But Europe is not to be saved by any single man. England has saved herself by her exertions, and will, as I trust, save Europe by her example." That pageant was a sort of State funeral, for he was never seen in public again.

A month afterwards (December 7) he set out for Bath. Austerlitz, the battle of the Emperors, had been fought on the 2d. One Emperor was in flight, the other sullenly sustained defeat; their armies were scattered; a peace was being negotiated; amid the shattered ruins of the Coalition, Pitt alone remained. But even in the wreck of his life, his intrepid foresight survived. Nothing, he said, but a war of patriotism, a national war, could now save Europe, and that war should begin in Spain. Melville and Ulm had borne heavily on Pitt; Austerlitz killed him.

He was at Bath when he received the news. Tradition says that he was looking at a picture gallery when he heard the furious gallop of a horse. "That must be a courier," he exclaimed, "with news for me." When he had opened the packet he said, "Heavy news indeed," and asked for brandy. He hurriedly swallowed one or two drams; had he not, says an eye-witness, he must have fainted. He then asked for a map, and desired to be left alone.

He had gout flying about; the shock of the tidings threw it back on some vital organ. From this day he shrank visibly. His weakness and emaciation were painful to witness. Still, he did not abate his high hopes, or his unconquerable spirit. He wrote cheerfully to his friends. He was better, but wanted strength: Bath was of no further use; he would return to the house which he had hired at Putney—a house still existing, and locally known as "Bowling Green House." There, in a spacious and sunny room, from which one may still look out on Pitt's green lawns and avenue of limes, he was destined to die. On the 9th of January he set out home. So feeble was he, that it took three days to compass the journey. He arrived at his villa on the 12th. As he entered it, his eye rested on the map of Europe. "Roll up that map," he said; "it will not be wanted these ten years."

On the 14th Wellesley, just returned from his great proconsulate, had a long interview: the last, for no one again saw Pitt but his immediate family, among whom Rose and Tomline may be included, and his physicians. He fainted indeed, while Wellesley was in the room. That old friend felt it his duty on leaving Putney to go to Lord Grenville, and warn him that Pitt was at the point of death. Wellesley found him drafting resolutions of censure, and concerting the fiercest opposition to the Minister. On learning the news Grenville broke into a passion of grief. It is difficult to test the temperature of tears, but it is easy to believe that these were both bitter and sincere.

Party hostilities were at once suspended. There was, indeed, nothing left to fight against. Fox displayed a generous emotion: "Mentem mortalia tangunt," he said. The address to the Crown was agreed to, and the House adjourned. As the Speaker and members were proceeding with this address to the palace on the 23d (January 1806), they learned that Pitt had died early that morning.

From the time that he saw Wellesley, he had gradually declined. He could take little or no nourishment. Early on the morning of Wednesday the 22d, Tomline had thought it his duty to warn his old pupil that death was imminent, and to offer the last sacrament. Pitt declined, as he had not strength; but he joined earnestly in prayer. He threw himself, he said, on the mercy of God, and trusted that the innocence of his life might plead for him: the same thought which had solaced the last moments of the Emperor Julian. He then bade a solemn farewell to Hester Stanhope, the niece who had kept house for him, and who was to develop so fierce an eccentricity. To her he gave his blessing; "Dear soul," he said, "I know she loves me." All Wednesday night he was delirious. His wandering mind revolved round the mission of Harrowby, whom he had sent, as has been said, to fix the fickle energies of the Court of Berlin, the last hope of Europe. He constantly asked the direction of the wind. "East, that will do, that will bring him quick," he murmured. At midnight the end was near; at half-past four it came. A short time previously, with that strange recovery which so often precedes death, he said with a clear voice, "O my country! how I leave my country!"[1] After that last note of anguish he neither spoke nor moved again.

A motion was at once brought forward to provide a

[1] Mr. Disraeli, in the more genial and less majestic days before 1874, used to tell a saturnine story of this time. When he first entered Parliament, he used often to dine at the House of Commons, where he was generally served by a grim old waiter of prehistoric reputation, who was supposed to possess a secret treasure of political tradition. The young member sought by every gracious art to win his confidence and partake of these stores. One day the venerable domestic relented. "You hear many lies told as history, sir," he said; "do you know what Mr. Pitt's last words were?"—"Of course," said Mr. Disraeli, "they are well known. . . . 'O my country! how I love my country!'" for that was then the authorised version. "Nonsense," said the old man. "I'll tell you how it was. Late one night I was called out of bed by a messenger in a postchaise, shouting to me outside the window. 'What is it?' I said. 'You're to get up and dress and bring some of your meat pies down to Mr. Pitt at Putney.' So I went; and as we drove along he told me that Mr. Pitt had not been able to take any food, but had suddenly said, 'I think I could eat one of Bellamy's mutton pies.' And so I was sent for post-haste. When we arrived Mr. Pitt was dead. Them was his last words: 'I think I could eat one of Bellamy's meat pies.'" (Mr. Disraeli mentioned the meat—veal or pork I think, but I have forgotten.)

State funeral, and a public monument in Westminster Abbey; it was agreed to by 258 to 89 votes. Fox, in spite of a personal appeal from Grenville, deemed it his duty to oppose it. Such an opposition was in the highest degree distasteful to a nature eminently generous. But, after a parliamentary opposition of twenty years, he could not stultify himself by paying honour to Pitt as an "excellent statesman." No one can blame such a course, though abstention had been perhaps less painful and more dignified.

He had, however, an opportunity of showing the purity of the principle on which he proceeded. It was proposed to vote £40,000 to pay Pitt's debts, to award life pensions of twelve hundred a year to Lady Hester Stanhope, and of six hundred a year to each of her two sisters. "Never in my life," said Fox, "did I give a vote with more satisfaction than I shall do this night in support of this motion." No wonder such a man had such friends.

A month after his death Pitt was laid in the Abbey by his father's side, amid a splendid pomp of public grief. "The statue of the father," said Wilberforce with fine feeling, "seemed to look with consternation at the vault that was opening to receive his favourite son." "What sepulchre," exclaimed Wellesley, who was also present, "embosoms the remains of so much excellence and so much glory?"

The Ministry, as Rose had predicted, crumbled instantly to pieces. Hawkesbury was content with the Cinque Ports as his share of the great inheritance. Portland was not thought of. Castlereagh had the courage, but neither weight, nor standing, nor speaking power.

The Sovereign appealed to them in vain; they were unanimously of opinion that their headless body contained no principle of vitality. The King, without hope or resource, succumbed helplessly to fate. So was formed the ministry of "all the Talents," and, it may be added, all the incongruities. Fox and Addington, Grenville and the Lord Chief Justice of England, were the strange chiefs of this dubious fellowship. It is not now possible to discover the burning principles which had impelled these eminent men to fight Pitt to the death; for they at once abandoned the Catholics, and proceeded with the war. In any case, their Administration, after an inglorious year, came to a guileless end. Then succeeded a long government of which Portland was the first nominal head; and twenty years of much glory without, and utter darkness within.

CHAPTER XV

CHARACTER AND POSITION OF PITT

So passed Pitt. Cromwell and Napoleon yielded their breath amidst storms and tempests; but no natural convulsion could equal the political cyclone that raged round that lonely bed at Putney. All Europe lay at the feet of the enemy. The monarchs whom Pitt had leagued together in a supreme alliance were engaged either in negotiation or in retreat. The Prussian minister, ready for either event, had also hurried to the conqueror's tent to secure his friendship and a share of the spoil. There was not the vestige of a barrier to oppose the universal domination of Napoleon, but the snows of Russia and the British Channel. Well might Pitt, in a moment of despair, roll up the map of Europe.

At home his prospects were no brighter. He had to meet Parliament, with Trafalgar indeed to his credit, but with Nelson dead; with Ulm and Austerlitz as the result of his continental combinations; with a scanty and disheartened following. Arrayed against him, and thirsting for his overthrow, were the legions of Fox and Grenville, and the domestic circle of Addington. His friends had no conception of any resource that could save him. Rose and Long competed in dismay. Pitt, however, did not seem greatly to trouble himself. He had defeated a more formidable coalition before, and he believed in himself. His calculation was probably right. With health he would have maintained himself. His last reception in the city showed that he had preserved or regained his popularity with the people at large. He had a working majority in Parliament. And though his colleagues of the Cabinet were flaccid and null, he had a boundless resource in Canning, his political son and political heir. Fox was not to live long; and, after his death, even had Pitt once more failed to induce the King to receive him as a minister, the long desired Administration of all the capacities must have been formed.

Of the private life of Pitt there is not much to be said. There are constant attestations of his personal fascination in that intimate and familiar intercourse which was the only kind of society that he enjoyed. He seems to have liked that country house life, which is the special grace of England; we find him visiting at Longleat and Stowe, at Wycombe and Dropmore, at Cirencester and Wilderness, at Buckden and Short Grove, at the villas of Hawkesbury, and Rose, and Long, and Dundas, and Addington. Here we find him indulging—*proh pudor*—in a game of cards; the once fashionable Speculation or Commerce, now relegated to children. In all these societies he seems to have left but one unfavourable impression. A high-born spinster, who met him at Dropmore, says: "I was disappointed in that turned-up nose, and in that countenance in which it was impossible to find any indication of the mind, and in that person which was so deficient in dignity that he had hardly the air of a gentleman. If not tropes, I fully expected the dictums of wisdom each time that he opened his mouth. From what I then heard and saw I should say that mouth was made for eating." This is a harsh judgment. On the other hand, one of the choicest ladies of the French aristocracy, who met him during the Revolution, expressed her delight in his grave and lofty courtesy, and long recalled the patient pleasure with which he heard French books read aloud. To the purity of his French she also paid a tribute. Butler records that his talk was fascinating, full of animation and playfulness. Pitt said of Buckingham that he possessed the condescension of pride. It was said of his own manners in society that he possessed the talent of condescension; than which, if it means that he made condescension tolerable, there is perhaps none more rare.

Curiously enough, he seems to have preserved his boyish spirits to the end. Miss Wynn when she met him at Dropmore, and drew the crude portrait just quoted, records the competition of unearthly howls which disturbed her rest and possibly gave her an unfavourable bias, caused by Pitt and the other assembled statesmen chasing a bird out of the drawing-room. And Sir William Napier, who as a young ensign first knew Pitt in 1804, has recorded the romp when he and the young Stanhopes and Lady Hester succeeded in blacking the Prime Minister's face with a burned cork. The struggle was interrupted by the arrival of Hawkesbury and Castlereagh; and Napier graphically records the change that came over their playfellow as he received them; how the "tall, ungainly, bony figure seemed to grow to the ceiling," while the Secretaries of State bent like willows before him. Few, without these testimonies, would have suspected Pitt of being addicted to those sports known to the present generation as "bear-fights." But it is certain that nothing could be more easy and familiar than the footing of that little set of people with whom he habitually lived, and who seem to have been known among themselves as "the firm" or "the gang."

His friendship, although, like all worthy friendship, not lavishly given, was singularly warm and was enthusiastically returned. Nothing in history is more creditable and interesting than his long and brotherly intimacy with Wilberforce, so widely differing from him in his views of life. Hardened politicians like Rose and Farnborough were softened by their intercourse with him, and cherished his memory to the end of their lives with something of religious adoration. This indeed was the posthumous feeling which he seems to have inspired more than any other person in history. Sidmouth, who had loved him little during the last lustre of his life, felt this, and boasted that he had destroyed every letter of Pitt's which could cause the slightest detriment to Pitt's reputation. Canning, Pitt loved as a son. There is nothing more human in Pitt's life than the account of his affectionate solicitude and absorption at Canning's marriage. Canning's love for Pitt was something combined of the sentiments of a son, a friend, and a disciple.

The usual epithet applied to him is "haughty." A truer light is thrown by the conversation which is recorded to have taken place as to the quality most required in a Prime Minister. While one said Eloquence, another Knowledge, and another Toil, Pitt said Patience. Rose in a close intimacy, private and official, of twenty years, never once saw him out of temper.

His family affections were warm and constant. His letters to his mother are pleasant to read; he was indeed the most dutiful of sons. His grief at the death of his favourite sister, Lady Harriet, and her husband, Mr. Eliot, was beyond description. His kindness to his oppressed nephews and nieces, the Stanhopes, was constant and extreme; the father who harassed them had long quarrelled with him. It was truly remarked that he unselfishly made a great sacrifice and cheerfully ran a great risk, when, after a life of bachelorhood, he took his niece Hester to keep house for him. She led him an uneasy life with her terrible frankness of speech; but he bore all with composure, and she repaid him with the rare devotion of that vain, petulant nature, which fretted off into something like insanity.

Once, and once only, he formed an attachment which might have led to marriage; though he liked women's society, and is even said to have drunk a toast out of the shoe of a famous Devonshire beauty. But in 1796 his feeling for Eleanor Eden, the eldest daughter of Lord Auckland, went so far that he wrote to her father to declare his affection, but to avow that his debts made it impossible for him to contemplate marriage. Auckland was obliged to take the same view; Pitt discontinued his visits; and the lady married Lord Hobart, afterwards Lord Buckinghamshire. Lady Hester said that this nearly broke Pitt's heart; but Lady Hester's statements do not impress one with conviction. Lord Holland, also an indifferent authority on this subject, says that Pitt paid attentions to Miss Duncan, who was afterwards Lady Dalrymple Hamilton. But there seems no further confirmation of this statement. However, though we cannot imagine a married Pitt more than a married Pope, it is clear that he did seriously contemplate the married state; and cynics may remark with a smile that he afterwards showed a certain dislike of Lord Buckinghamshire, and a reluctance to admit him to the Cabinet; though other reasons might well account for that.

His life was pure; in an age of eager scandal it was beyond reproach. There was, indeed, within living recollection a doorkeeper of the House of Commons who from some chance resemblance was said to be his son; but Pitt's features, without the intellect and majesty which gave them life, lend themselves easily to chance resemblance and ignoble comparison. Wraxall hints at a licentious amour; but even Wraxall expresses his scepticism. The austerity of his morals inspired many indecorous epigrams, but also a real reverence.

His one weakness, it is said, was for port wine. We have seen that he was reared on port from his childhood; and, when he arrived at man's estate, he was accustomed to consume a quantity surprising in those days, and incredible in these. The habits of that time were convivial; but it is not till Pitt's health was broken that the wine which he took seems to have had more effect on him than a like measure of lemonade. Bishop Tomline has left a memorandum stating that never before 1798 did he see Pitt the least affected by wine. Addington, when questioned on this point, declared that Mr. Pitt liked a glass of port very well, and a bottle better. Sometimes, indeed, the Speaker, who himself was decorously convivial, had to stop the supplies and say, "Now, Pitt, you shall not have another drop;" though Pitt's eloquence would usually extract another bottle. Addington, however, averred that never had he seen Pitt take too much when he had anything to do, except once when he was called from table to answer an unexpected attack in the House of Commons. It was then so clear that he was under the influence of wine as to distress his friends. One of the clerks of the House was, indeed, made ill by it; he had a violent headache. "An excellent arrangement," remarked Pitt; "I have the wine, and he has the headache."

We read of hard drinking at the Duchess of Gordon's; of Thurlow, Pitt, and Dundas galloping home, after a dinner at old Jenkinson's, through a turnpike, the keeper of which, in default of payment, discharged his blunderbuss at them; and of Stothard, the painter, being told by an innkeeper, as Pitt and Dundas rode off, "I don't care who they are, but one of those gentlemen drank four, and the other three bottles of port last night." But all this must be judged by the habits of that time and not of ours;—when Scottish judges sat on the bench with their stoup beside them; when at least one Viceroy of Ireland could die of drink; when Fox and Norfolk would after a debate get through a *great deal* of port wine, (and what this last meant by a *great deal* it is scarcely possible to compute); when the English clergy are said to have considered their cellars more than their churches; when a great Scottish patron only stipulated that the ministers whom he chose should be "good-natured in their drink"; when a university common room could only be faced by a seasoned toper; when Lord Eldon and his brother could drink any *given* quantity of port. It is hardly conceivable, if Pitt had been guilty of habitual excess, that Wilberforce should have been his constant host or guest at dinner. There is, however, little doubt that, if he dined with a party now, it would be thought that he drank a good deal; and, while the Tories said that he died of a patriot's broken heart, the Whigs averred that he died of port. But in this, as in so much else, it must be constantly reiterated that he must be judged by the temper of his own times and not of ours.

He was tall and slender in appearance. The early portraits by Gainsborough represent a face of singular sweetness and charm; the last portrait by Lawrence, who only saw him a few weeks or months before his death, represents a figure of rare majesty, with gray if not white hair. Of this picture a replica was painted for the King, and hangs in the great Gallery at Windsor. One who had sat with him in Parliament, and who survived until some score of years ago, said that "he had a port-wine complexion, but the most brilliant eye ever seen in a human face": much the same description as is given of Sheridan's appearance. Hoppner, who painted Pitt from the life for his colleague Mulgrave in 1805, gives him tints of this kind; as Wilberforce said, on seeing Hoppner's portrait, "His face anxious, diseased, reddened with wine, and soured and irritated by disappointments. Poor fellow, how unlike my youthful Pitt!" Fox said that he could see no indications even of sense in Pitt's face—"did you not know what he is you would not discover any." Grey thought otherwise; but Wraxall agrees with Fox. "It was not till Pitt's eye lent animation to his other features, which were in themselves tame," says Wraxall, "that they lighted up and became strongly intelligent. . . . In his manners, Pitt, if not repulsive, was cold, stiff, and without sincerity and amenity. He never seemed to invite approach, or to encourage acquaintance. . . . From the instant that Pitt entered the doorway of the House of Commons he advanced up the floor with a quick and firm step, his head erect and thrown back, looking neither to the right nor to the left; nor favouring with a nod or a glance any of the individuals seated on either side, among whom many who possessed five thousand pounds a year would have been gratified even by so slight a mark of attention. It was not thus that Lord North or Fox treated Parliament." His nose, said Romney, was turned up at all mankind. How many a vote he and Peel and Lord John Russell may have lost by this shy self-concentration of demeanour, or how many have been gained by the sunny manner of Palmerston, or the genial face-memory of Henry Clay, must remain a permanent problem for the student of politics and man.

His action as a speaker, that might have been supposed to resemble the majestic stateliness which a later generation admired in Lord Grey, was vehement and ungraceful, sawing the air with windmill arms, sometimes almost touching the ground. Unfriendly critics said that his voice sounded as if he had worsted in his mouth; but the general testimony is that it was rich and sonorous. Fox never used notes, and Pitt rarely; a specimen of these is given by Lord Stanhope.

His eloquence must have greatly resembled that with which Mr. Gladstone has fascinated two generations, not merely in pellucid and sparkling statement, but in those rolling and interminable sentences, which come thundering in mighty succession like the Atlantic waves on the Biscayan coast,—sentences, which other men have "neither the understanding to form nor the vigour to utter." It seems, however, to have lacked the variety and the melody; the modulation of mood, expression, and tone, which lend such enchantment to the longest efforts on the least attractive subjects of his great successor.

"To Pitt's speeches," says a contemporary by no means prejudiced in his favour, "nothing seemed wanting, yet there was no redundancy. He seemed as by intuition to hit the precise point, where, having attained his object as far as eloquence could effect it, he sat down." This is high praise, indeed; but it can hardly be believed that Pitt was never open to the charge of diffuseness. In those days the leader stood forth as the champion of his party, and stated every argument in a speech of exhaustive length; private members had little to do but to cheer. It was, however, calculated as an almost certain matter of proportion that, if Fox were three hours on his legs, the reply of Pitt would not exceed two. Butler says, not untruly, that, as Fox was verbose by his repetitions, so was Pitt by his amplifications. Neither had before him the terror of the verbatim report, and the coming spectre of that daily paper in which the evening's speaking bears so ill the morning's reading. Had it been otherwise, they must have condescended to compression; and probably to those notes which guide and restrain argument. Sheridan, indeed, said of Pitt that his brain only worked when his tongue was set agoing, like some machines that are set in motion by a pendulum or some such thing; but this opinion bears the stamp of a certain envy of Pitt's ready and spontaneous flow of speech, felt by one to whom laborious and even verbal preparation was necessary.

Lord Aberdeen, who had heard all three, preferred the oratory of Canning to that of either Pitt or Fox. Sheridan made a more famous speech than either. But no criticism can now affect Pitt's place as an orator. Wilberforce, himself no mean orator, writing in 1825 spoke of the brilliancy of the speaking at that time, when Brougham and Canning and Plunket were at their best, but said also that it was on a distinctly lower level than that of Pitt and Fox. The stupefaction produced by Pitt's Slave Trade speech on the greatest minds of the Opposition has already been recorded; Dudley, the most fastidious of judges, breaks into enthusiasm in speaking of him. Fox did not seek to disguise his admiration. He said that, although he himself was never in want of words, Pitt was never without the best words possible. His diction, indeed, was his strongest point. His power of clear logical statement, so built up as to be an argument in itself, was another. And as a constant weapon, too often used, he had an endless command of freezing, bitter, scornful sarcasm, "which tortured to madness." This gave him a curious ascendancy over the warm and brilliant natures of Erskine and Sheridan, over whom he seemed to exercise a sort of fascination of terror. We can scarcely conceive an assembly in which there were greater orators than Erskine, Windham, Sheridan, Grey, and even Burke. But all contemporaries placed Pitt and Fox on a level apart. This alone enables us to compute their genius. And when we consider their generation and those that preceded, we cannot but arrive at the belief that eloquence and stenography are not of congenial growth; and that in an inverse ratio, as the art of reporting improves, the art of oratory declines.

It is said that Pitt did not read much or care to talk about books. It is probable that he had no time to keep abreast of modern literature, though we know that he delighted in Scott. But we possess a graphic account of the little sitting-dining-room at Hollwood, with the long easy chair on which the weary minister would throw himself, below the hanging shelf of volumes, among which a thumbed and dog-eared Virgil was specially paramount. His rooms at Hollwood and Walmer, says one of his friends, were strewn with Latin and Greek classics. Lord Grenville, a consummate judge, declared that Pitt was the best Greek scholar he ever conversed with. He was, adds Wellesley, as complete a master of all English literature as he undoubtedly was of the English language. He especially loved Shakespeare and Milton, and recited with exquisite feeling the finer passages of *Paradise Lost*. It is unnecessary to multiply testimony of this kind. But it is also, somewhat unexpectedly, recorded that he relished the *Adventures of Telemachus*, and especially enjoyed the speeches of the dreary Mentor in that too didactic tale. His well-known anxiety to possess a speech of Bolingbroke's seems to have arisen, rather from curiosity as to an orator so consummate, than from any peculiar admiration of his style. He considered, we are told, *Gil Blas* the best of all novels.

All this does not amount to much. Few Prime Ministers are able to give much time to literature, when in office; especially at a period when an interminable dinner took up all the leisure that could be snatched from work. As an author he did little; his collected works would scarcely fill a pamphlet. During his last stay at Bath two of his colleagues committed a crime worthy of the lowest circle of the *Inferno* by sending him their poems to correct. What, perhaps, was venial in Canning was unpardonable in Mulgrave; but it shows that he was considered as great an authority in literature as in politics. Of his own poetic faculty nothing remains but the dubious reputation of having contributed a verse to the "University of Gottingen"; two couplets which he bestowed on Mulgrave, and of which it suffices to say that they are not to be distinguished from Mulgrave's own; a translation of an ode of Horace; and some lines not less insignificant. They are on the same level as the stanzas which we unluckily possess of Chatham's. In prose we have only the political articles which he wrote for the *Anti-Jacobin*, of which those on Finance in Numbers II., III., XII., XXV., as well as the Review of the Session in XXXV., are by him. At least Canning has so ascribed them, in his own handwriting, in his own copy.

He has been loudly blamed for his insensibility to literary merit; so far, at least, as such sensibility is shown by distribution of the funds and patronage of the Crown. We do not know what were his principles as to such matters, for during his twenty years of government he was, though assailed by Mathias and Montagu, never taken to task in Parliament on that subject. This fact, while it deprives us of his explanation, throws so remarkable a light on contemporary opinion as possibly to illustrate his own. If he was convinced that literature, like war, thrived best upon subsidy, he was culpable indeed. But it is conceivably possible that he may have thought differently. He may have believed that money does not brace but relax the energies of literature; that more Miltons have remained mute and inglorious under the suffocation of wealth, than under the frosts of penury; that, in a word, half the best literature of the world has been produced by duns. Pensionless poetry may at least bear comparison with that which has flourished upon bounties. Under the chill rays of Pitt, we had Burns, Wordsworth, Cowper, Southey, Scott, Coleridge, Canning, Crabbe, Joanna Baillie, Rogers; and even under the tropical effusion of twelve hundred a year, dispensed in heat-drops of fifty or a hundred pounds apiece, we have had nothing conspicuously superior. It is not easy at any rate to cite the names of many eminent men of letters, who have received material assistance from the State since the time of Pitt. Hook and Moore had reason even to curse the ill-judged bounty of their country, and yet they were provided with lucrative offices. Nothing, Pitt may have thought, is so difficult as for a Parliamentary Government to encourage literature. It may begin by encouraging a Shakespeare, but it is far more likely to discover a Pye. You start with a genius and end with a job. Apart from these arguments, a more practical and pressing plea can be urged for Pitt. Government then rested largely on patronage—he lived in that respect from hand to mouth; and, when he had but half satisfied the demands of politics, there was no surplus for literature.

His exercise of patronage has been attacked on another point. He is said to have advised the creation of too many peers. He did, indeed, ennoble with unsparing hands. During the first five years of his ministry, he bestowed forty-eight peerages; in two subsequent years (1796 and 1797) he created and promoted thirty-five; and when he resigned in 1801 he had created or promoted a hundred and forty. He nearly, in fact, doubled the peerage as it stood at the accession of George III. This profusion had the strange result that the Reform Bill of 1831 was, it is said, rejected by Mr. Pitt's peerages against those of older creation.

Pitt had a triple reason for this excessive bounty. In the first place, the economic measure of reform in the civil list, which had been passed in 1782, had so crippled and confined the patronage of ministers, that a profuse creation of peerages was almost the only resource of government, as carried on in those days. But his own reductions of this kind were enormous, and with this special distinction. Burke had reduced the patronage of the Crown and of ministers. Pitt as Prime Minister laboured faithfully and indefatigably to reduce his own. Between 1784 and 1799 he abolished eighty-five absolute sinecures in the Customs with salaries of from £2000 a year downwards. He collected a revenue of twelve millions with 747 fewer officials than it had taken under previous governments to collect a revenue of six. All this was done in the service of the public to make enemies for himself, and diminish the opportunities of rewarding his followers and strengthening his government. Conduct of this kind was unique in those days, and has not been too common since.

He desired, secondly, to recruit and refresh the House by large additions from various classes—from the old landed gentry and the commercial, banking aristocracy. And, thirdly, it was necessary for the security of his own and any future governments to render impossible combinations of great peers to overset the Government. He had to destroy the Whig oligarchy, which had so long wielded a perilous and selfish power. It was on this ground that he secured the cordial co-operation of the Crown in the creation of peers; though to the end of life he called himself a Whig; a term which it must be remembered was then the only one to describe every shade of what we call Liberalism—the Radicalism of Chatham, or the selfish oligarchy of the Revolution families.

One thing more must be said on this head, which is essential to a right understanding of the subject. The main reason which prevailed, consciously or unconsciously, with Pitt in his creation of peers was his disdain of the aristocracy. His sympathies, his views, his policy were all with those middle classes, which then represented the idea of the people. By a strange accident, he became the leader of the nobility; but they supported him on their necks, for his foot was there. They were the puppets through which he conducted the administration of the country; but he scorned them, and snubbed them, and flooded their blue blood with a plentiful adulteration of an inferior element. Read, for example, the anguish of the Duke of Leeds under his treatment; read his letters to the brother of Cornwallis and the son of Chichester, both noble bishops, discreetly ready for the enlargement of their spiritual opportunities. Pitt and the aristocracy had not an idea or a sentiment in common; his attitude to them resembled the earlier relations of the late Lord Beaconsfield to the magnates of the party. He was willing to give a peerage to any decent possessor of ten thousand a year; as for his baronets, their name was legion, and his knights were as the sand of the sea. But he had no sympathy with their sympathies, and regarded their aspirations with a sort of puzzled scorn. His mission to appease Buckingham, when that potentate was raging over a distribution of Garters from which he was excluded, must have been one of the most solemn farces on record, for he could not understand the feelings he had to soothe. He considered the peers as his election agents; therefore the more the better. And as regards their further objects of promotion or decoration he would, had he had the power, have satisfied them all. A minister of this temper may gratify, but he is not likely to strengthen, an aristocracy.

To estimate Pitt as a statesman, to sum up his career, to strike his account with history, one must take adequate means and scales. Jauntily to dismiss him as a superannuated prodigy, with an account of the reforms he projected and abandoned, with a summary record of his loans and gagging acts, with a severe gaze at the corruption of the Union and the horrors of the Irish Rebellion, with an oblique glance at port wine; to consider him as a trained liberal who became one of the King's tools, and then held power by prerogative in some form or another; to regard him as a man infirm of purpose and tenacious only of office; is to take a view, justified by passages and aspects and incidents of his career, but one neither adequate nor comprehensive.

Men will long canvass his claims and merits as a minister, for the subject matter is so unparalleled. Lord Beaconsfield, for example, who delighted in political paradox, wrote a letter in 1873 to Sir William Harcourt, (whose kindness affords me the opportunity of printing it), which contains his view of Pitt:

"I do not at all agree with you in your estimate of Pitt's career. It is the first half of it which I select as his title deed to be looked upon as a Tory Minister. Hostility to boroughmongering, economy, French Alliance, and commercial treaties, borrowed from the admirable negotiations of Utrecht — the latter half is pure Whiggism, close parliaments, war with France, national debt and commercial restriction—all prompted and inspired by the Arch-Whig Trumpeter, Mr. Burke."

These sentences express perhaps rather the light scoff of a bantering spirit than the cold results of historical research. But they represent an opinion always worth reading, even when given partly in jest; and one which derives colour from the confusion caused by the necessary change between Whiggism and Toryism before and after the sure establishment of the Protestant Succession.

The various classes of opinion have crystallised, roughly speaking, into two schools of thought. The first—the most common and the least informed—is that which honours Pitt as one who became Prime Minister at the age of an ensign, who achieved the Union with Ireland, and who was the great antagonist of the French Revolution. The other—the more recent and scientific school—is that which severely divides the life of Pitt into two parts; the first embracing his Administration up to 1793, which was entirely praiseworthy, and which might from its character deserve the commendation of Peel or Cobden; the second the remainder, which was entirely and conspicuously blameworthy.

It may be permitted to hold aloof from both parties; the one does not go sufficiently into detail, the other draws a distinction which is not natural. If you take two portraits of a man, one at the age of three, and the other at threescore and ten, you will trace no resemblance whatever between the faces depicted. And yet the change from the one to the other is so gradual, that there is no one day of his life at which you could say that a man was unlike what he was the day before. As with the natural, so it is with the political man. A politician may make a sudden and complete retractation, and so abruptly change his historical aspect; just as an individual may meet with an accident that entirely changes his personal appearance. But, putting such catastrophes on one side, it is not possible to draw a line across the life of a statesman with the declaration that all is white on one side and all is black on the other. With Pitt, at any rate, it was the circumstances that changed, and not the man. And the circumstances resolve themselves mainly into one—the French Revolution.

No man can understand Pitt without saturating

himself with the French Revolution, and endeavouring to consider it as it must have seemed at its first appearance. In the first five years he had not to deal with it, and they were fruitful years for England. He found our average imports in 1784 £11,690,000; in 1793 they had risen by seven millions. In the same period our exports of British merchandise had risen from ten to eighteen millions, and of foreign merchandise from £4,330,000 to £6,560,000. In December 1783 the Three per Cents stood at 74; in 1792 they stood at over 96. But the new element clouded the whole firmament. It is safe to say that there was not a sane human being then living in Europe so exalted or so obscure or so dull as not to be affected by the French Revolution; except perhaps that traditional Marquis de l'Aigle, who snapped his fingers at it, and went on hunting at Compiegne without interruption. Was it possible that Pitt, and Pitt alone, should remain heedless and insensible? Was it desirable?

We are now able to fix epochs in the French Revolution, to fancy we can measure its forces, to point out exactly what, in our philosophical opinions, might have modified, or turned, or arrested it; just as we calculate what would have happened if Hannibal had captured Rome; or as men of powerful imagination have composed eloquent dialogues showing what eminent personages would have said to each other, had they happened to meet. It is all cut and dried; a delicate speculation of infinite science and interest, though critical minds may differ as to its value. But Pitt could only perceive the heavens darkened, and the sound of a rushing mighty wind that filled all Europe.

Seeing and hearing that, he formed perhaps a juster judgment than those who discussed the matter as an elegant question of political balance. He saw that uncontrolled it was overwhelming, and he did not pause to reason as to what might be its eventual effect when another century had passed. An earthquake, or the movement of snows surcharged, or the overflow of some swollen river, may cause absolute ruin for the moment, and great subsequent benefit. But the philosopher who is speculating on the fifth act will disappear in the first. Pitt faced the cataclysm, and made everything subservient to the task of averting it. All reforms were put on one side, till the barometer should rise to a more promising level. It is impossible, said Windham, to repair one's house in the hurricane season. It is impossible, it may be added, to put Pitt's French Revolution policy in a form more terse and more true. Many may profess to regret that we did not allow full play to the agitation, that we did not sit still to receive what should be prescribed from Paris. They may be right. But those may also be right who, without dogmatising one way or the other, feel unable to estimate the result of the sudden flow of so fermenting a vintage into the venerable vessel of the British constitution.

It is probable that most people will think that Pitt was right in his forecast of the Revolution, and in his inability to accept it as a boon for a country of such different conditions. For there was no middle course; the Revolution had to be accepted or repelled. But if his view be right, a large latitude must be given for his acts of repression, and suspensions of *Habeas Corpus*; for the enemy he had to fight was as much subterranean as external. The French fought not less by emissaries than by armies; and so, Pitt would say, if the thing had to be done at all, it had to be done with all possible might and main; there could be no refinement as to means, any more than in a storm with much mutiny on board. His case for his repressive acts depends on the reality and extent of the alleged conspiracy. It is common now to think that it was exaggerated. That is always the case with regard to such efforts when they have been baffled. It was so said in the case of Catiline, and so in the case of Thistlewood. What has been rendered abortive it is common to think would never have possessed vitality. But it must be remembered that what Pitt did was not a vain imagination of his own, but founded on the solemn, anxious inquisition and report of Parliament itself. It was Parliament that instructed the Executive: it was Parliament that ordered repressive measures. It is impossible to carry the matter further than this, and there it must be left.

Had he lived now, his career would of course have been different. Instead of being a majestic and secluded figure, supreme in the House of Commons and supported by the direct, incalculable influence of the Crown, he must have looked outside to great democratic constituencies with his finger on their pulse. He would have addressed mass meetings all over the country; he must have lived not so much in Parliament, as with a nation outside, and a nation vastly larger than that with which he had to deal. That, however, was not his position, or the position of any minister then, or for long afterwards. He had to deal with powers we neither know nor understand; on the throne, an active and ardent politician, buying boroughs by the dozen, and contributing £12,000 at each dissolution to the election fund of every minister he approved, besides what he might spend at bye elections; whose personal party in the House of Commons numbered perhaps a third of that assembly, and whose party in the House of Lords controlled that body. Secondly, he had to deal with the boroughmongers, who required to be fed as regularly as the lions at the Tower.

These are the vanished factors of Government. But because he was supported by them, it is not to be supposed that he was not supported by the people. The people were then, politically speaking, the middle classes, and he was the man of the middle classes. When he took office he did so by the act of the King, but the King was clearly the interpreter of the national will. The petitions, the municipal resolutions, the general election clearly proved this. And the nation seem, so far as we can judge by the limited but sole expressions of their will, by elections and by acclamations, to have followed Pitt to the end of his long administration. Wilkes, who was himself no bad test of popular feeling, followed him from the beginning. He had, it is true, the King and the aristocracy with him; but he truckled to neither the one nor the other. Indeed, it is one of his singular merits that he managed to combine into a solid array of support king, lords, and people. But it is no real charge against him that he utilised as an aid the King and the aristocracy, for there was no possible Government without them. Nor, when the Whigs succeeded him, did they dream of introducing any other system. They only complained that the King withheld his election contribution from them.

It is perhaps unnecessary to say more of the circumstances and surroundings of Pitt. But it is impossible to complete any sketch of his career, or indeed to form an adequate estimate of his character, without setting him, if only for a moment, by the side of Chatham. Not merely are they father and son; not merely are they the most conspicuous English Ministers of the eighteenth century; but their characters illustrate each other. And yet it is impossible for men to be more different. Pitt was endowed with mental powers of the first order; his readiness, his apprehension, his resource were extraordinary; the daily parliamentary demand on his brain and nerve power he met with serene and inexhaustible affluence; his industry, administrative activity, and public spirit were unrivalled; it was perhaps impossible to carry the force of sheer ability further; he was a portent. Chatham in most of these respects was inferior to his son. He was a political mystic; sometimes sublime, sometimes impossible, and sometimes insane. But he had genius. That flame it was, fitful and undefinable though it be, that gave to his eloquence a sublime and terrible note which no other English eloquence has touched; that made him the idol of his countrymen, though they could scarcely be said to have seen his face or heard his voice or read his speeches; that made him a watchword among those distant insurgents whose wish for independence he yet ardently opposed; that made each remotest soldier and bluejacket feel that when he was in office there was a man in Downing Street, and a man whose eye pierced everywhere; that made his name at once an inspiration and a dread; that cowed even the tumultuous Commons at his frown. Each Pitt possessed in an eminent degree the qualities which the other most lacked: one was formed by nature for peace, the other for war. Chatham could not have filled Pitt's place in the ten years which followed 1783: but, from the time that war was declared, the guidance of Chatham would have been worth an army. No country could have too many Pitts: the more she has the greater will she be. But no country could afford the costly and splendid luxury of many Chathams.

To sum up: it is not claimed that Pitt was a perfect character or a perfect statesman. Such monsters do not exist. But it may be confidently asserted that few statesmen and few characters could bear so close a scrutiny. He erred, of course; but it is difficult to find any act of his career which cannot be justified by solid and in most cases by convincing reasons. It may be said that his party acted more on him than he on them; but the relations of a successful leader with his party are so subtle that it is difficult to distinguish how much he gives and how much he receives. It is, no doubt, true that the changed conditions of the world compelled him to give up his first task of educating his followers, and to appeal rather to their natural instincts or prejudices. It may be alleged that he clung to office. This is said of every minister who remains long in power. Office is, indeed, an acquired taste, though by habit persons may learn to relish it; just as men learn to love absinthe or opium or cod-liver oil. But the three years which Pitt spent out of place and almost out of Parliament seem to have been the happiest of his life; and his resignation was almost universally condemned as groundless and wanton. It may, however, be conceded that unconsciously he may have become inured to office, and as leaving it implies at any rate a momentary defeat, he may have been unwilling to face this. Men who pine for unofficial repose dread the painful process of leaving office—the triumph of enemies and the discomfiture of friends and the wrench of habit—as men weary of life fear the actual process of death. It may also be said that, though he generally saw what was right, he did not always ensue it. What minister has or can? He has to deal not with angels but with men; with passions, prejudices, and interests, often sordid or misguided. He must, therefore, compromise the ideal, and do, not the best, but the nearest practicable to the best. But let us remember what is indisputable. No one suspected his honesty; no one doubted his capacity; no one impeached his aims. He had, as Canning said, qualities rare in their separate excellence, and wonderful in their combination. And these qualities were inspired by a single purpose. "I am no worshipper of Mr. Pitt," said Wilberforce in the House of Commons, long after Pitt's death, "but, if I know anything of that great man, I am sure of this, that every other consideration was absorbed in one great ruling passion—the love of his country." It was this that sustained him through all. For he ruled during the convulsion of a new birth at the greatest epoch in history since the coming of Christ, and was on the whole not unequal to it. There let us leave him; let others quarrel over the details. From the dead eighteenth century his figure still faces us with a majesty of loneliness and courage. There may have been men both abler and greater than he, though it is not easy to cite them; but in all history there is no more patriotic spirit, none more intrepid, and none more pure.

APPENDIX A

Year.	Foreign State or Potentate.	Amount of Subsidy.		
1793	Hanover	£492,650	17	11
	Hesse Cassel	190,622	16	5
	Sardinia	150,000	0	0
1794	Prussia	1,226,495	0	0
	Sardinia	200,000	0	0
	Hesse Cassel	437,105	1	9
	Hesse Darmstadt	102,073	0	0
	Baden	25,196	5	7
	Hanover	559,375	11	3
1795	Baden	1,793	15	3
	Brunswick	97,721	13	9
	Hesse Cassel	317,492	11	2
	Hesse Darmstadt	79,605	5	6
	Hanover	478,347	17	6
	Sardinia	150,000	0	0
1796	Hesse Darmstådt	20,075	13	8
	Brunswick	12,794	9	5
1797	Hesse Darmstadt	57,015	3	4
	Brunswick	7,570	11	6
1798	Brunswick	7,000	0	0
	Portugal	120,013	13	0
1799	Prince of Orange	20,000	0	0
	Hesse Darmstadt	4,812	10	0
	Russia	825,000	0	0
1800	Germany	1,066,666	13	4
	German Princes	500,000	0	0
	Bavaria	501,017	6	0
	Russia	545,494	0	0
1801	Portugal	200,113	15	4
	Sardinia	40,000	0	0
	Hesse Cassel	100,000	0	0
	Germany	150,000	0	0
	German Princes	200,000	0	0
1804	Sweden	20,119	4	11
	Hesse Cassel	83,303	19	5
1805	Hanover	35,340	14	6
	Total .	£9,024,817	10	6

APPENDIX B

I.—ACCOUNT showing the amount of stock created in respect of loans raised and Bills funded from the commencement of the French Revolution war till the end of Mr. Pitt's first administration in March 1801; and also the amount of stock purchased by the Sinking Fund during that period:—

Financial Year.*	Loans of which the Charge was borne by Great Britain.			Loans of which the Charge was borne by Ireland.*		Sinking Funds.	
	Raised for Supply Purposes.	Raised for assistance of Foreign Powers.	Raised in respect of Bills funded.	Funded in Great Britain.	Funded in Ireland (but expressed in British currency).	Great Britain.	Ireland.
1793–4 . .	£6,250,000	...	...	...	£323,077	£2,174,405	...
1794–5 . .	†13,750,000	...	£1,926,526	...	‡950,446	2,804,945	...
1795–6 . .	†50,095,800	§£3,833,333	1,609,898	...	‡1,469,231	3,083,455	...
1796–7 . .	†30,918,669	...	26,026,900	...	‡890,769	4,390,670	...
1797–8 . .	†25,350,000	3,669,300	...	† £2,925,000	‡1,047,692	6,716,153	£73,870
1798–9 . .	†35,624,250	...	...	†4,000,000	1,886,723	7,858,109	244,766
1799–1800 .	21,875,000	...	...	5,250,000	1,846,154	7,221,338	269,169
1800–1 . .	29,045,000	...	...	3,140,000	2,307,692	7,315,002	363,950
1st Feb. 1801 to 17th March 1801 . . .	44,816,250	...	...	4,393,750	...	...	...
Totals . . .	£257,724,969	£7,502,633	£29,563,324	£19,708,750	£10,721,784	£41,564,077	£951,755
	£325,221,460					£42,515,832	

II.—ACCOUNT showing the amount of stock created in respect of loans raised and Bills funded during Mr. Pitt's second administration; and also the amount of stock purchased by the Sinking Fund in that period:—

Financial Year.	Loans on which the Charge was borne by Great Britain.			Loans on which the Charge was borne by Ireland.		Sinking Funds.	
	Raised for Supply Purposes.	Raised for assistance of Foreign Powers.	Raised in respect of Bills funded.	Funded in Great Britain.	Funded in Ireland (but expressed in British currency).	Great Britain.	Ireland.
1804–5 . .	£18,200,000	...	...	£8,190,000	...	£9,137,515	£107,980
1805–6 . .	34,400,000	...	..	{ 4,300,000 †360,000	£2,566,154	12,972,913	255,352
Totals . . .	£52,600,000	...	...	£12,850,000	£2,566,154	£22,110,428	£363,332

Total of loans: £68,016,154 — Total of sinking funds: £22,473,760

* The financial year (for debt purposes) of Great Britain ended on the 1st February, and the financial year of Ireland ended up to and inclusive of 1800 on the 25th March, and subsequently on the 5th January.

† With long terminable annuities expiring in 1860.

‡ With short terminable annuities of various currencies.

§ With an annuity for 25 years.

III.—ACCOUNT showing the Estimated Capital Value of

(NOTE.—*Rate of Interest*

GREAT

Financial Year.	ANNUITY											
	£62,791 13 4			**£85,500**			**£58,500**			**£20,582 7 6**		
	£	s.	d.	£	s.	d.	£	s.	d.	£	s.	d.
1794–5	1,205,663	18	5	......			......			......		
1795–6	1,203,155	7	10	1,638,271	9	8	......			......		
1796–7	1,200,521	5	8	1,634,684	15	2	1,118,468	10	5	392,610	9	0
1797–8	1,197,755	18	9	1,630,919	6	10	1,115,892	3	7	391,658	10	3
1798–9	1,194,851	16	6	1,626,964	19	4	1,113,186	11	1	390,659	0	8
1799–1800	1,191,802	13	2	1,622,813	1	8	1,110,345	15	11	389,609	14	11
1800–1	1,188,601	10	10	1,618,454	5	8	1,107,363	9	4	388,507	15	4
1801–2	1,185,239	13	6	1,613,876	12	6	1,104,231	7	6	387,350	16	7
1802–3	1,181,710	3	2	1,609,070	13	5	1,100,943	1	10	386,136	1	2
1803–4	1,178,004	3	10	1,604,024	9	2	1,097,490	8	5	384,860	7	3
1804–5	1,174,112	7	4	1,598,725	3	5	1,093,864	11	10	383,521	1	4
1805–6	1,170,026	10	3	1,593,161	13	8	1,090,057	19	11	382,114	13	6

IRELAND

Financial Year.	ANNUITY											
	£4500			**£4916 13 4**			**£9504**			**£16,670**		
	£	s.	d.	£	s.	d.	£	s.	d.	£	s.	d.
1794–5	......			......			98,648	5	9	......		
1795–6	......			......			94,076	13	8	173,028	18	8
1796–7	......			......			89,276	10	4	165,010	6	11
1797–8	85,837	17	2	......			84,236	6	11	156,590	17	3
1798–9	85,629	14	8	93,558	5	9	78,944	3	2	147,750	8	2
1799–1800	85,411	4	4	93,319	10	8	73,387	7	5	138,467	18	5
1800–1	85,181	16	1	93,068	17	8	67,552	14	5	128,721	6	5
1801–2	84,940	17	6	92,805	12	11	61,426	7	6	118,487	7	10
1802–3	84,687	18	7	92,529	5	7	54,993	13	9	107,741	15	2
1803–4	84,422	6	7	92,239	2	0	48,239	7	6	96,458	16	9
1804–5	84,143	8	7	91,934	7	3	41,147	7	0	84,611	15	8
1805–6	83,850	12	4	91,614	8	9	33,700	14	4	72,172	7	7

3—*continued*

erminable Annuities created during Mr. Pitt's Administrations

ken at 5 per cent.)

RITAIN

F												Total Estimated Capital Value of Annuities set up in Great Britain, at the end of each Year.		
£39,000			£36,875			£75,000			£230,000					
£	s.	d.	£	s.	d.	£	s.	d.	£	s.	d.	£	s.	d.
......			......			...			......			1,205,663	18	5
......			......			...			3,241,606	4	0	6,083,033	1	6
......			......			...			3,173,687	4	0	7,519,972	4	3
743,928	2	5	......			...			3,102,371	2	0	8,182,525	3	10
742,124	7	5	701,688	2	1	...			3,027,490	0	0	8,796,964	17	1
740,230	10	7	699,897	9	1	...			2,948,864	10	0	8,703,563	15	4
738,242	6	2	698,017	11	4	...			2,866,308	6	0	8,605,495	4	8
736,154	5	0	696,043	5	7	...			2,779,623	12	0	8,502,519	12	8
733,962	1	2	693,970	10	9	...			2,688,605	14	0	8,394,398	5	6
731,660	5	7	691,794	3	6	...			2,593,036	2	0	8,280,869	19	9
729,243	1	2	689,508	13	3	...			2,492,687	2	0	8,161,662	0	4
726,705	6	7	687,109	4	2	1,397,510	0	0	2,387,321	16	0	9,434,007	4	1

F									Total Estimated Capital Value of Annuities set up in Ireland, at the end of each Year.			Total Estimated Capital Value of Annuities set up in Great Britain and Ireland, at the end of each Year.		
£7385			£14,250			£16,731								
£	s.	d.	£	s.	d.	£	s.	d.	£	s.	d.	£	s.	d.
......			......			......			98,648	5	9	1,304,312	4	2
......			......			......			267,105	12	4	6,350,138	13	10
76,653	15	9	133,858	8	4	......			464,799	1	4	7,984,771	5	7
73,101	9	3	126,301	6	10	202,199	9	9	728,267	7	2	8,910,792	11	0
69,371	10	9	118,366	8	0	195,578	10	7	789,199	1	1	9,586,163	18	2
65,455	2	4	110,034	14	6	188,626	9	4	754,702	7	0	9,458,266	2	4
61,342	17	4	101,286	9	3	181,326	14	7	718,480	15	9	9,323,976	0	5
57,025	0	3	92,100	15	8	173,662	1	10	680,448	3	6	9,182,967	16	2
52,491	5	4	82,455	16	4	165,614	3	3	640,513	18	0	9,034,912	3	6
47,730	16	7	72,328	12	3	157,163	17	5	598,582	19	1	8,879,452	18	10
42,732	7	3	61,695	0	11	148,291	1	5	554,555	8	1	8,716,217	8	5
37,483	19	8	50,529	1	7	138,974	12	3	508,325	16	6	9,942,333	0	7

APPENDIX B—*continued*

IV.—SUMMARY of preceding Accounts.

	Total Amount of Stock created in Mr. Pitt's Administrations.	Estimated Capital Value of Terminable Annuities at close of Mr. Pitt's Administrations.	Total Capital Liability.	Amount of Stock purchased by Sinking Fund during Mr. Pitt's Administrations.	Total Net Capital Liability.
Additions to debt in Mr. Pitt's first administration	£325,221,460	£9,323,976	£334,545,436	£42,515,832	£292,029,604
Additions to debt in Mr. Pitt's second administration	£68,016,154	£9,942,333	£77,958,487	£22,473,760	£55,484,727
Total additions to debt for which Mr. Pitt was responsible . . .	£393,237,614	£9,942,333	£403,179,947	£64,989,592	£338,190,355

APPENDIX C

FOR this Appendix, and much besides, I am indebted to my friend Mr. E. W. Hamilton of the Treasury.

Mr. Pitt's income derived from official sources is generally stated to have been about £10,000 a year. It may be interesting to show how these emoluments, somewhat understated, can be arrived at :—

1. *First Lord of the Treasury.*

(1) Salary as a Lord of the Treasury, charged on Civil List	£1600*	
Less deductions on account of Land Tax and other duties . .	380	
Making net salary .		£1220
(2) Salary as First Lord, likewise charged on Civil List	4022†	
Less deductions amounting to .	242	
Making net salary .		3780
So as to bring total receipts of First Lord to		£5000

* Cf. Fifteenth Report from Select Committee on Finance, ordered to be printed 19th July 1797 ; and other House of Commons Papers, No. 147 of 1803, No. 309 of 1806, No. 17 of 1830, and No. 366 of 1869 (pp. 586-90).

† Cf. Fifteenth Report from Select Committee on Finance, ordered to be printed 19th July 1797, etc.

2. Chancellor of the Exchequer for Great Britain.

(1) Salary as Chancellor of the Exchequer charged on Civil List .	£1800‡	
Less deductions on account of duties	148	
		£1652
(2) Exchequer fees, amounting to about		800‡
Total receipts of Chancellor of the Exchequer		£2452

3. Warden of the Cinque Ports (or Constable of Dover Castle).

(1) Salary as Warden, charged on Civil List	£4100	
Less deductions on account of duties and salaries to subordinate officers, amounting to (about) . .	1300	
Making net salary .		£2800§
(2) Further salary, charged on Army Votes, amounting to (about) .		280§
Total receipts as Warden of the Cinque Ports		£3080

4. Summary of Mr. Pitt's Emoluments.

(1) First Lord of the Treasury	£5000
(2) Chancellor of the Exchequer for Great Britain	2452
(3) Warden of the Cinque Ports	3080
Total emoluments	£10,532

Note.—Prior to 1797, the First Lord and Chancellor of the Exchequer had a share in (what was called) "New Year's Gifts," of varying but trifling amounts, which may be put at

‡ House of Commons Paper, No. 322 of 1831.

§ Cf. Appendix to Report on Select Committee of Finance, ordered to be printed 19th July 1797.